THE HAPPENING WORLDS
OF JOHN BRUNNER

The moral of this is that heretical teaching must be made irresistibly attractive by fine art if the heretics are not to starve or burn. I have to make my heresies pleasing as plays to extract the necessary shillings from those to whom they are also intensely irritating.

—Bernard Shaw, *"Postscript: After Twenty-five Years," to* Back to Methuselah

Kennikat Press

National University Publications

Literary Criticism Series

General Editor
John E. Becker
Fairleigh Dickinson University

THE HAPPENING WORLDS
OF JOHN BRUNNER

CRITICAL EXPLORATIONS
IN SCIENCE FICTION

Edited by **Joe De Bolt**

Preface by **James Blish**

Response by **John Brunner**

National University Publications
KENNIKAT PRESS • 1975
Port Washington, N.Y. • London

Manufactured in the United States of America

Published by
Kennikat Press Corp.
Port Washington, N.Y./London

Library of Congress Cataloging in Publication Data
Main entry under title:

The happening worlds of John Brunner.

    (National university publications: Literary
criticism series)
    Bibliography: p.
    Includes index.
    1. Brunner, John, 1934–   –Addresses, essays,
lectures. I. De Bolt, Joe.
PR6052.R8Z7   823'.9'14   75-31968
ISBN 0-8046-9124-X

TO JAMES BLISH
1921 - 1975

Acknowledgments

The creation of this book, begun in the Summer of 1973, has been a long and difficult task and many persons have given me their help. Indeed, the book represents a combined effort from all segments of the world of science fiction—fans, professional writers, and academics. Fanzine editors William Bowers, of *Outworlds,* and Richard E. Geis, of *The Alien Critic,* provided useful material on Brunner, as did long-time science fiction fan and "huckster" Howard DeVore. Helpful comments came from Tom Clareson, editor of *Extrapolation,* Darko Suvin, co-editor of *Science Fiction Studies,* and Donald Wollheim, publisher of DAW books; also Peter Nicholls, editor of *Foundation: The Review of Science Fiction,* contributed out-of-print biographical material on Brunner.

Closer to home, Denise De Bolt, my wife, served admirably as an editorial assistant, as well as typist for the nearly half million or so words that went into the several drafts of the manuscript. English professors John Pfeiffer, Norman Rasulis, and Ronald Primeau, my informal "editorial board," rendered invaluable services in both the writing of the following essays and in the manuscript's final preparation. The fine cover photograph of Brunner was created by David Britten, a photographer with Central Michigan University's Information Services. The efforts of all these persons are deeply appreciated, and I give them my thanks.

Above all, I am grateful to those two excellent writers, James Blish and John Brunner, whose works stand like sentinals at this volume's beginning and end; their presence helped to keep all of us honest. Finally, John Brunner, whose complete cooperation lent immeasurably to whatever merit this book may have, deserves special praise for his patience and forebearance as I poked and pried into the chambers of his life and work. He never closed a single door to me.

October 8, 1975
Mt. Pleasant, Michigan

Contents

5 RESPONSE
When I was halfway up who should I bump into but myself coming down
               or
We have met the eminent and he is us

THE HAPPENING WORLDS
OF JOHN BRUNNER

A BIBLIOGRAPHIC NOTE

In the interest of conserving space and simplifying references, frequently cited and quoted works by John Brunner have been abbreviated throughout the text, except for their initial appearances in each selection. These abbreviations along with the specific editions to which page citations refer in those cases where multiple editions exist, are listed below. Complete bibliographic information for all of Brunner's works can be found in the bibliography at the rear of this book; all non-Brunner sources are referenced at the conclusion of the selection in which they are used.

AJB   "About John Brunner"

DSFW   "The Development of a Science Fiction Writer"

EFP   *Life in an Explosive Forming Press*

EWJB   "An Evening With John Brunner"

FTDF   *From This Day Forward*

GSOZ   "The Genesis of *Stand On Zanzibar* and Digressions into the Remainder of its Pentateuch"

OOMM *Out of My Mind* (Ballantine, 1967).

SOTC   *The Squares of the City* (Ballantine, 1965, 1970, 1973).

SOZ   *Stand On Zanzibar* (Ballantine, 1969, 1970, 1972, 1974).

TJO   *The Jagged Orbit* (Ace Books, 1969, 1972).

TRIP   *Trip: A Sequence of Poems Through the U. S. A.*

TSLU   *The Sheep Look Up* (Harper & Row, Publishers, Inc., 1972).

TWM   *The Whole Man* (Ballantine, 1964, 1970, 1973).

JAMES BLISH

John Brunner: A Colleague's View

In this essay I shall discuss briefly the unique beauty and promise of the works of John Brunner, especially what is probably his greatest virtue—being the foremost exponent of an important new sub-genre of science fiction. This will require me to talk a little about science fiction's history, and then about the things Brunner has written which I think to be works of art, each to be considered on its own terms. I shall probably do this badly, in part because I speak as a writer from my own taste, and in part because I am irritated that this author in particular so well deserves being made the center of this project and yet is so seldom spoken for here *as an artist.* That has been left to me, and since it must be done, I do not feel entirely presumptuous in taking it on. Nor, in his final essay, will Mr. Brunner hold back from telling me where he thinks I've gone astray, for we have been among each other's most merciless critics since we first met, over a decade ago.

Not long after the late John W. Campbell took over the editorship of *Astounding Stories* in 1937, magazine science fiction—which in those days was the only kind of science fiction being published—underwent a major change in character at his direct command. (He had started another major change earlier by auctorial example.) He announced, both personally and editorially, that the stories he wanted were those which might have appeared in an ordinary household magazine *of the period in which the stories were set,* stories which might have fallen into his hands, as it were, by time machine. He wanted stories with lived-in backgrounds, not stories in which the backgrounds dominated the characters.

The result, eventually, was something which came to be called sociological science fiction: stories which projected a whole future society and made it seem real and consistent. As a side-effect, the requirement brought about a rebirth of the science-fiction novel—for creating a society is difficult in five or ten thousand words.

This, as it turned out, was the work at which the then-unknown Robert Heinlein excelled, and still excels. Critics who today lash out at the increasingly conservative (some say fascist) nature of his projections must simply be unaware that Campbell never required any given author to stick to a projected future after inventing it; he never even required that the projected future seem likely, but only that it seem to be lived in. To use the example immediately at hand, Heinlein wrote a major novella ("The Man Who Sold the Moon") rooted essentially in the exploitative, Adam Smithian economics of early American railroading, driving the point home by naming his hero after the most notorious predatory president of the Union Pacific; he then promptly wrote another ("Beyond This Horizon") in which the economy was totalitarian, based upon the Social Credit theories of Douglas and Gesell as modified by Jerry Voorhis. Campbell published both; any immediate future satisfied him if the author made it sound viable within the confines of the story itself.

Campbell also continued to publish stories set so far in the future that the societies involved could not possibly have been extrapolated from the present because the data were too few. He also published stories, or series of them, by authors who adopted cyclical theories of history (both Isaac Asimov and A. E. van Vogt retold Roman history in a far-future setting, and I was allowed to see some of my far futures through the eyes of Spengler). And, of course, he also continued to publish stories of the previously standard kind, such as tales of slam-bang interplanetary action—what we now refer to contemptuously as "space opera"—because many readers liked such tales, and many still do. But the sociological science fiction story had been invented, and quite rapidly became the dominant mode. It still is, although it has undergone a sea-change, primarily but not solely because of the auctorial example of John Brunner; mainstream writers venturing into science fiction adopt it almost instinctively and parlay it into best-sellers.

In learning to produce this kind of story, both then-new authors such as Robert Heinlein and Lester del Rey, and old-time specialists in slam-bang such as Jack Williamson, found as a matter of course that the characters in a lived-in society must talk a natural speech and have real emotions. On the one side, lectures and orations would no longer serve; on the other, neither would stock reactions by stereotypes. Some pulp habits lived on, and not entirely damagingly, either—the pulps at least insisted upon tight plotting, an almost lost art now—but most of them became increasingly fossilized, and confined to minor and short-lived magazines (though the rise of the "monster" movie and of the paperback novel, both addressed to new audiences, revived them as zombies for a distressingly long while). Essentially, however, these formulae had been thrown out.

As a beginner, and an extraordinarily young beginner at that, John Brunner thus faced a field which had changed significantly from the one which had been faced by the older writers. Standards in science fiction had risen with the introduction of lived-in backgrounds, stylistic polish, characterization and emotion into what had become a literary backwater. There was still a market for slam-bang, and Brunner's early novels, some recently revised and reissued, fall into that category; the short stories of the same period are a little more sophisticated, but in hindsight are ingenious though unpopulated notions. They were not simply hackwork and some still read well today. Even then he wrote well, knew how to plot *ab initio,* and gave the customers value for money. But they were hardly memorable. (I then asked another newcomer whose start I much admired, "Why have you been silent lately? If you don't resume publishing soon, I'll be reduced to reading the Collected Works of John Brunner." As prophecy, never did I choose a verb more badly, but I think it was excusable at the time.)

This situation was soon to change. I first became aware of the change in the novel published in the United States as *The Whole Man* (in England, as *Telepathist*; the publishing history of this seminal work is complex and it would serve no purpose of mine to lay it out here, but I much prefer the wealth of ironic implications in the Stateside title). The protagonist is a man who, though physically handicapped himself, has telepathic powers which he uses for healing other people. Telepathy had been given a hundred different uses before, but this one occurred only to John Brunner, as far as I have been able to find. In any case, *pace* Poe, originality is not the main issue here, indicative though the choice proved to be. What counts is that the novel showed powers of insight and compassion previously unsuspected (by me, anyhow) in this author—the powers of an artist, not just the technician being celebrated by some of the essayists whose pieces follow this.

These powers were promptly shown again in almost unbearably concentrated form in "The Totally Rich," a novelette first published in an ephemeral American magazine of 1963 but since reprinted in a Brunner collection. Ostensibly the story's subject is longevity vs. death, but filtered through the Brunner sensibility it turns out to be about love, and the overall effect almost approaches high tragedy. It baffles me that this beautiful work, which despite its length is in no sense minor, is not far more widely known.

These same powers are now abundantly evident in his recent work, and most particularly in his present penchant for choosing protagonists the reader can barely like at the outset and making them grow into full-fledged human beings worthy of love as well as respect. This was implicit in "The Totally Rich"; it reaches full maturity in the 1972 novel *The Sheep Look Up,* along with much else.

But we have not quite made our way to *TSLU* yet. In the interim, something else was happening to science fiction, something called the New Wave. I have no intention of attempting to describe again here that rather inchoate sub-movement, but two aspects of it relate directly to John Brunner: a dominant concern with the problem of today rather than the far future; and freedom to try any stylistic experiment no matter how wild (or, in the mainstream, old hat). John Brunner had shown an intense social consciousness before, both in his writing and in his personal life. It fused with stylistic experiment in the monumental *Stand on Zanzibar,* about which mountains of comment have been written and this book contains still more. I shall say only that I publicly misjudged it as an attempt (Hollywood orchestration) to blind the reader with sheer technical virtuosity and missed the artistic substance. The following novel, *The Jagged Orbit,* is also stylistically idiosyncratic—for instance, it is divided into a hundred "chapters," two of which consist of single syllables—but though Brunner did not pioneer this freedom in modern science fiction, he remains to date one of the very few (I would adduce Aldiss and Disch as others) who has subsumed it to artistic purpose.

The ultimate issue we have seen is *TSLU,* surely his finest work thus far. It is again a sociological science fiction novel, but one with the sea-change of immediate concern with imminent social problems. It is technically brilliant, not only experimentally but in the way it does not scorn the old pulp ideal of tight plotting and beyond that the older ideal of being well-made and in balance. It is long, but not a word is wasted—on the contrary, it is one of those novels like Gaddis's *Recognitions* where as the pages left to be read dwindle the reader regrets that it does after all have to come to some end. (It is not the masterwork *The Recognitions* is—Brunner has yet to give us that—but it is a novel one is equally reluctant to stop reading.) There are scores of characters, all vividly brought to life and treated with sympathy, even the obvious villains. And it has nevertheless the most merciless happy ending I've ever encountered: the burning down of the entire United States. This may not strike you as happy at all, but it is the inevitable solution for the multiplex problem posed, and the only one. The work has beauty, compassion, power, precision, and immediacy. It is not science fiction as we used to know it, but we are all the better off for that.

This, I hope, has been a brief overview of John Brunner the artist—not John Brunner the sociologist, the philosopher, the politician, the computer-man, the editorialist, or the futurologist (and what an ugly word that is). It cannot be said fairly, in my view, that he has fulfilled his early promise, because very little promise was visible at the beginning; but once he found his real voice, the outcome was not so much a promise as a sort of aesthetic explosion.

I am most pleased to have this chance to speak about this John Brunner, the artist and the craftsman. And if prediction is one of the roles of a science fiction writer, however minor a role it is, then I shall repeat that there are prodigies still to come from him.

PART 1

BIOGRAPHY

JOE De BOLT

An Introduction to
John Brunner and his Works

1. THE CAREER

Origins. John Kilian Houston Brunner was born in Oxfordshire, England, on September 24, 1934, the first child of Anthony and Felicity Brunner.[1] Two sisters followed, but young John, reared in the tradition that a boy's world was different from a girl's, never was very close to them emotionally. Further underscoring this isolation was the socially limiting atmosphere of the Brunners' rural family life. As John Brunner recalls, "My parents had almost literally no friends, never entertained, never held parties and never took me anywhere on holiday." ("The Development of a Science Fiction Writer," p. 7.) It is not surprising, then, that John invented an imaginary playmate when he was about three or four years of age.

Illness, too, marred the whole of his childhood. Not only did John experience the complete repertoire of typical ailments such as whooping cough, mumps, measles, chicken pox, and repeated tonsillitis, he also fell victim to more esoteric and serious diseases. At the age of three he developed dysentery from lettuce that an ignorant gardener had contaminated with raw sewage. Two years later an attack of rheumatic fever went undiagnosed until it was over, followed in a year by an infection stopped just short of the meningeal membrane by one of the new sulfa drugs. As if these weren't enough, there were outbreaks of scarlatina, conjunctivitis, and even cattle ringworm. Despite these occurrences John was anything but a placid child; between bouts with illness, he was always active. But misadventure dogged his explorations, culminating in a fall from a haystack onto a brick threshing floor about his eighth year resulting in a short confinement in a wheelchair.

11

These disasters have physically marked the adult John Brunner—recurrent digestive trouble from the dysentery, a weak ankle due to the fall, a ringworm scar that dictates, to some extent, how he combs his hair—but their psychological impact on the child may have been of greater significance. The foundations for Brunner's future literary development may have been laid by the nearly continuous illness and isolation of his early years. Children caught in such an environment often turn to fantasy, as John clearly did with his make-believe companion. Coupled with this was an early passion for reading, a means for further enlarging his imaginative worlds. He was proud of having read completely the unabridged *Robinson Crusoe* when he was six years old.

It was thereafter, perhaps while recovering from one of his ailments, that the young Brunner discovered a copy of H. G. Wells's *War of the Worlds* in his nursery. The fact that it was a rare first edition owned by his grandfather did not deter the child from sketching on its endpapers his daydreamed fusion of Robinson Crusoe's defense against the cannibals, invading Martians, and the vague "war machine" so much in the news of those World War II days. His fantasy compass had found its north, and, as Brunner has frequently pointed out, this nursery episode was to lead eventually to his life's work—the writing of speculative fiction.

For the next few years John sought out appropriate fodder for his voracious reading appetite. All handy Wells and Verne tumbled into the maw, along with any available pulps, comics, even pop science works—anything that fed the hunger of his imagination—but there was never enough. So, at the age of nine he began his first original story. He soon found that getting "Gloop, the Martian" into trouble was easier than getting him out, and the tale was never finished. The story may have failed, but its young author's resolve had been galvanized: John Brunner would become a writer.

There were two ironic elements in this decision. Writing replaced an earlier childhood ambition, hatched against the background of the Battle of Britain, to be a fighter pilot; Brunner's later military service was to prove the most distasteful experience of his life. Also, his final, firm commitment to writing was unwittingly abetted by his father Anthony, who pointed out the April, 1947, British reprint of *Astounding,* a science fiction magazine, on a Wallingford bookshop counter and said, "That looks like fun"; in hindsight, considering the Brunners' plans for their son, it looked much more like "disaster."

The Brunner family had long been associated with the large chemical company Brunner-Mond Ltd, which had been founded by John's great-grandfather but incorporated in 1927 into the vast conglomerate Imperial Chemical Industries. Although the huge fortunes, and even the titles of nobility, to which the company had given rise were not in John Brunner's branch of the family, it seemed reasonable to expect that any bright young Brunner might find a secure future assured for him in the firm which bore his name. Anthony and Felicity had decided on this course for John and mistook his interest in science for a step in that direction. Following traditional British practice, his own opinions on the matter could be, and probably were, ignored. Once laid, parental plans, buttressed with the appropriate educational institution, formed the mold; the fluid youthful substance need only be poured in and left to cool and harden.

And so, at nine and a half years of age John was sent off to be appropriately educated in "boys' only" boarding schools, first to a prep school and then to Cheltenham College, to which he was transferred when he was thirteen. It was just as well that he was not interested in pursuing a career in science, for the prep school offered not a single science course outside of elementary nature study. Moreover, at Cheltenham John's "extraordinary ineptitude" in mathematics was pointed out by his senior science master as grounds for keeping his work concentrated in language and letters. Thus, John Brunner, author of scores of science fiction novels and stories, can truthfully say, "I've never had a science lesson in my life." Moreover, although his marks were no problem, he was far from being a tractable student. He describes his relations with his teachers as involving

. . . veiled but genuine mutual hostility. They kept insisting that I read stuff which didn't speak to me. Whereas I was—still am—a voracious reader, I resented having to waste valuable reading time on stuff that was just going to get me through an examination when I wasn't enjoying it, knowing perfectly well that there were things on the library shelves that I would enjoy far more and get considerably more benefit from. This was particularly the case with the so-called classic Victorian novels, things like Hardy's *The Woodlanders,* which I had to struggle through very painfully. Hardy simply was not talking to me because his subject matter and his characters were so completely outside my experience. On the other hand, I would read great chunks of Milton for pleasure, he being somewhat unfashionable at that time.

What did speak clearly to him was science fiction, and it told him that he must become a writer. Thus, at thirteen he collected his first rejection slip because the British *Astounding* bought no original material. But just past his seventeenth birthday Brunner made his first paperback novel sale. It was retitled and issued under a house pseudonym by its British publisher, which suited its author very well. The novel's quality was so poor that it remains the only publication which Brunner refuses to acknowledge.

Meanwhile constant pressure was being applied to deflect Brunner from his decision to be a writer. At school housemaster and form-master lectured "on the patent foolishness of such an ambition, warned of the insecurity I would risk and of the utter improbability of my ever making a living that way" (*DSFW*, p. 6). Similar objections came from home. Actually, such concerns were not entirely unwarranted; both teachers and parents most likely had vivid memories of the Depression and the war, events more than catastrophic enough to make them security minded. Certainly the Brunner family was not opposed to having a writer in the family per se; Anthony's mother had written novels and published them at a vanity press, and he himself had a continuing ambition to be a playwright. Rather, John's parents just didn't believe that their son had the talent needed to write professionally and to support himself wholly from that writing.

This mounting dispute over writing, coupled with a general disenchantment with his formal education, forced Brunner out of school. Knowing that the doors of Oxford had been opened for him in the summer of 1951 as the result of a state scholarship must have heightened his awareness of the seriousness of abandoning the academic track. Yet, it was a decision he claims never to have regretted. "I am still discovering that I was told lies or offered half-truths or a distorted version of the facts from start to finish of my schooling" (*DSFW*, p. 7). However, this is not the course he would recommend for everybody:

There is exactly one good reason for dropping out of school if you have the chance of higher education, and that is you honestly believe you can educate yourself better than it is being done for you. But you'll have to prove it, otherwise you may regret it in later life. I've been very lucky; I happen to have that inquiring cast of mind which has enabled me to go on mortaring up the gaps in my formal education right up to the present day—I still haven't finished.

And so, just past his seventeenth birthday, John Brunner left Cheltenham and purchased his first typewriter with the money earned from the sale of that first novel, −£ 27 10 s.

First efforts. Brunner's first major break occurred when John Campbell bought the novelette "Thou Good and Faithful" for *Astounding,* then the world's leading science fiction magazine. This was his first American magazine sale. It appeared in the March, 1953, issue as the lead and the cover-illustrated story. "It's one of the few stories whose genesis I recall with absolute clarity. It stemmed from a passing remark in a novel of Clifford Simak's—a retired robot had run off to homestead a planet. And the rest followed in smooth succession" (*Now Then!* p. 10). "Thou Good and Faithful" still reads well today. In many ways it can be taken as embodying many of the essential thematic elements Brunner would continue to use in his work up to the 1960s and the end of his "Ace period." But a still insecure Brunner, hedging against the possibility that his family's dire predictions about his ability as an author might be true, had the story appear under the name of "John Loxmith," a pseudonym he never used again.

During this same period Brunner made his first American novel sale. Originally entitled "Duel over Argus," a literal description of the plot, it was re-titled "The Wanton of Argus" and printed in *Two Complete Science Adventure Books* (summer, 1953). A good swashbuckling yarn that blends elements of sword and sorcery with science fiction, it was to appear again in 1963 as *The Space Time Juggler*. Writing speculative literature requires boundless imagination, but it is somewhat more finite as a business; so the fact that this first American purchase of a Brunner novel was made by Malcolm Reiss, the man who was to become Brunner's American agent a score of years later, even though a coincidence, was not a great one.

Likewise, it is not surprising to find members of the same family with similar names. The young science fiction author John K. H. Brunner was confronted with a cousin five years his senior named John H. K. Brunner. Moreover, this older cousin was also a writer, a journalist specializing in economic and trade union affairs, and both Johns moved in similar political circles. To avoid the inevitable confusion, Brunner published several of his science fiction works, including "The Wanton of Argus," under the name of "Kilian Houston Brunner." But this practice was soon ended when a reader quipped in a letter to one of the magazines in which a "Kilian Houston" story had appeared that if he wrote under such a name, he would expect it to fall on him one day and do some damage. The eventual emigration of the other John Brunner (H. K.) to Western Australia at last solved the problem.

Considering the quality of these early, 1953, works, it might seem that Brunner appeared spontaneously as a competent writer. Not so; many other pieces had been written and had failed to sell. Those that saw print were, of course, the best of the lot. This author, like any other, was learning his craft, as evidenced by a growing pile of rejection letters.

There was one letter of acceptance that was far from welcome; Brunner was drafted. Even though he received a commission in the RAF, the young man who as a boy dreamed of being a pilot found his military experience bitter indeed (*DSFW*, p. 7).

My two years of Air Force service were the most futile, empty, and in general wasted period of my life. I was bored by the routine; I was disgusted by the company of professional killers; and I drew from it perhaps only one advantage, a conviction which endures to this day that the military mind constitutes the single greatest handicap under which the human race is condemned to labor, inasmuch as these people without imagination or compassion have been given the power to destroy our species. My detestation of them increases with every passing year, a fact which I suspect could easily be deduced from a study of my writing, as could my distrust of politicians who sacrifice honesty to the exercise of personal power and my loathing of those so-called Christians who bless weapons of war and condone such abominations as the use of atom bombs, the napalming of Vietnamese children and the sectarian hatreds afflicting Ulster.

John Brunner the misfit officer fared no better than the earlier obstinate student or incorrigible son. A common denominator is apparent: those institutions or practices which attempted to constrain his will, in effect to own him and channel his actions for the "good" of others rather than for his own self-actualization—either through reward or punishment—were all rejected.

As if further to emphasize his repudiation of the "establishment," Brunner refused a second university scholarship in the winter of 1953. While at recruit training camp, he had received a letter from an uncle offering Imperial Chemical Industries support provided he study those subjects chosen for him by the company. "I was heartily sick of being told what I ought to learn. I had a sneaking suspicion that there were other and more important things from which my attention was meant to be diverted" (*DSFW*, p. 7). In a strange freak of historic time, Brunner found himself facing the same set of existential dilemmas that American youth would come to know so well. Given the place and times, his own responses were not so different from what theirs would be a decade later.

The Siamese-twin themes of the destruction of one's will and the corrupting power of affluence are woven throughout Brunner's works and probably reach their clearest and most powerful statement in *The Devil's Work* (1970). But in the early 1950s they were issues to be faced and solved by a young and very inexperienced, aspiring writer. A few more sales added courage, and Brunner left his Berkshire home for London in 1955 to begin a career as a free lance writer. "I was damn well going to prove that I was right and they were wrong—and I did." But not immediately.

He earned £4 a week, spent half of it for rent, and ate potatoes frequently. The Nova Publications, *New Worlds* and *Science Fantasy,* Britain's only non-reprint science fiction magazines at the time, were his major market, but their rate was only two guineas per thousand words—about one-sixth of American pay. In an attempt to grind out a living at those rates, he placed multiple stories in many issues, hitting a high of three in the February, 1956, *Science Fantasy.* Nova editor Ted Carnell, facing great difficulty in filling his magazines, invented the names "Keith Woodcott" and, once, "Trevor Staines" for Brunner in an attempt to maintain the illusion of variety on his contents pages.

Not only was Brunner going broke, but the sharpening of his writing skills was difficult under such a load. This condition troubled him increasingly and even appeared to preoccupy him as time went on. Even so, he turned out good stories. "Fair" (1956) is probably the most noteworthy, combining a vision of Cold War anxiety and international idealism with personally innovative and, for science fiction, "avant-garde" writing techniques. Just as a mindless, automatic conveyor belt running in circles tries to toss off the story's protagonist, so the free lance treadmill, requiring Brunner to run ever faster just to stay aboard, threatened to dislodge the story's author. "Fair" won readers' praises, but that was not enough.

After five months of daily work Brunner was ready to admit that he was wrong; he could not make a living writing, and nothing remained but to creep back to his parents' home with his tail between his legs. Then one morning the phone rang. Christopher Samuel Youd (known to science fiction readers as "John Christopher") was on the line and looking for one of Brunner's acquaintances. Youd's boss at the *Bulletin of Industrial Diamond Applications* was ill, and Youd needed a temporary replacement for himself while he filled in for his boss. The acquaintance wasn't to be found, but John Brunner was. He took the job of technical abstracter and bought six more months of time away from home.

For the first time since he had struck out on his own, his pay was adequate. He learned to use the Patent Office Library, a useful aid for a science fiction author. There was time for writing on weekends and in the evening. Still, being employed by another was not the independence Brunner sought, but the alternative, surrender, was more distasteful than the expediency of this temporary truce. It seemed quite natural, therefore, when the technical abstracter's position was reassumed by Youd, for Brunner to pick up a second job as "an editorial dogsbody" with Books for Pleasure, one of London's big pop publishing houses.

This could have been the first step toward a career in publishing; after all, it was a field that used literary skills, it offered the potential of security and big money, and Brunner could and did continue to write in his spare time. During 1957 and 1958 several Brunner short stories appeared in both British and American magazines, although their combined number was only half the heavy output of the short free lance period in 1956, Brunner's peak year for short story publications. More importantly, he had sold two novels, "Threshold of Eternity" to *New Worlds* (1957-58) and "Earth Is But a Star" to *Science Fantasy* (1958).

"Threshold of Eternity" is a complex, van Vogt style story of alien invasion and the unified human solar system's defensive war fought through both time and space. Of very different style is "Earth Is But a Star," a quest story with strong fantasy elements where the protagonist, Creohan, perceiving the forthcoming destruction of Earth by a rogue star, sets out to find others who love the planet at least enough to mourn its demise. Creohan has little luck in those future times of decadence.

Among Brunner's early novels "Earth Is But a Star" is a particular favorite of mine, and considering its later publishing history, its author must share this sentiment. Ace released it in 1959 as *The Hundredth Millennium,* and again in 1968, after extensive revision and expansion, as *Catch a Falling Star.* It is the earliest of Brunner's novels to be later revised after initial book publication, a practice Brunner has engaged in eight times to date.

But life was not too enjoyable at Books for Pleasure (*DSFW*, p. 8):

I cannot say that I invested my entire attention in that job; the atmosphere of the company was so whole-heartedly commercial that on one occasion I recall hunting in vain for a copy of a book entitled *Prehistoric Animals* in which I'd written elaborate directions to the printers concerning essential corrections—the paintings were marvelous but the text was hopelessly obsolete, so I'd gone to some trouble to revise it for a new edition . . . and it transpired that it had been sent out by the sales department along with a batch of mint ones. We only got it back because the woman in (I think) Nottingham who had bought it complained about the way it had been scribbled on.

However, the job did have some advantages: it exposed Brunner to a great many books he hadn't previously known he had an interest in and taught him to read and correct proof to a high standard—both of which were to be future assets, although the proof correcting did drop his reading speed from over one thousand to about three hundred words a minute. But above all, the steady paycheck made it possible for Brunner to remain in London, mix with the science fiction community there, including his own boss, the author John F. Burke, and keep alive his writing ambitions.

It was while Brunner was with Books for Pleasure that he married Marjorie Rosamond Sauer. Having lived together for more than a year, they decided that if it had stuck that long, it was likely to stick indefinitely. The wedding took place on July 12, 1958.

Ace period. Three months later, in November, Ace Books bought *Threshold of Eternity;* this event launched Brunner on a new phase of his career, his Ace period, which would last until the mid-sixties and carry him across the threshold of mature writing. He was in the hospital at the time, having his appendix removed, but after two distasteful years as an editorial assistant, this first American book sale seemed the proper omen. He resigned his job from his hospital bed and returned to free lancing, this time permanently.

The Ace science fiction line, then under the editorship of Donald A. Wollheim, was of particular utility to new writers (*DSFW*, p. 8):

I acknowledge as do many SF writers, a debt to the Ace Doubles, where a beginning author like myself could "ride on the back" of a better known personality—I shared sales in my early days with Poul Anderson, A. E. van Vogt, and other famous names—and then in turn serve as a prop to launch further novices. Thanks to this system, I was able to earn my bread-and-butter comfortably by about the age of 25 or 26 [about 1959].

Further, these paperbacks, printed in lots of nearly a hundred thousand copies, provided the exposure needed to attract a solid readership. As the market shaped the producer, Brunner turned increasingly to longer fiction and wrote twenty novels for Ace between 1958 and 1963. Counting revisions, his total Ace books to date number thirty-five. Another advantage of this system was that novels could first be serialized in magazines and then released in book form, thereby earning more financial return from any given wordage—a general practice among science fiction writers. Finally, Brunner's Ace period provided writing experience needed for further development of his art and craft.

Wollheim, now publisher of DAW Books, aptly summarized the significance of these early novels:[2]

I only regret that no one seems to be able or have the data to do a real in-depth analysis of Brunner's earlier works, those one might term light space-opera, which I published way back ten, fifteen years ago at Ace Books. Very readable, very enjoyable; in these books too, though written rapidly for a quick turnover, you would find the elements of all of Brunner's social themes and crusading attitudes. In spite of light plot movement, those earlier novels carried their morals structured into the texts.

Free lance writing was still far from lucrative for the Brunners, and Marjorie continued to work for the first few years after that November Rubicon. Her salary, plus the slightly greater amount earned by John through constant writing, produced earnings in 1958-59 of £2,400.[3] Thus, not for the first time, nor for the last, did Brunner find himself required to be enormously prolific out of economic necessity.

In addition to the Ace novels Brunner began to sell stories to all the major American science fiction magazine markets in this period. Having already appeared in *Astounding,* he made his first sale to *Galaxy* with "Silence" (1959); 1962 found him in the *Magazine of Fantasy and Science Fiction* with the widely reprinted "Such Stuff," followed by "Protect Me from My Friends." "Singleminded" (1963) marked Brunner's debut in *If,* and the inclusion in 1964 of a novel in *Amazing,* "Bridge to Asrael," and a short story in *Fantastic,* "An Elixir for the Emperor," rounded out his initial American magazine appearances.

By 1962 Brunner had produced more than enough short science fiction to justify the first collection of some of his better stories: *No Future in It* appeared with its entirely unprophetic title. Meanwhile he moved into fresh areas of writing: *The Brink* (1959) stands as a solitary outpost of his ventures into contemporary fiction until 1964, when *The Crutch of Memory* appeared. In 1960 "The Gaudy Shadows," a mystery story with science fiction overtones, was printed in *Science Fantasy*, the same magazine which carried the fantasy story "Father of Lies" in 1962. However, such excursions merely foreshadowed the diversity that awaited Brunner in the late 1960s and early 1970s.

Amidst all the quantity of Brunner's Ace period, and building upon such previously successful works as "Puzzle for Spacemen" (1955), "Fair" (1956), "Two by Two" (1956), and "Substitute God" (1958), a substantial body of quality science fiction began to develop. First major honors went to the mock-serious "Report on the Nature of the Lunar Surface" (1960), which won a slot in Judith Merril's *Sixth Annual Edition, The Year's Best SF* anthology and remains Brunner's most reprinted story. Other works that received recognition include "Badman" (1960), "The Analysts" (1961), "Father of Lies" (1962), "Protect Me from My Friends" (1962), "A Better Mousetrap" (1963), "Singleminded" (1963), "See What I Mean!" (1964), "Coincidence Day" (1965), "Nobody Axed You" (1965), "Speech Is Silver" (1965), and "Wasted on the Young" (1965). Four other stories from this period deserve special mention: "Some Lapse of Time" (1963) was dramatized on the BBC series *Out of the Unknown*, as was "The Last Lonely Man" (1964). This latter work, included in both Judith Merril's and Wollheim and Carr's year's best anthologies, along with "Such Stuff" (1962) and "The Totally Rich" (1963), probably constitutes Brunner's best short fiction published between 1958 and 1966.

A second important group of works from this period consists of story series that were later developed into novels. The earliest and most successful of these was the *Whole Man* series, consisting of two stories, "The City of the Tiger" and "The Whole Man" (American title "Curative Telepath"), which were published in 1959. The following year "Imprint of Chaos" (1960) appeared, the initial episode in the *Traveler in Black* series; although the remaining three stories did not see print until after the end of Brunner's Ace period, the origins of this excellent fantasy are certainly here. The third and final story series, involving "The Society of Time," ran throughout 1962 and consisted of "Spoil of Yesterday," "The Word Not Written," and "The Fullness of Time"; they were collected that same year as *Times without Number*.

These superior works of short fiction stand in sharp contrast to the many undistinguished novels from the same period, especially *The Super Barbarians* (1962), *The Skynappers* (1960), and *Echo in the Skull* (1959), although the latter has been substantially improved in a recent enlarged version, *Give*

Warning to the World (1974). However, one cannot conclude from this that Brunner, best known today for his novels, was not then producing superior works of larger form; there are three good reasons for this conclusion—*The Squares of the City, Manalive* (unpublished), and *The Whole Man*. SOTC was finished in May, 1960, but not published until 1965. It was his longest and most ambitious novel at the time, and remained so among his published works until *Stand on Zanzibar* in 1968. As one of his best and most popularly received works in the field of science fiction, *SOTC*'s failure to appear in the early 1960s marked the most serious setback in Brunner's entire career as a writer. Major recognition in the field of speculative literature was unnecessarily delayed for five years. It was my reading of *SOTC* when it finally did appear, with its contemporary setting in an underdeveloped nation's ultramodern capital and its writing disciplined by the moves of a classic chess game, that first fixed Brunner in my mind as a major science fiction author.

The second major contribution to Brunner's development as a novelist during this period was a setback as well, perhaps an even more serious one. After years of involvement in the British nuclear disarmament movement, Brunner summed up his experience in a massive mainstream novel, *Manalive*. His London agent thought it the best novel of his he had yet read, and Brunner himself considered it "far and away the best thing I'd done" up to that time. Unfortunately, it was "sat on from springtime to November by a famous left-wing publisher in the year before the last Aldermaston March," and "the Society of Authors did not get [it] back for me until after its topicality had been destroyed forever."[4] Perhaps an appearance of *Manalive* at the height of international concern over nuclear war would have established Brunner as an economically successful author years earlier, allowing him to polish his work and pick his projects, and would have facilitated an early escape from the ghetto in which science fiction was trapped in those days. He now claims that *Manalive* will never see print.

Throughout his Ace period Brunner continued to work at improving his writing. From his very first sales it was never enough to be merely a writer; he must be the very best writer he could become.[5]

I was always conscious [Brunner wrote in 1971] that even the items I was proudest of in those days were nothing more than practice for what I hoped eventually to write . . . what, to be exact, I had already shown I could write in the form of books like *The Squares of the City* and *Manalive* . . . At least, however, I was getting paid for those quickies, saving like fury to buy myself enough time to tackle major projects on the grand scale.

Brunner's continuing concern with craft is well illustrated by the development of *TWM*. Originally conceived in 1958 as a formula for the infinite production of sword-and-sorcery adventures, all set in the mind of a physi-

cally deformed telepathic psychiatrist seeking to escape his corporal limitations, the central character, Gerald Howson, became a source of fascination
for Brunner. Rather than continuing the series after its first installment as
originally planned, the author decided to write Howson's biography instead,
and it, combined with the preceding story and a great deal of additional
material, became the final book. Thus, a routine adventure series was con-
verted into a study of the character of a crippled but still very human person,
who carried his deformity within as well as without. Brunner's involvement
with Howson led him to further his concern for character development, a
fact displayed in the works following *TWM*. Meanwhile readers were treated
to one of the more sensitive and developed portrayals of character to come
out of science fiction in the early 1960s.

This quest for excellence was surely stimulated by the London scene in
which the Brunners were deeply involved. Perhaps the most basic of these
activities was their role in educating the public to the dangers of nuclear war.
The late 1950s and early 1960s found both John and Marjorie Brunner ac-
tivists in the Campaign for Nuclear Disarmament. His talents as writer and
musician led to his composing "The H-Bombs' Thunder" (recorded as Selection JEP 3003), which was dubbed "the national anthem of the British peace
movement." Both Brunners pooled their skills to prepare a four-language
version of the CND exhibition "No Place to Hide" and took it on the road to
Sweden, Denmark, West Germany, Switzerland, France, Belgium, and Hol-
land. This trip left its mark (*About John Brunner*):

Living night and day with images of horror and destruction stamped permanently on my mind the truth that we inhabit a planet too small to be further
shrunk by nationalism, intolerance and prejudice. Those of my future worlds
which are not dystopias, "awful warning stories," tend to be unified and pacified—less from wishful thinking than because, writing mainly about the future, I have a vested interest in there being a future for me to write about.

In 1962 Brunner journeyed to Russia as a CND observer at the Moscow
Peace Congress, where he met Yuri Gagarin, the first man in space. "Now
that was an awfully nice guy." Back in London the Brunners were on the
Russian embassy's guest list and attended parties there; but it wasn't long
before Brunner wore out his welcome by getting arrested and fined for sit-
ting-in outside the embassy in protest against Russia's explosion of the 100-
megaton bomb. After that they were not invited back. "A shame really—
they used to serve beautiful vodka."

The year of his Russian trip Brunner wrote of himself: "I play guitar,
recorder and other instruments rather badly. Am a folknik. Have been described as 'the most socially conscious of British science fiction writers.'
Suits me."[6] Brunner had known a number of outstanding jazz musicians

when he first moved to London. Later he and Marjorie became involved with the London folksong scene, and performers such as members of the Ian Campbell group would gather at their house after closing time and sing and play for hours. Other house guests included Mbiyu Koinage, spokesman for African nationalist Jomo Kenyatta. And then there were conversations with double Nobel Prize winner Linus Pauling, whom they had first met in Stockholm when he had opened the "No Place to Hide" exhibit in July, 1959, and Paul Robeson, another guest at the Russian embassy parties. For vacations the Brunners toured Britain and the Continent in their current sportscar. Above all, there were the monthly meetings at the Globe pub of the London SF Circle, a twenty-one-year-long tradition. Meetings presently continue on the first Thursday of each month at the One Tun, following the Globe's recent demolition. Besides the regular British crowd of Arthur C. Clarke, William F. Temple, Walter Gillings, E. C. Tubb, and others, visiting American writers frequently dropped in. Such communication, and subsequent cooperation, is prevalent among science fiction writers, perhaps more so than with any other category of authors. Such interaction must have served both as stimulus and information source for the maturing Brunner.

The established pro. Nineteen sixty-four marked the end of Brunner's Ace period; the tentative free lancer had become the established pro. Publication of Brunner's major works began that year, starting with *TWM*, which was nominated for the Hugo (the Science Fiction Achievement Award), a new high point in his career. Riding the book's success wave, a more economically secure Brunner made his first visit to the United States, long since the major market for his writings.

The upswing accelerated in 1965; Ballantine finally bought *The Squares of the City* ("for what I thought then and still do think was a derisory advance, lower than I was by then receiving for routine SF novels," *DSFW*, p. 9), and it, too, was nominated for the Hugo and ran second in the voting. "It was a great success" (*DSFW*, p. 9).

Seven other novels were published that year, including the mystery adventure *Wear the Butcher's Medal*, along with a collection of novelettes, *Now Then!* and twelve magazine appearances. This output, plus a decade of accumulated work, was making an impact on the consciousness of the science fiction field. In September, 1965, Judith Merril included John Brunner with J. G. Ballard and Brian Aldiss as the "stimulus center for the rather more subjective, perhaps more thoughtful, certainly more literary, direction of British s-f in the mid-sixties." She went on to say, "Of the three, Brunner is probably the most conservative in terms of literary technique and adherence to the 'science fiction conventions.' "[7] Within three years Brunner would completely invalidate this observation.

It was for his general record that Brunner received the first British Fantasy Award, presented by the British Science Fiction Association, on Easter, 1966. But this was also a time to strike out in new directions as well as to be honored for past accomplishments. Brunner spent four weeks in the United States, traveling from coast to coast, his longest visit to date. The sights of the tumultuous mid-1960s filled his mind with visions first exorcised in a series of poems, his first major venture into that form, and later in the festering society of *SOZ*. Meanwhile a wedding of contemporary and speculative fiction was being arranged by Brunner in "The Productions of Time" and their honeymoon suite prepared in *Quicksand*.

It was an era of optimism; great works were being planned, new economic decisions made. Brunner Fact & Fiction Ltd was founded, with codirector Marjorie as the business side. She became responsible for keeping accounts, the filing and analysis of contracts, and the general implementation of the small family business. Formed to administer John's copyrights, the company provides future economic protection of the Brunner estate, present-day tax advantages, and lots of room for expansion.

The optimistic, even romantic, tone rings clearly in Harlan Ellison's *Dangerous Visions* where Brunner has himself described as living in Hampstead, driving a Daimler V-8 convertible (successor to a Jensen), having previously visited fourteen countries, and cherishing the ambition of building a villa in Greece to escape the wet English winters. The villa dream was given up when the Greek military took power. Perhaps Brunner took his revenge in *Good Men Do Nothing* (1970), a novel that attacks the police state that developed under the Greek colonels.

Final remnants of the past appeared in a third collection, *Out of My Mind* (1967), the mention of *A Planet of Your Own* (originally "The Long Way to Earth," 1966) and *The Productions of Time* (1966) in the first Nebula (Science Fiction Writers of America Award) ballot for 1967, and Brunner's appearance as guest of honor at the British Science Fiction Convention in Bristol. But his career was about to reach a third plateau of achievement, one that would make his past efforts pale. *SOZ* had been wrapped and mailed to Doubleday on February 5, 1967, and this blockbuster of a book, filled with almost a quarter of a million words, was ready to be tossed into the lap of the unsuspecting science fiction community.

Bringing forth a major classic in speculative literature wasn't easy. In fact, John had faced the toughest writing task of his career.[8] For two or three years he had been thinking about a story set in a world of enforced eugenics legislation, but postponed it time and again under the pressure of producing simpler and faster-income-generating works. Meanwhile a mound of clippings from *New Society* and *New Scientist* accumulated on subjects such as population pressure, urban violence, cell structure, genetics, and new drugs. Given this mountain of data, a second obstacle became apparent—the manner of presentation. How does one go about creating a convincing world with all its supporting elements in which a story of technogenetic breakthrough could be laid?

The convergence of two events in 1965 and 1966 made *SOZ* a reality. The first was a contract obtained by Brunner's London agent from a British paperback company for two books. Brunner thought, "Now's my chance to write as well as I know how!" His ideas for the two books were accepted, and all of 1966 and early 1967 were occupied by their writing.

The first was *Quicksand* (1967), a fine book in its own right and one of Brunner's best. Was Urchin, the young girl discovered naked in a woods after battling a would-be attacker, simply psychotic or was she a visitor from another time? Rich in characterization, this novel represents Brunner's most successful effort at fusing contemporary and science fiction story elements in a single narrative. Unfortunately, it was practically buried in the *SOZ* landslide the following year.

Now that time was available in plenty, the problem of form was just as neatly solved. During the farewell party at the British equivalent of the Milford SF Writers' Conference, Brunner had an insight. Why bother inventing a technique for the creation of new worlds—a difficult task at best—when an already existing one, from outside science fiction, could be easily borrowed? After all, Brunner reasoned, many writers had portrayed worlds changed by new technology, political turmoil, and war. Hemingway and Vance Bourjaily came to mind—and especially Dos Passos. The model existed. Add to it McLuhan's observations of the impact of media and the informational milieu of the twentieth century, and it all came together.

The actual writing of *SOZ* took five full months. The pile of clippings was ignored—Brunner's flypaper memory had already stored the information away where his subconscious had had a good two years to work on it. Breaking with his usual working methods, he filled sixty pages of a school exercise book with notes and began typing. The words formed a torrent.

I got to the 120,000 word mark which was the length specified in the contract, and I realized I'd only said about half what I wanted to say, so in a big panic I got on the phone to my, then, London agent and explained the problem and he said, "Oh, not to worry. I was talking to Anthony Blond, the London publisher, and he said his novels sell on the basis of weight regardless of quality," so I went ahead and finished the book.

In December, 1969, nearly two years after finishing *SOZ*, a still awed Brunner recalled that creative experience in these words ("Genesis of *Stand on Zanzibar* and Digressions into the Remainder of its Pentateuch," p. 37):

I got high on that book, I walked around six inches off the ground for weeks on end! It was a very tough but also a very rewarding job. And, incidentally, an exhaustive one. I say, deliberately, "exhaustive" rather than "exhausting," because it seems to have drained my entire stock of things I wanted to say about the immediate future (the section in which, as has been rightly said, it behooves us all to be interested because that's where we're going to spend the rest of our lives) to the point where during the past summer I realized with a shock that for the first time since I set up in business as a freelance writer I had *no* science fiction awaiting first publication, not even a magazine story.

The euphoria soon ended, and so did the optimism. The publisher that had originally commissioned them, having changed editors, rejected both *SOZ* and *Quicksand*. Further delay occurred when the publisher sat on *Quicksand* for a longer period of time than it took to write it! Brunner finally "unloaded" both books on Doubleday, to that company's advantage. *Quicksand* outsold every other of the twenty-four science fiction books issued that year by Doubleday, while *SOZ*, obtained for a mere $1,500 advance, achieved international attention in the field of speculative literature.

But the damage was done. Both books failed to pay their author a full year's income until a long five years later, while their writing had consumed all of John's savings and had bitten into Marjorie's as well. As the accolades started to pour in, a drained Brunner found himself celebrating his greatest triumph by turning out another rush of less satisfactory works. Four earlier novels were revised and published in quick succession: *Into the Slave Nebula* (formerly *Slavers of Space*) (1968); *Catch a Falling Star* (formerly *The Hundredth Millennium*) (1968); *The Avengers of Carrig* (formerly *Secret Agent of Terra*) (1969); *Times without Number* (1969). Also, two new light works were written, *Double, Double* (1969) and *Timescoop* (1969). Surprisingly, two books of high quality did emerge from this conglomerate, *Bedlam Planet* (1968), Brunner's best space exploration novel, and the intentionally experimental *The Jagged Orbit* (1969). For a brief while it looked as if the new plateau had become a pinnacle, and a new Ace age lurked on a downhill slope.

But the *SOZ* explosion had occurred, and the flying pieces could not be put back together again. Reactions began soon after *SOZ*'s September, 1968, appearance. J. B. Post said in *Science Fiction Times;* "Words fail when one has to describe one of the most important, if not *the* most important, pieces of fiction in or out of science fiction, to be published recently."[9] Norman Spinrad in *Science Fiction Review: "Stand on Zanzibar* is a brilliant and dangerous book. Brilliant because with it Brunner has invented a whole new way of writing book-length SF. Dangerous because what he has done looks so damned easy."[10] Judith Merril in the *Magazine of Fantasy and Science Fiction:*[11]

In a sense, Brunner has written the first true science fiction novel. That is, he has taken a true novel plot, developed it in proper novelistic style, and at the same time extrapolated fully in accordance with all the basic science fiction rules, a future environment whose initial assumptions provide not only the background for the story, but an essential component of its central conflicts.

Professor Dale Mullen put it most strongly: "In my opinion *Stand on Zanzibar* is the most important work to come out of the science-fiction ghetto since it first formed itself in the years following 1926" (*AJB*). Raves weren't limited to the science fiction audience. In Britain Edmund Cooper wrote in the *Sunday Times;* "Mix a dash of *Ulysses* and a splash of *Brave New World* into a sprawling television script, then attempt to rewrite some of it as a novel. You might—if you had John Brunner's intensity, imagination and undisciplined creativity—end up with something like *Stand on Zanzibar*" (*AJB*). And the *Manchester Evening News;* "A book that must go into the 'classic' archives of SF" (*AJB*).

Likewise, in the United States the *Dallas Times-Herald* wisely observed: "A fascinating McLuhan-influenced novel of some considerable merit . . . deserves some literary attention it probably won't get because of its SF label" (*AJB*). *The Library Journal* described it as "highly recommended for any kind of reader" (*AJB*).

Later the French were to be even more ecstatic. *Actuel;* "At once twisted like a Borges story, flashy and vivid like the ingeniously frenzied analyses of McLuhan, jerky and baffling like the cut-ups of William Burroughs" (*AJB*). And *Le Combat;* "Never, perhaps, has science fiction given rise to such a success. This book . . . justifies all by itself the existence of what is becoming less and less a fringe genre" (*AJB*).

But one can't spend praise; half a year after its publication Brunner had received not a penny outside of the advance for the book. And *SOZ*'s audacity was costing its author in other ways, too. Not everyone found the massive and difficult book to their liking, and the science fiction subculture buzzed with controversy. Charles Platt complained, "Compare the contrived world of *Stand on Zanzibar* with the horrific vision in William Burroughs's *Naked Lunch*. Everything Brunner talks about Burroughs *feels* in his drugged, terrified guts."[12] Some more traditional critics were also unimpressed; James Blish's first reaction was to call it "a novel of apparatus."[13] Fans complained that it was "laborious," "confusing," "too long," and a burgeoning fight over the value of "new wave" writing in science fiction focused on *SOZ*. One of the most serious blows was delivered by the influential critic Brian Aldiss, himself an outstanding writer, in an *Oxford Mail* review in which he said, "Still, *Stand on Zanzibar* is not all dross."[14] A more reasoned summation was offered by Professor Willis McNelly: "It may be a nonnovel or an antinovel, it may be the ultimate 'New Worlds' novel, the *Ulysses* or *Finnegan's Wake* of the New Wave, but one can hardly be indifferent to it. Indeed, *Stand on Zanzibar* may be the most important science fiction novel of the last decade. Unfortunately it may also be the most difficult."[15]

Meanwhile the Science Fiction Book Club released *SOZ* to its members in 1969, Ballantine followed with a paperback edition, and MacDonald and Company brought out a British edition that same year. The awards began. Nineteen sixty-nine saw both Hugo and Nebula nominations, and although *SOZ* lost the Nebula award to Alexi Panshin's *Rite of Passage,* the Twenty-seventh World Science Fiction Convention in St. Louis did award the Hugo for the past year's best novel to John Brunner, the first Englishman to be so honored. He could not, unfortunately, be at the convention, and his trophy was accepted by Gordon Dickson. Although not the equal of Hollywood's Academy Awards in splendor, the Hugos take no back seat in emotional intensity. They are the highest popular honor in speculative literature, a demonstration by the hundreds of fans who vote their preference.

Spring of 1970 brought the British Science Fiction Award, presented by the British Science Fiction Association at the Royal Hotel in London. Back in the states Ballantine ran a second printing, followed by a third in 1972 and a fourth in 1973; a British paperback edition finally arrived from Arrow in 1971. *SOZ* was assured a long run in print, an infrequent situation in the science fiction world of magazines and paperbacks. Meanwhile *SOZ* began its exposure to non-English audiences with an excellent French translation, *Tous à Zanzibar* (1972); Swedish and German translations are under way, and Japanese, Portuguese, and Italian rights have been sold. *SOZ* won its latest award in 1973, the French Prix Apollo. In all, the Zanzibar explosion lasted five years, and its fallout changed John Brunner's career.

Post "Zanzibar" period. *SOZ* had not brought wealth, but it did lead to a new plateau in Brunner's career; it earned him a major reputation in the field, and the critical response to it further sharpened his literary sensibilities and increased his discontent. Following the writing of *SOZ* Brunner began a period of expansion, setting new and increasingly difficult goals for himself. His restiveness with the narrowness of the science fiction field increased, pulled by his long-standing drive for excellence and pushed by economic necessity. It was not that a totally new Brunner emerged; rather, previously existing tendencies were strengthened. What once had been itching now began to burn.[16]

But ... God damn it, andy offutt is *so* right when he says that in our 'millpond' even a biggie doesn't give the author the chance to spend a year on a

28

single book. I wish to heaven it did; I have things simmering in my mind
that could be tremendous—I'm sure of it— if only I could devote sufficient
time to them.

I am seriously thinking of quitting sf altogether. Can you blame me?

Writing a masterpiece at the age of thirty-two can leave one feeling empty,
particularly if the financial rewards are not commensurate. In 1968 Brunner
sought a teaching post in the United States, especially in the San Francisco
Bay area. He didn't find one. The following year he went to Hollywood
and acquired an agent, hoping to find film markets for his work; unfortunately, this didn't work out either.

Meantime there were the frontiers of speculative literature to be widened,
an interest of Brunner's for the past several years and one which he had begun to carry out in *The Productions of Time* and *Quicksand,* where conventional fiction was infused with science fiction elements. His next effort in
this direction had been *SOZ,* which brought mainstream experimental fiction forms to a science fiction story. But neither attempts were the breakthrough to a mode of expression unique to science fiction. Could Brunner
be the one to do it? In the fall of 1969 he thought this way:[17]

I would, naturally, like to be the through-breaker myself—but my problem
is the opposite: I write, and always have written, too much to achieve the
lapidary precision the task will clearly call for. If I ever achieve anything
spectacularly personal, it will be on the level of that superlative drawing of
Picasso's, dashed off in a few minutes on the wall of a landing. . . .

I don't mean I'll be a Picasso, baby. I mean it'll be a unitary thing. I'm
not an original on the grand scale; I'm a synthesist and a dilettante, and I
recombine borrowed elements into a new pattern, rather than inventing *per
se.* I may, though, just possibly, come up one day with a brand-new idea. . . .
Wish me luck.

That winter he carried this theme further in his talk to the science fiction
seminar at the Modern Language Association meeting in Denver. Consider
that scene: the thirty-five year old Brunner receiving the full attention of a
body of scholars devoting that segment of their professional meeting entirely to one book, *Stand on Zanzibar.* Brunner gets nervous just speaking before students; he must have been nearly petrified before that audience. But
there he stood, urbane as ever, though fortified by a few drinks and tran-
quilized by chain-smoked cigarettes (an overindulgence characteristic of his
trips, so it's little wonder he frequently returns home with throat and respi-
ratory problems). At that time he wore his brown hair to the base of his
neck, combed straight back, with the ends forming small curls. This emphasized his hawk-beaked nose and bushy goatee worn at chin point and down
the throat. With a medium stature, not an imposing figure. Still, the polished

speech would be delivered clearly in a slightly hoarse announcer's voice with a clipped British accent, augmented with frequent digressions and enlivened with sophisticated humor. There's a bit of a Barrymore in this Brunner.

In the talk itself he spoke of accepting the increased challenge involved in writing closer to the present (*GSOZ*, p. 40).

... I have found that writing about the arbitrarily far future is too damned easy. I said before that I'm a fluent writer, and my chief danger is of becoming glib. It's facile to jump a million years ahead and talk about planets as though they were small towns which one could travel between as if by Greyhound. ...

The closer one comes to the present, the more one's material is conditioned by—what can one say?—honesty, perhaps: by the evidence of one's own reason, which is forever struggling (without much success) to make sense of the forces busy altering our environment. The more intractable the material is thereby rendered, the more satisfying is the sense of achievement when one finally has it licked into shape.

Therefore, the real challenge for the sf writer is to do precisely what Judy Merril calls projecting the mores and emotional responses of realistic human beings into a realistically different environment. It's very difficult, because to introduce that degree of reality into what is by definition a work of fantasy involves a paradox.

These statements in 1969 provide the groundwork for Brunner's next major accomplishments in speculative literature.

Beginning with *SOZ*, Brunner's science fiction has been dominated by the dystopia, or "awful warning" story. This resulted in part from a growing desire on Brunner's part to interpret in fictional form some of his personal opinions. *The Jagged Orbit* (1969) attempted to do this by examining the institutionalized paranoia present in Western society. The separation of person from person, and therefore race from race, resulted in violence and decay. Likewise the dystopian element is strong in the less successful *The Wrong End of Time* (1971), where fortress America is locked into a rigid and dangerous "soft" fascism. But *The Sheep Look Up* (1972) is the latest, and best, of Brunner's dystopian novels. In it Brunner assumed, fairly accurately, that "ecology" would be just a passing fad, an outcome assured by public apathy, private greed, and governmental stupidity. The resulting unconstrained environmental destruction grows to irreversible proportions.

While Brunner's production of nonnovel fiction remained low, several stories of merit were published in this post-Zanzibar period. Among the best are "The Vitanuls" (1967), "Judas" (1967), "Factsheet Six" (1968), "Out of Mindshot" (1970), "Dread Empire" (1971), "The Inception of the Epoch of Mrs. Bedonebyasyoudid" (1971), and "Easy Way Out" (1971), this latest story being included in Frederick Pohl's *Best Science Fiction for*

1972. With the exception of the fantasy "Dread Empire," all these stories contain some strong dystopian, or at least socially critical, elements. Themes include consumer fraud, overpopulation, technological domination, and opposition to the Vietnam War. Even "Easy Way Out," set in the distant future and involving two survivors of a spaceship crash on an uninhabited planet, takes swings at the spoiled super-rich and at mankind's willingness to welcome a pleasant illusion rather than face a distasteful reality.

Race came center stage in 1969 not only in *TJO* but in a series of spy thrillers as well. Brunner invented Max Curfew, a Jamaican black, and suspended him between East and West, oppression and freedom. *Blacklash* (1969; British title, *A Plague on Both Your Causes*) was followed by *Good Men Do Nothing* (1970) and *Honky in the Woodpile* (1971). Another novel, combining contemporary fiction, the occult, and race appeared in 1969; *Black Is the Color* (an expansion of "This Rough Magic") involved race relations in Britain and featured one of the most explicit sexual scenes in Brunner's work up to that time.

Climaxing his most extensive foray into contemporary fiction is *The Devil's Work* (1970), not one of Brunner's better-known novels, but worth taking very seriously. In it he undertook a major exploration of the nature of evil, using elements from his personal experience and many of the writing techniques pioneered in *SOZ*. In 1970, the year of *The Devil's Work* and *Good Men Do Nothing,* Brunner published *no* science fiction novels, the first time since 1956, and only about a half dozen shorter pieces. He might almost have left science fiction altogether.

He turned increasingly to poetry in 1970 and 1971 with the publication of *Life in an Explosive Forming Press* and *Trip,* which contained the poems written after his 1966 American visit. He stepped up his reading appearances, which included not only shows in London but a 1970 visit to the Dayton, Ohio, Living Arts Center, where he was to return in 1972 as part of an effort to rescue the Center financially. Besides the poetry readings he made frequent appearances on TV and radio in three languages and at least seven countries.

But the pull of speculative literature was strong. Brunner found time to do a word-by-word critique[18] of a draft of "Aye, and Gomorrah" for Samuel Delany and of Tom Disch's "The Asian Shore," both of which received critical recognition. He continued his contacts with fandom, to whose amateur magazines he had long volunteered letters, by reviving a column, "Noise Level," which "memorializes, as they say, an amateur magazine which I, myself, used to publish for the 'Off Trail Magazine Publisher's Association' in Britain. This was one of the things which helped to keep me sane while I was in the Air Force." The column ran in Richard Geis's Hugo-winning fanzine *Science Fiction Review,* and the first installment was a lengthy defense of *SOZ* and *TJO* and Brunner's ambition to transcend the science fiction ghetto. Later it appeared in Bill and Joan Bowers' graphically excellent *Outworlds*. When Geis founded his new magazine *The Alien Critic*, Brunner returned "Noise Level" to it in November, 1973, where it continues to appear.

The Science Fiction Foundation was another new area of Brunner's involvement. Founded on October 22, 1970, the Foundation is housed in the Department of Applied Philosophy at the North East London Polytechnic and is dedicated to the study and advancement of science fiction. Arthur C. Clarke is its patron and John Brunner, along with authors James Blish and Kenneth Bulmer, are among its vice presidents. The first issue of its journal *Foundation: The Review of Science Fiction* contained an autobiographical sketch of Brunner; and subsequently his work has appeared in its pages many times.

As one might expect in such a period of stocktaking and housecleaning, Brunner changed his American agent in January, 1970. Currently he is represented by Paul R. Reynolds, Inc., in New York, and has other agents in London and Hollywood as well. But the end of 1970 seemed to signal the beginning of a more settled time in Brunner's career; the frantic twisting and turning of the post-Zanzibar period were ending and a yet more mature Brunner emerging.

Overlapping this period of personal development and turmoil, and continuing to the present, was a series of professional activities, honors, and accomplishments. Brunner was on the go as never before. He was vice chairman of the Committee of the British Science Fiction Convention in 1969, and traveled to Brazil that same year for the first Rio Symposium on Science Fiction. In 1970 *TJO* received a Nebula nomination in the United States and took the British Science Fiction Award in 1971, giving Brunner two consecutive wins of this honor.

While the *Traveler in Black*'s final segment "Dread Empire" was receiving a Hugo nomination in 1972, Brunner was off to Trieste as both guest of honor at the First European Science Fiction Congress and as a member of the jury for the annual Science Fiction Film Festival. Then it was to Stockholm as guest of honor at the Seventeenth Scandinavian Science Fiction Convention. Back at home he became chairman of the British Science Fiction Association. Busy 1972 also found Brunner as guest writer in residence at the University of Kansas in Lawrence. In Kansas City he addressed the annual meeting of the Cockefair Chair. Then off to Philadelphia November 17–19 as the guest of honor at the Philadelphia Science Fiction Conference.

TSLU received a Nebula nomination the next year, and Brunner returned to the North American continent, first as a featured speaker at the World Science Fiction Convention in Toronto and then as a Visiting Scholar of the School of Arts and Sciences, Central Michigan University. It was guest of honor time again in March 1974, this time in Clermont-Ferrand for the first French National Science Fiction Convention. In May Brunner returned again to the United States to participate in "Science Fiction: Fantasy and Fact," a conference at Kean College, New Jersey. At least in terms of the field of speculative literature, John Brunner, the honored celebrity, was clearly a success.

In 1972 the total sale of Brunner books passed the two-and-a-half-million-copies mark. Income for 1971–72 totaled £6000, of which £1300 came from British sources. The British portion increased to £1600 in 1972–73, but the Brunners still depended on foreign sales for survival.

When he compared his 1973 income in constant pounds with that of his first year of free lance (1958–59), he did find improvement: an annual increase in purchasing power of just under one and a half percent. Also, in 1958 the Brunners were renting half a house. In 1973 they were purchasing a whole one in a nicer district and had only nineteen years of mortgage payments left. Brunner Fact and Fiction Ltd had grown and occupied three rooms, whereas Brunner once worked in half of a bedroom.

But the economic pinch that followed *SOZ* was soon to repeat itself. The Brunners were rudely surprised by a tax problem: "The highly reputed firm of accountants whom I hired precisely because I know I'm not businesslike amalgamated with another company, and somewhere we got lost in the shuffle." Taxes for 1969, 1970, and 1971 went partly unpaid, and by the time the 1970 and 1971 taxes were sorted out, the 1972 ones were about due, also:[19]

I was only able to pay half of it; the rest had to be spread over the next twelve months ...

Curing this financial malaise, however, is involving me in the writing of about three novels I don't want to write; I don't mean they're bad books— on the contrary, Doubleday fell on the first of the three with cries of joy— but I do mean they're superfluous. They're not in any sense an advance on what I've done before, just competent stories competently told, forced on me to make ends meet at a juncture when I have a couple of really ambitious books in mind, now obligatorily postponed until next year, or the year after.

One again John Brunner had to fall back on "routine space-opera," as he had in 1960 after the initial rejection of *SOTC* and again in 1967 after the original *Quicksand* and *SOZ* contracts were negated. But being the writer he had now become, *The Stone That Never Came Down* (1973), *Total Eclipse* (1974), and *Web of Everywhere* (1974) are a good deal more than the "routine space-opera" of his Ace period.

The Brunners' Hampstead home was another casualty of the new financial squeeze. In 1973 his mortgage rate was raised to eleven and one-quarter percent. "We decided this is *it*, let's sell up and move to the West Country where we can escape the thumbscrews."[20] They moved to South Petherton, Somerset, in early November. The London scene was rather distant, but the Brunners settled in comfortably:[21]

We have what originally seem to have been the servants' quarters of a house built some 100-odd years ago by a guy who, having made his pile in Australia, shipped home the timber for a house and proceeded to retire in it. The house is not all timber-built—that went into the roof-tree, the floors, the windows, shutters and so on. It's what they call Ham stone, from Hamden Hill, a few miles away to the south. Great stuff once it mellows, and ours is nicely mellowed after a century.

The psychological effects of the economic let-downs were not so easily surmounted.[22]

But the only means I've found to escape from falling behind the explosive rise in the cost of living is one which candidly I don't at all enjoy. I have to shamelessly exploit what's sometimes termed "gall," but in the North of England—where my father was born—is frequently called "brass." That also, incidentally, means "money."

Were it not for the fact that I push myself, hard, into blowing my own trumpet, at the risk of boring people by saying over and over who and what I am, then no matter how excellent my writing I couldn't keep afloat as a freelance. I know this to be true because so many of my colleagues who, in the objective sense, are more talented than I have to depend on external support.

Inevitably, there is resentment: "What I deeply envy in some other writers and haven't acquired is the sense of total financial security needed for me to wrap and mail only—I mean *only*—those items which I truly believe reflect my capability as an author."[23]

Even though accurate, it doesn't help at all when critics observe that he's a very talented writer who is unfortunately caught in the commercial bind and writing four or five times too much stuff for his own good. Talent doesn't spend any better than praise.

The contemporary Brunner. So what of Brunner today? At forty the same sense of humor is still there, but so is a somberness accentuated by a cool aloofness. The bushy goatee remains, but the hair is now a long page-boy with short bangs edging the high forehead—and perhaps covering a receding hairline. The body is a little more stocky and the bottom buttons of his vest pull tightly. The energy and intensity remain, and the polish, if anything, is

even more bright, and there is a tremendous sense of presence—especially
during a formal reading when there's just Brunner and the words . . .

My head's as full of words as a hive of bees,
and they buzz the whole damn time!

He continues to break new ground in his writing. His next major book,
The Shockwave Rider, was released in January, 1975, although it was finished on December 30, 1973. It's large, over 100,000 words, but, as the
critics will surely say, not another *SOZ.* The work grew out of Brunner's
concern that society may not be able to adapt to the present rapidly increasing pace of change as described in Alvin Toffler's famous work. "I found
Future Shock enormously stimulating and provocative, and, almost at once,
I could see characters developing logically out of Alvin's suggestions. When
I thought about it for a little longer, I discovered that I had the meat of a
hell of a strong story." The book should be a success. On April 22, 1974,
Alvin and Heidi Toffler drove down from London to lunch with the Brunners. "Al likes *The Shockwave Rider* and said it was fascinating to see how
his ideas were transformed by a different approach."[24] A new collection
of his works from DAW, *The Book of Brunner* (1975), will include, in addition to stories, samples of his original verse, translations, and a number of
limericks.

One thing is certain: Brunner is as uncompromising in his principles today as he was as a child defying the career demands of his family and teachers and as a young man acting to prevent nuclear war. This applies to money
matters as well: "I would prefer to have a small, but perhaps more sensitive
audience and stick absolutely to my principles than to compromise my beliefs for the sake of getting a mass audience." Brunner has held this tenet
for some time:[25]

I received, a few years ago, a letter from East Berlin inviting me to submit
some of my books for possible publication in the German Democratic Republic—a notion which of course pleased me very much—but also warning
me that they would be purged of corrupting and debasing influences. Naturally I wrote back saying I'd be delighted to see my work published in the
GDR, but that I was not a purveyor of corrupting and debasing influences
and took it as an insult that the guy had assumed I must be.
I heard nothing further, by the way. . . .

In 1968, shortly after Martin Luther King's assassination, Brunner founded
a memorial literary prize in King's name and he still administers it. He remains on the board of editors of *Sanity,* the journal of the Campaign for
Nuclear Disarmament, and on the steering committee of the Family Planning

International Campaign, for which he revises and polishes publicity material. From time to time he contributes articles to journals like the *Tribune,* a British weekly with Labour party ties.

How does Brunner see himself today?[26]

The best way to sum up how I feel about my situation (predicament) as a writer is to quote the title of one of my favorite Child ballads and say, "Lang a-growing!" I have been obliged by force of outside circumstances to attempt —and to my surprise find I could handle—a huge range of styles, themes and formulae I would not *a priori* have imagined were to my taste. In particular I was astonished and delighted to find that my supreme talent is as a *pasticheur,* and that I can put on and take off dozens of literary hats almost at will . . . or at any rate with the reasonable certainty that any which I decide to wear in public will suit me for the purpose I intended.

So I'm still very much a developing, not a finished writer. Which can't be bad.

Indeed, one of Brunner's major goals is to write a book with which he'll be perfectly satisfied. He believes that it would most likely be in the area of the dramatization of societal problems. For such an effort an economic "breakthrough" would help—perhaps an especially large advance or a film contract; in fact, it is probably a prerequisite if he is to continue (*DSFW,* p. 12).

Does it therefore follow that a science fiction writer with pretensions must inevitably be squeezed out of the field?

I doubt it. On the contrary, my suspicion is that long ago science and its applied counterpart, technology, have so deeply affected our attitudes and our patterns of social behavior that you can't go anywhere and escape them. For a brief while, SF became isolated in what Dr. Dale Mullen has called a "ghetto." But this was an anomaly. There was no wall dividing the readership of "The War of the Worlds" from that of "Tono-Bungay"; nor that of "The Sign of Four" from that of "The Lost World"; nor that of "Brave New World" from that of "Antic Hay." Equally today, an admirer of Anthony Burgess accepts without question that this talented author should now and then hit on a science fiction theme and treat it with the same seriousness and conviction as his other novels.

It makes, in the upshot, no difference from which direction one approaches the central question of our time: will we, or will we not, survive the consequences of our own ingenuity? Both alternatives remain open. Having explored each quite extensively over the past several years, I find I can imagine either coming to pass. So, plainly, can a great many of my colleagues on both sides of the SF fence.

Here we are, then. And tomorrow is another day.

2. THE WRITER

John Brunner has written much science fiction, but prefers to be called simply a writer—no limiting adjectives, please (*GSOZ*, p. 35).

... I'm one of those writers whom publishers appear to hate, because I refuse to be inserted into a nice tidy pigeonhole; I write almost literally everything that one can expect to get paid for, bar technical manuals and advertising copy, and if you count jacket blurbs as ad copy I've even done that. I've never regarded myself as a quote/unquote "creative writer," but rather as a working writer, a craftsman—if you like, a wordsmith, a person whose trade is arranging words on paper. I've sold fiction in all lengths from 700 words to nearly a quarter of a million, and as well as that I write a lot of topical songs, one of which was once recorded by Pete Seeger, and lately—to my great surprise—I seem to have acquired a certain reputation as a poet, too, having been invited to read at various arts festivals and even at the Poetry Society in London.

Although spoken in late 1969, these words are just as accurate today. Brunner writes much out of a sheer love of the English language, feeling the prose and poetry streaming out and reveling in the interplay of words.

Awed by Brunner's vast and varied output, a fledgling writing student asked him how he forced himself to write so much. Brunner answered this way:

From an entirely personal point of view, I feel that one is not even within shouting distance of becoming a writer unless one finds that one would rather sit down at the typewriter than call up that attractive bird met at last night's party, or go to a movie, or whatever. Everybody I know whose work I generally admire has this demon riding behind him. When you've encouraged your demon to work on your behalf rather than against you, you'll probably begin to understand what I mean.

Another question frequently asked of Brunner when he appears before writing classes is, "Who influenced your writing the most?"

I've developed my own approach to the writing craft very eclectically; I've borrowed wherever I thought something might be useful to me. Of the writers who influenced me most when I was starting out, I would have to put Rudyard Kipling above all, whom I regard as *the* most completely equipped writer to ever tackle the short story in the English language—so good that he outran his critics and became unfashionable long before his death.

Some of the influences which he has left on my writing are perfectly submerged and digested and I couldn't point to an example in my recent work. But I am very conscious of the fact that my early short story writing was

37

very, very much influenced by my great admiration for Kipling's skill as a craftsman.

More recently, I think I've begun over the past five or ten years to find my own voice, but I still consciously borrow techniques that have been used by other writers because one of the advantages of being human is that you don't have to make all your own mistakes! And if somebody's got it right previously there's no reason you shouldn't take it over, adapt it—this is what they call standing on the shoulders of giants. I can't say I feel aware of any influence in my poetry. Certainly so far as technical devices are concerned, I acknowledge a good deal of influences in my novels. Above all, I would cite John Dos Passos, whose technique of intermingling factual exposition and fictional narrative in the U.S.A. trilogy I quite shamelessly borrowed, and it proved to work very, very well in SF. And Sterne in *Tristram Shandy,* because he was the ultimate master of random divagation without actually losing track of what he was going to say. He was helping to invent the modern novel and you can see just how much fun he was having doing it. If I could get that kind of excitement into my own writing, I'd be well away.

Brunner usually composes easily and writes rapidly. He can carry the development of a book of 60–70 thousand words in his head, setting down to work with as few as half a dozen notes. Novels of 100,000 words and up do require some detailed advanced planning; *SOZ* required almost a notebook full of data on the characters and their settings.

Actual composing time varies, but his record is a 71,000-word novel completed in one week, one day, and one and a half hours; he hopes never to have to do it that way again. His longest book, *SOZ,* took five months, but *TSLU* holds the record for length of time devoted exclusively to one book—seven months. He doesn't see speed of composition as a particular virtue—rather, it is a necessity imposed by economics.

Brunner attributes this ease of composition to a highly disciplined subconscious mind, one trained not to bother him until the material is pretty much in the form in which it will finally go down on paper.

Long before I've formulated a novel completely, I have a pretty damn good guide to the kind of data I'm actually going to need to draw on. What does take the time, and the longer and more complex the book the more time it requires, is mulling it over in the subconscious. *Stand on Zanzibar* (Doubleday's count was 240,000 words) was two years in the thinking before I had a single word of it on paper; quite literally I didn't even have a note. But I knew that someday I was going to write a novel around this particular theme. Similarly, in the case of a more recent novel, *The Stone That Never Came Down,* I'd had the idea at the back of my mind for something like six or eight years without being able to see quite how I was going to turn it into a fully dramatized work of fiction. However, once I did spot it, it went pretty damned quickly—about two and a half, three months. But reckon in how much of the previous six to eight years I spent looking at this particular card from my ideas index, thinking isn't it about time I sorted that one out, then an hour or two later thinking, no, not today.

Like many professional writers, Brunner follows a fairly routinized schedule when he's working, which is most of the time unless he's traveling or engaged in a research project. An ideal day begins with Brunner reading the morning mail while he finishes his coffee. He answers the most urgent of the letters. This is followed by a short stroll down to the post office for a bit of exercise. At about 11 A.M. he sets to work in his study, shutting the door and pushing down the bell-off switch on the phone. After the typewriter is switched on, no one, not even Marjorie, is allowed to come into the study.

Brunner will then work through until a late lunch, beginning again in the afternoon and, occasionally, continuing into the evening until he has about five thousand words, a customary day's output. He doesn't like to quit unless he's got to a point where he knows clearly what he wants to say next; then he can safely go away and be distracted, even sleep on it, without losing the thread.

Despite the scores of successful short stories and novelettes to his credit, he prefers to write novels, presently his major output, where there's more chance to develop an idea, to evolve it, and to examine its relationships to the characters. He considers the most difficult task in writing science fiction to be the creation of characters who would look on us in the present as old-fashioned, a necessary ingredient for a successful work. Likewise these characters must be four-dimensional, not the cutouts of much speculative fiction, lacking depth, motivation, and individuality.

Brunner's great emphasis on form and craft naturally leads him generally to reject stream-of-consciousness or free associational writing.

I prefer to impose as few barriers as I can between my meaning and what goes on in the reader's head. But, I do like, for special purposes, to dramatize a particular high point in the narrative by using an unconventional mode of presentation. In *Stand on Zanzibar* there are passages where I quite deliberately set out to use free associational techniques, but for a very special reason—to give an impression of the life style of a future world, I montaged snippets of conversations, advertising, bits from the news and so forth. I looked at the world picture I had in my mind and set down these items in the order in which they occurred to me. But this was for a particular effect and it's not something I would ordinarily expect to succeed with any reader picked at random. It had to be within the context of a much more developed and formalized framework, where it stood out by contrast.

Brunner gets miserable when he's kept away from writing. It should be obvious from what was pointed out above that he tries to equip himself as best he can to keep mere physical inconveniences from disturbing him. But what of word block, that infamous occupational hazard that frustrates many writers?

I'm not very often afflicted by word block, but on those occasions when I do have one I set myself some sort of task I know will take a week or more like doing over a room, or go away somewhere . . . and after a few days I can pretty well rely on the old itch coming back to the point that I have to force myself to finish the task I set. When I go back to the typewriter, it's not out of a sense of duty, but of relief. It doesn't invariably work, but it works nine times out of ten.

It is another tenet in Brunner's approach to writing that an author's job is not finished once the manuscript is wrapped; he must pay attention to every single stage a work goes through on the way from the typewriter to the public. For example, there are galleys to contend with, and copy editors sometimes do strange things with an author's words. He feels his own experience working at editorial jobs has stood him in good stead.

Although the minutiae and fringe problems of writing may be tedious or downright boring, I'm afraid they have to be dealt with, and the real mark of somebody who's going to make a go of it as a writer is not reliance on somebody to do the chores for you, but a willingness to do the chores for yourself because you care sufficiently about what you've written to get it across to the public in the best possible form.

And Brunner does care about his readers, a concern that goes beyond mere sales. His works, although highly entertaining, frequently carry statements of social concern; in his major novels it's the world itself which is made the protagonist. If such literature is to succeed, the reader must assume prime importance.[27]

I have no conception of a "faceless mass" out there—even though I couldn't memorize the names and faces of a fraction of the people who've bought my work. Hell! A hundred thousand of them, even for an Ace paperback? For me there is always an imaginary audience waiting; if it's something trivial I'm doing, nonetheless it might make the impact of a joke told at a party, and if it's something serious, on a subject I regard as important or involving some deep emotional commitment on my part, it might (hopefully will) have the impact of winning a soberly conducted argument. At the very least it will leave a trace on the mind of the other person; a telling phrase, a vivid episode, a dramatization of something which previously was nothing but empty words.

The thing that strikes one most about Brunner is his continuing pursuit of excellence. It has become an overriding factor in his development—and has led to what he considers his major problem. In the past he frequently was forced to send off manuscripts which he felt needed more work. Growing income over the years has reduced the frequency of such occurrences, but they have not been completely eliminated. Brunner believes himself capable of doing better work. Many critics and scholars in the field of speculative literature agree with his self-evaluation. Meanwhile, with the resources available to him, Brunner continues to perfect his craft.

This process is evident in his comments on negative critical reaction to his work.[28]

It is, in essence, a question of temperament how one reacts to reviews; I draw a lot of data from them, and try to discipline my reaction and learn from them instead of flying off the handle. (I confess I did blow my top once over a review, but I shall try not to be so foolish a second time). As it were, I try to couch my response not so much in terms of "The idiot's missed the point" as of "How could even an idiot miss the point? *What did I do wrong?*"

Finally, above all, there is the exhilaration of the whole writing process, the ultimate reward for a man who loves writing, who must write, who would make his living and his life no other way.

For me, one of the chief joys about writing is that it is a genuinely mind expanding process. Ordinarily I live very much in my head; my body is a vehicle for moving my *self* from place to place. When I'm working, I come out the tips of my fingers. It's almost as if there is no interface between me and the typewriter. Precisely because I become so caught up in the flow of words which is going down on the page, I don't feel in any sense that I'm just getting the better of the words for the time being. I feel that they and I are working in efficient harmony.

And that's why John Brunner wants to be called simply—a writer.

3. THE WORKS

A brief overview. Brunner's fiction output is summarized in tables 1 and 2 below; a complete listing of all his writings, including nonfiction, can be found in the bibliography which concludes this book. Table 1 does not include expansions and revisions, except in those few cases where a work was predominantly new in content. Since the mid-sixties Brunner generally has produced fewer works in any given year, but the works he did turn out have tended to be longer. Science fiction and fantasy constitute the overwhelming majority of all his works, although a much larger percentage of nonscience fiction can be found when book publication is considered separately (table 2). Peaks in the production of short fiction occurred in the mid-fifties and early to middle sixties; the output of longer fiction was most numerous in the early to middle sixties, too, making this Brunner's most prolific period. However, those comparatively less numerous works of the late sixties and early seventies include the bulk of Brunner's best writing.

Table 1

FIRST APPEARANCES OF BRUNNER FICTION
by length and year*

	Short stories	Novelettes	Novellas	Novels
1953	1	0	1	1
1954	0	0	1	0
1955	6	2	0	0
1956	12	2	2	0
1957	2	2	1	1
1958	0	2	2	0
1959	2	1	2	2
1960	3	2	2	4
1961	0	1	0	3
1962	5	3	3	4
1963	2	2	1	4
1964	4	0	2	3
1965	7	1	0	6
1966	3	1	2	2
1967	3	0	0	1
1968	2	1	0	2
1969	1	0	0	5
1970	4	1	0	3
1971	1	2	0	3
1972	1	0	0	1
1973	0	1	1	1
1974	2	0	0	2
Forthcoming	0	1	0	1
Total	61	25	20	49
Yearly averages	2.8	1.1	.9	2.2

*Excluding expansions and revisions

Three of Brunner's works have been sold to television. "The Last Lonely Man" and "Some Lapse of Time" appeared as part of BBC TV's "Out of the Unknown" series, and "Such Stuff" was sold to America's "Night Gallery" series. Brunner has written one film script; *The Terranauts* (Amicus Productions), which was adapted from a Murray Leinster story, "The Wailing Asteroid."

Recently he took up translating, beginning with Gerald Klein's *The Overlords of War* (1973). Translations of poems by Rilke, Stefan George, Ausonius, and others are now in press. Besides his fiction Brunner has two books of poetry and several factual and critical articles to his credit, and some two to three hundred contributions to science fiction fanzines.

Brunner's books have appeared in English under thirty-six different publishers' imprints, with Ace Books being the single largest market: thirty-five titles. Most of these were early novels; later works have been published in America by Ballantine, Bantam, DAW, Dell, Doubleday, and Harper & Row.

Table 2
BOOKS BY BRUNNER
Novels and Novellas

SF and fantasy		Non SF		Translation		
Original book appearances	= 50	Mystery–thriller	= 6	SF	=	1
Expansions of previously published books	= 8	Contemporary fiction	= 3			
	58		9			1
		Total Group = 68				

Collections

SF	= 11		Poetry	=	2
	Total Group =	13			
	Grand Total =	81			

Brunner's fiction has been translated into eight languages, of which German is the most common. Not all of these translations have been to Brunner's liking, particularly the German ones. He has complained that "often I don't even glance at a German edition . . . for fear that I shall burst a bloodvessel. . . ."[29] The German translation of *TJO* he considers especially bad; it includes only thirty-two out of an original one hundred chapters. Exceptional among the translations are *Times without Number* in Dutch, which happens to have been done by a Jesuit, and the French translation of *SOZ*. As a result of these translations Brunner is widely recognized in science fiction circles throughout Europe, perhaps more so than in Great Britain.

In terms of quality, Brunner's novels exhibit great variation. In my analysis of his science fiction and fantasy, I find that two groups of novels can be distinguished and rated as superior and very superior. The superior works are: *The Dramaturges of Yan; The Long Result; The Productions of Time; The Stone That Never Came Down; Timescoop; Total Eclipse; Web of Everywhere; The Wrong End of Time.* The very superior novels include: *Bedlam Planet; The Jagged Orbit; Quicksand; The Sheep Look Up; The Squares of the City; Stand on Zanzibar; The Traveler in Black; The Whole Man.* From among these *The Jagged Orbit, The Sheep Look Up,* and *Stand on Zanzibar* deserve special attention as Brunner's most ambitious novels and the core of his dystopian works.

I find the best of his nonscience fiction novels to be *The Devil's Work.*

The major dystopias

Among the umpty-dozen other things I've written, I've tackled over the past few years a group of novels which attempt to dramatize in fictional form some of the major problems facing mankind today. It used to be, back in the 30s and 40s, that your typical SF writer was a guy who graduated in one of the hard sciences or in engineering and who was primarily concerned with the technological aspects of change. I never had a science lesson in my life, and in this sense I suppose I may have been one of the precursors of the contemporary trend in SF, which is that the majority of the good young writers coming into the field come in through the arts and the humanities. If they took science, they took it as a minor. This reflects a change in our perception of the probable future world that we are all willy-nilly being deported to by the flow of time. Around the time it became obvious that mankind could destroy itself, SF writers started asking the question, "If we are smart enough to liberate nuclear energy, why aren't we smart enough to live in a sane society?" This is the crucial question which provides the dynamics for virtually all the good SF of our day. As my contribution to this particular strand of argument, I've tackled three of the major problems confronting our species. In *SOZ*, I attempted to dramatize the extreme psychological pressures resulting from acute overpopulation. In *TJO*, I tackled the problem of institutionalized paranoia—the separation of man from man which results from the building into social systems of distrust, and much to my regret I seem to sense some of the atmosphere I tried to generate in the book now here in the US. I know I sense a lot of it in Britain. Of course, the division between man and man is most obvious when there's a different skin color involved. And in *TSLU*, I attempted to analyze a polluted world, on the assumption that interest in ecology was a passing fad and that people would slump happily back into their old wasteful ways thinking that the passage of a few items of legislation was all that was necessary to cure the problem.

With these words Brunner gives us his own summary of the books which many consider his finest works. Similarities exist among the three: all are large and complex books; all are highly believable dystopian visions; all were written in the latter half of Brunner's career. But each in its conception, execution, and impact shows important differences. They form neither a trilogy nor any part of a planned series, and each must be examined separately.

When *SOZ* first appeared in 1968, it hit the field of speculative literature with explosive force. Content was not the issue; Brunner possesses a masterful understanding of urban decay and violence, and vividly generates the feeling of overcrowded city centers where the individual constantly fears that the guy around the corner is out to get him. But others had written on population concentration and even eugenics. What stunned readers was the form of the work:

Of my books, *SOZ* is my favorite, primarily because in the course of writing it, I discovered that I could handle a great many literary forms I didn't know I could. There's all sorts of stuff in there—regular narrative, dislocated narrative, collage, montage, free and strict verse, parodies of popular songs—oh, stacks of stuff. I just had so much fun discovering how many types of forms I now knew how to handle.

It is a difficult book for many readers and Brunner has offered some advice for those who have yet to discover it.

Forget that *SOZ*'s got the shape of a novel and remember it's actually a newspaper. You think nothing of reading about a dozen different subjects on the front page of a newspaper before you turn to page 2. In this sense *SOZ* is much closer to a newspaper than it is to a regular novel; things are interlayered which, believe it or not, one does actually need to *know* before understanding the action of the novel at a later stage. So my strong recommendation to anybody who may be tempted by this book is just to hold your nose and jump in. After a while, you may find you're swimming.

Dennis Livingston, then a social scientist at Case Western Reserve University, had no trouble finding it intelligible: "*Stand on Zanzibar* is an attempt to envision a realistically complex society and is perhaps the most sophisticated social and political description of a future world yet to appear in science fiction."[30] Similarly impressed, I have used the book in my own university classes on social change as an example of future scenario writing.

Such scenario development should not be confused with prophecy, a point with which Brunner strongly agrees: "... my chief target was no more than plausibility, which is a very common goal of sf writers" (*GSOZ*, p. 37). What Brunner did do was to take images of America in the mid-sixties, of which the press was full, combine them with his own experiences obtained while visiting here, and extrapolate these within the context of what was then being discussed in the scientific literature on the effects of population pressure and the likelihood of new scientific developments in genetics.

It may come as a surprise to some readers, but the image of the future portrayed in *SOZ* was made deliberately positive by Brunner (*GSOZ*, pp. 37-38):

. . . I found myself compelled—when structuring my future world—to take the most *optimistic* set of plausible assumptions I could find. In other words, the argument of the book is predicated on the premise that nothing has become very much worse than it is today—excepting naturally the central pivot of the theme, the intensive pressure of population. This applies particularly to the episodes set in the States. Returning to this country, irregularly over about six years, I've already noticed that some of the things I was afraid I might have over-emphasized in the book have outstripped my most pessimistic imaginings. Your crime-rate; the increase in urban violence here is, I'm told, incredible, and I heard recently that in at least one New York school the incidence of drug-use among the pupils is estimated at twenty-five percent. Consequently, I foresee that the future of the United States will be infinitely worse than I envisaged for the novel.

These words date from December, 1969; Brunner had already written *TJO*, which contains just such a darker American future.

He cannot recall when he actually started work on *TJO*, but he does recall when he had the basic idea—at NYCON, the Twenty-fifth Annual World Science Fiction Convention in New York City in 1967. It proved to be a long, difficult book to write.[31]

It's almost unique among my books in that it went through four or five total re-thinkings from the original conception, growing less and less recognizable all the time, and the problem basically was that I was still too close to *SOZ*—a genuinely new plateau of achievement in my work—to be able to tell whether if I incorporated an unconventional element this was dictated by the needs of the novel or a subconscious attempt to imitate myself. I think the diffidence I felt as a result shows in the final version; I think there are great weaknesses which mar the parts I'm proud of, like the presentation of a divided society in which barriers are erected between even husband and wife in the name of "privacy," or "individuality."

Brunner's self-critical tone is very evident; indeed, of all his major work, he seems most dissatisfied with *TJO* and most conscious of its flaws.[32]

I should have created a much deeper and more convincing picture of Flamen's relationship to his employers; this rings hollow. I should have shown, rather than merely talked about, the suspicion—the institutionalized paranoia—which led to contract law mushrooming into a bigger industry than advertising. I deliberately chickened out on the rest of the world, bar such sidelights as the

46

intrusion of Morton Lenigo and the pirate TV satellite, because there simply wasn't room ... yet there should have been, and if I'd had time for one more complex re-think of the argument, one more complete revision, I could have eased in crucial details to round out the planet-wide picture, and not added more than a few thousand words to the book.

But one has to stop work on a book at *some* stage and what came out from Ace represents the situation where I felt myself going stale, and knew I must exploit my last few weeks of strong concern with the book to improve what I already had on paper, rather than attempting any extensive reconstruction jobs.

Brunner considers *TJO* the most baldly experimental work that he ever undertook, and that is another cause for self-criticism.

Another reason I have reservations about *TJO*, compared to *TSLU* and *SOZ*, was my use of real newspaper clippings. I'm not entirely sure it worked. This was a genuinely experimental technique; each day I sat down at the typewriter, I'd look in that morning's newspaper to see if there was an item directly relevant to the theme of the book. If there was, I'd clip it, copy it in, and let it dictate the course of that day's work. What I was trying to do was to pull the reader back from the world of the future narrative to his own present day real world; I'm not sure this technique was especially successful. It didn't pay off the way I hoped.

Brunner's ambivalence about *TJO* was reflected in the readers' reactions. Two back-to-back reviews in Richard Geis's *Science Fiction Review,* one positive and one negative, illustrate this. Ted Pauls concluded his review with "*The Jagged Orbit,* in short, is one hell of a good book, and one which you should not miss"; Richard Delap dissented, "*The Jagged Orbit* is tracking an erratic but weary path around a dead planet."[33]

Perhaps *TJO* was too close to *SOZ,* whose creation left Brunner more than a little drained. But it is a bridge with Brunner's latest major dystopian novel, *TSLU,* showing his increasing anger at the world scene and his resultant radicalization. True, *TJO* has a "happy ending," but Brunner claims that was just a coincidence: "By the time I got to the end of it, I needed cheering up." No such self-indulgence was allowed in *TSLU.* Like the two previous works, *TSLU* was a difficult novel to write.[34]

The trouble I'm having with it isn't due to difficulty in making the words flow, but the exact opposite—I have enough material for an encyclopedia, and every day I find something in the papers that I ought to have considered when I plotted it. .... Well, I guess that's the penalty you pay for selecting a topical subject.

The wait was well worth it. *TSLU,* with its meticulously researched scientific content, presents an overpowering atmosphere of imminent disaster unequaled in Brunner's work. The concluding catastrophe is as inevitable as a loosened boulder's fall down a mountainside.

But the political winds in the United States have changed directions sharply since the tumultuous 1960s. Dystopian pieces are not as fashionable as they once were. It is ironic that the book has been somewhat a victim of its own premise, the decline of the ecology fad. Thus, response to the book has been divided.

On the whole, Brunner reports that critical response to *TSLU* has been better than for most of his work, although seldom as euphoric as that of Richard Lupoff:[35]

It's a book that should be read by every Federal department chief, every congressman, every administrative or judicial agency head who hears environmental cases, and every top executive of a large corporation in the country—if not the world. It'll scare the daylights out of them, but it could literally save the world.

More typical of the reviews in science fiction magazines were those that accuse Brunner of preaching, of letting polemics get in the way of his literary sensibilities. Despite its many good qualities, the book won no awards in America and was not even nominated for a Hugo.

Not the least of these good qualities are the excellent examples of poetic pastiche which stand in ironic opposition before each of the chapters. These illustrate Brunner's considerable achievement in the medium of poetry.

In accordance with his desire to write as closely to the present as possible, *TSLU* is set only a few years ahead in time. Inevitably, events have outrun the book, making some things now dated, while new problems (e.g., the energy "crisis") are missing. But, as Brunner has observed, ". . . that's the penalty you pay for selecting a topical subject."

Other selected works. *SOTC* (1965), coming swiftly on the heels of *TWM* (1964, discussed below), won Brunner a major position in speculative literature. It is a large book, and the setting is in the very near future: in these respects it is a precursor of *SOZ, TJO,* and *TSLU.* It also shares the high degree of internal complexity common to most of Brunner's major works. But the complexity here is one of plot rather than narrative; as Judith Merril has pointed out, *SOTC* ". . . is a Games book—a novel about the many kinds of games that people play, and the many levels on which they play them, written by a shrewd gamesman and games analyst, for gameplayers and game-watchers both."[36] The fact that the story follows a classic chess game is provided in a note. Within the story itself the characters are being moved as living chess pieces by a dictator, Vados, and his chief political challenger, Diaz, with the winner taking the country. To accomplish their ends, advanced techniques of thought control such as subliminal suggestion are used. The characters, too, pursue their own games, including the hero, Boyd Hakluyt, a traffic analyst imported by Vados to rid his ultramodern Brasilia-type city of squatters. But in terms of the larger game, Hakluyt is played as Vados's knight.

Although *SOTC* was described by Merril as "a first-rate science fiction novel," the book has defects. They were discussed at length in a six-page analysis by Algis Budrys, whose opinion of the book was a good bit lower than most. "Read as a story for its own sake, this is a confusing, overpopulated, almost unidentifiable-with story set in a city which seems to have been created for the sole purpose of letting Brunner set a 'human chess game' in motion."[37] Budrys's description of Brunner in 1966 is also interesting and reflects the image of his Ace period: "Brunner is a workaday technician with an exaggerated sense of how much of his intelligence and awareness of the world gets translated into the prose he turns out."[38] The readers of *SOTC*, however, were more enthusiastic, and the book is still in print to date.

Quicksand appeared in 1967, and it, more than any other of Brunner's books, deserves more attention than it has received. Brunner himself was disappointed: "I regard it as one of my two or three best-turned novels, i.e. having the best combination of sheer writing with well-rounded character."[39] Besides its being overshadowed by *SOZ* in 1968, part of the reason for its neglect could have been that *Quicksand* may *not* be science fiction at all. Its style, plot, characterization all point to contemporary rather than speculative fiction. A psychiatrist, Paul Fidler, is caught between the bureaucratic demands of the hospital where he works and pressures from both his superior and wife for career advancement, and his sincere desire to treat his patients and govern his own life. The balance is tipped against the status quo when Urchin appears, an apparent amnesiac and victim of a fantasy that she is not from Earth, but a visitor from some make-believe utopia. Fidler becomes personally involved with her, finding her to be an exquisite sexual partner, and flees with her from career and marital pressures. But beneath Urchin's utopian fantasy lies a second—an ugly, brutal future world where girls are sterilized and specially trained in erotica to please despotic and decadent rulers. By the novel's end, the doctor has come to accept the second fantasy, and, driven by the jealousy and despair it inspires, murders Urchin and takes his own life. But is it only a fantasy? The novel is left open-ended on this point; perhaps Urchin really is a time traveler.

Similar elements of contemporary fiction can be found in *The Productions of Time*, which appeared about the same time as *Quicksand*. In it an alcoholic actor, Murray Douglas, is ostensibly hired, along with several other actors and actresses with problems, to do a play by a brilliant and eccentric playwright, Manuel Delgado. Actually, the cast is being manipulated by Delgado and others posing as his servants to orchestrate dramatic conflict; what Douglas took as a comeback becomes a struggle against a relapse into drunkenness. All this is being secretly recorded for viewing by a jaded audience located somewhere in the future. As in *Quicksand,* the psychological aspects of the characters and their interpersonal relations are emphasized. The story ends with Douglas victorious and the sadistic manipulators from the future destroyed.

Oddly, it was *The Productions of Time* and not the superior *Quicksand* which received a Nebula nomination. Further, the Signet paperback edition in 1967 was, in Brunner's words, "butchered" when compared with the original manuscript. As a final irony, *The Productions of Time* has appeared in Portuguese, Dutch, and German translations, while no foreign rights to *Quicksand* have even been bought.

Bedlam Planet (1968), which appeared the same year as *SOZ,* was a return by Brunner to the classic science fiction tale—space exploration. However, its central theme seems to be that the body is wiser than the mind. Rather than trying to re-create Earth on the alien world of Asgard, a few of the colonists discover how to live in harmony with their new world by becoming "poisoned" by local foodstuff. In a state akin to a psychological trance, their bodies pick out those foods they can live on, and reject the dangerous ones. Madness in this case is really sanity.

The story is made questionable from a scientific standpoint by its reliance on the concept of racial memory—"Your body is wiser than your mind; it's been around longer, and carries memories in its cells which we've barely begun to guess at" (*Bedlam Planet,* p. 147). And, of course, "Jungian" tenets are not far behind: "Something's been working like a leaven in human thinking, preparing us psychologically for the process of dying and being reborn as a different species. Asgard-Man is only the first of many, I'm certain" (*Bedlam Planet,* p. 148). Still, its central lesson, that man must adapt to an alien world rather than change it, is sound ecological thinking, as are its declarations of the relativity of sanity. "What sanity consists in is doing what *the planet you live on* will accept. And precisely because Asgard is not Earth, what is sane here may well seem crazy in Earthly terms" (*Bedlam Planet,* p. 146).

Nineteen seventy saw Brunner producing his most ambitious and best nonscience fiction and nonfantasy novel. This was *The Devil's Work,* which, according to George Bernard Shaw, is to break a man's spirit. Using symbolic names, short chapters, montages of popular song lyrics, ads and so on— techniques similar to those in *SOZ*—Brunner explores this theme allegorically through the destruction of Stephen Green, not quite eighteen and fresh from boarding school. His mother, to whom he was deeply attached, dead in an automobile accident, Stephen is left without funds and must live with his stuffy, divorced father, Victor. Their house is on a "No Through Road" in the village of Limborough. Stephen's destroyer is Baron Someday, a rich businessman with holdings in oil, armaments, aircraft, and chemicals. He is surrounded by a personnel staff that includes Felix Mauleverer, Harriet Lewer, and Hugo Vandeleur. Mr. Someday's mistress, advisor, and confidante is the strangely attractive Moira Morgan. All come to Limborough and buy an old estate, Helbury Hall, to make into an exclusive gambling casino.

The plot is set in motion when Stephen, identified through a community "survey," is hired by Mr. Someday, which allows him to escape his father's repressive house and feel useful and important. Meanwhile the village curate, Jimmy Lavender, who is suspected of being a homosexual by the local young people, has tried to involve Stephen in his church's youth club. This makes Stephen suspect, too. But Stephen has his eyes on the prospects of affluence and reneges on his promises of help to Lavender.

Mr. Someday's "hobby" is witchcraft; his coat of arms displays a spear whose wooden shaft is partly obscured by blood trickling from a closed-eyed, severed head impaled on its sharp metal point. It is the head of Christ. Back in the village cleaning ladies find the altar of the church tampered with and a red stain on the chalice. Lavender takes the evidence to his superior, P. R. Unthank. The rector disregards it. But Someday has something in mind for Stephen: participation in a black sabbath at the opening of the casino, carried out before the altar of an abandoned, though still consecrated, chapel on the old estate's grounds.

It is Halloween, and the thirteen guests wear half man/half animal costumes. Someday is dressed in a bishop's robes and sports a goat's head. Moira is a nun with a mask of pustuled flesh. Stephen is given an angel's outfit, in pink and white with little wings, and a purse-lipped effeminate mask. Moira seduces Stephen before the dark altar as the others watch, and while Stephen drinks a bloody communion, he sees the altar adorned with a spear upon which is impaled a monkey's head. As Moira attempts to feed him a stolen communion wafer with her tongue, Stephen flees in terror. But it is too late: Stephen belongs to Mr. Someday. He has nowhere else to go; he has broken with his father, Lavender represents a threat to his insecure manhood, and he is penniless, while Mr. Someday, satan-like, offers him everything.

This climactic scene provides a major image of Brunner's concept of evil. It is defined earlier in the book, however, through a conversation between Humphry Warden, manager of the casino, and Stephen: "All your freedom of choice taken away—like being sentenced to solitary confinement for life—

when you still had a lifetime before you. This is what you would do to someone you really hate." Stephen finds this frightening: "To be doomed in full possession of your faculties . . . to be rendered powerless for life, without even paralysis to blame . . ." (*The Devil's Work*, p. 272).

The Devil's Work never went into paperback and is now out of print. It was never published in Britain, though, as Brunner notes, "I wrote it in that frame of mind, and am still very sad that my hopes for it went unfulfilled."[40] Since this work Brunner has written no other contemporary novels.

Brunner's recent science fiction, with the exception of *TSLU*, although competent, includes none of his best works. *The Wrong End of Time* falls within the dystopian vein, between *TJO* and *TSLU*, and portrays a rigid America hiding behind its nuclear shield, while Russia has become more open and flexible. Race repression continues in the decayed cities of America, where a Russian agent must seek out a young black with special extrasensory powers. Otherwise, as the Russians have discovered, an approaching alien space ship threatens to trigger America's massive nuclear arsenal.

The novels of 1973 and 1974 were written rapidly during the Brunner family's most recent economic crisis. *The Stone That Never Came Down* tails out the dystopian emphasis that Brunner began with *SOZ*. It is set in Britain, the first time for one of his science fiction novels since *Quicksand*, and ends on an upbeat note, a fact perhaps responsible for its going into a second printing and setting a United States sales record for Brunner's hardbacks. Still, its author was dissatisfied:[41]

Given more time, I could have extended *The Stone That Never Came Down* and shown, more or less convincingly, a lot more of the new society emerging as people become better able to analyze and calculate with the total experience of their lives. As things stood, I had to fudge the ending. A terrible shame, but imperative from a purely monetary angle.

The story is set in the 1980s, and Britain and Europe are falling apart; cities have erupted into civil war and national armies mass on the borders; governments are caught between vested interests and intent on preserving themselves. A new discovery, VC (viral coefficient), has fallen into the hands of a small band led by Malcolm Fry, who set out to make things right with the world by spreading the virus. The effects of VC include amplifying intelligence, making selective inattention more difficult, heightening one's senses sharply, and providing total recall; once in the body, the virus grows and spreads to others. As people "wise up," world problems begin to diminish.

Web of Everywhere (1974) explores the aftermath of social collapse following the development of "skelters," instantaneous matter transmitters. The central character is blind Mustapha Sharif, the world's leading poet, and each section of the novel is introduced by one of Sharif's poems, designated by a letter of the alphabet. They end with "U." Despite the shortage of qualified leaders in the depopulated and disorganized world, Sharif spurns government offers of position and power. But Sharif has been breaking the law for years by selling the codes of abandoned "skelters," and an accomplice of his, Hans Dykstra, threatens to expose him. But Mustapha represents the development of a new order, a new way of thinking, a new hope for the world, and, after Dykstra's guilt-ridden suicide, the government, more enlightened and therefore more flexible in this age, forgives Mustapha's transgressions.

Brunner returns to space exploration in *Total Eclipse* (1974), a novel that contains some interesting similarities with *Bedlam Planet*. Both are set on a Sigma Draconis planet and both utilize qua-space for interstellar travel. Note the two passages: "After the disappointments of Tau Ceti, Alpha Centauri, Epsilon Eridani . . ." (*Bedlam Planet*, p. 9); ". . . in view of the disappointments of Proxima, Epsilon Eridaniand Tau Ceti . . ." (*Total Eclipse*, p. 1). These similarities are the only ones in these two books, which otherwise vary greatly. But the reasons for them give some insight into how a science fiction writer works:[42]

As to the overlap between *Bedlam Planet* and *Total Eclipse*—well, I was talking the other evening with some of the people responsible for the British Interplanetary Society's design for a starship, attainable with presently existing technology. (Not, by the way, with available money; it would cost about 1½ planetary GNPs, near as I can figure it!), and I mentioned the point you raise, about having to re-use Sigma Draconis. (To which one of them replied, with a sage if tipsy and owlish nod, "A very good star—a very good star!").

If you're trying to work within the confines of a real universe, you're stuck with available data. Poul Anderson has likewise set some of his stories at Sigma Draconis. I'm sure many other SF writers have done the same. Of all the stars near the sun, this happens to be the one that best matches Sol for size and spectral type. I spent three solid days trying to find an alternative for it when I was plotting *Total Eclipse;* I even pulled the useful strings I have which can get me data from the Royal Greenwich Observatory at Hurstmonceux!

No luck. That *is* the likeliest star in our neighborhood to father (mother) an earthlike planet.

So you have to give a degree of background, since it isn't the nearest—so you have to list the nearer stars and explain that they were let-downs—so you wind up (as you noted) with a virtual repetition of what you said last time. Damn. Like they say about the future: "When the real future gets here it'll be dull, because there's only one of it!"

As to qua-space—hell, that's my personal term, chosen to avoid the overused concept hyperspace. (The physicists are saying superspace now. Etymologically better perhaps—it doesn't mix Greek and Latin roots—but not so euphonious). Compare Murray Leinster's use, in many of his stories, of "overdrive" . . . one of which I have on my present car, and had on others dating back certainly to 1955. The phrase, regardless of whether it was coined in a Madison Avenue advertising office or in a writer's sanctum, presents a good evocative ring—OVER-drive. Mm-hm! I like it more than anything using ultra-, or even hyper-.

The plot involves a scientific expedition trying to find out why a once technologically advanced species of aliens became extinct. It is feared that the same could happen to man. But Earth has its problems—overpopulation, poverty, international tensions—and interstellar travel is *very* expensive. The colony may be abandoned at any time, especially since they have worked for years, requiring resupplying, and haven't found the answer. A brilliant young linguist, Ian Macauley, arrives and represents the best hope yet of solving the mystery; certain electronically imprinted crystals, may, if decoded, give the answers. This proves a dead end, and Ian tries another approach—empathy. A mechanical shell, a simulacrum, that duplicates the original alien is designed and built; Ian dons it and goes to live alone in an abandoned city. Eventually he perceives the solution: the aliens, trading in genotypes in order to achieve their conception of individual perfection, went bankrupt. "You mean that without realizing what they were doing, they restricted their genetic pool until it became dangerous, and then it was too late. Like fortunes being concentrated in the hands of a few ultra-powerful families? A sort of genetic capitalism?" (*Total Eclipse*, p. 167). But the story doesn't end here. Ironically, the relief ship from earth never returns, and the great discovery remains unknown to humanity. In the book's surprising and beautifully written final chapter, Ian, the lone survivor, contemplates the graves of his fellow scientists and writes a last testament. Mankind cannot adapt to the alien world; the invisible world of fungus spores, viruses, and dietary deficiency has slowly destroyed the colony—a complete reversal of the conclusion of *Bedlam Planet*.

Again Brunner is dissatisfied with his work. "I wish I hadn't had to write *Total Eclipse* in such a hurry; now, a few months later, I see ways in which I could have exploited the central idea (one of the two genuinely original ideas I ever came up with) much more effectively."[43]

Series. There are six series to be found among Brunner's works, three series of novels and three of shorter fiction. The earliest of these is the Galactic Empire series, founded in 1953 with "The Wanton of Argus," later retitled *The Space Time Juggler*. This was followed by a novelette, "The Man from the Big Dark," in 1958, while a second novel, "The Altar at Asconel," retitled *The Altar on Asconel*, appeared in 1965. Excellent space-opera, these stories are set during the fall of a vast interstellar empire which had arisen ten thousand years earlier, after humans discovered a billion-vessel space fleet abandoned by an earlier, and apparently extinct, race. The old imperial capital, Argus, governs a remnant of the empire, trying to maintain order with its disintegrating fleet. Barbarism has engulfed most worlds, while others have lapsed into authoritarianism and exploitative, petty, mini-empires. Out on the galactic rim are the homes of mutants and pirates; little is known of these distant places, but they were the only areas where humans ever built interstellar ships. The series abruptly terminates after a struggle over Asconel, one of the few planets holding its own against the general galactic decay, returns its rightful ruler to the throne; but the scholar Spartak and the warrior Vix, brothers of Asconel's ruler, and the mutant girl Eunora, in deadly danger from the antimutant policy of Argus, leave for the galactic rim. Two sequels were planned, but most likely will never be written.[44]

The first (to be called *A Planet of Puppets*) would have taken Vix and Spartak to the Rim where the mutants had been hounded, and portrayed them in contact with a society where paranormal powers were taken for granted. The villain would have been one of the space admirals of a defeated Imperial fleet, still hankering for a private holding of his own, be it no more than half a dozen stellar systems. After that, in a further sequel probably entitled *The Long Night and the Sudden Dawn,* there would have been a renaissance novel where the bits and pieces of the old human empire were picked up and re-assembled by the mutants. But frankly I got bored with trying to rationalize the argument. Much too much was happening around me, especially in the London of the "swinging sixties," for me to summon up the slightest smidgen of interest in that kind of plot. Now that I've discovered people like Gerard Klein are still happily writing novels of this type, I no longer feel impelled to produce any myself.

Given Brunner's great gift for this kind of story, one can't help feeling that science fiction is the poorer for having lost what might have become another classic space epic.

A second series of novels, the Zarathustra Refugee Planets, began in 1962 with *Secret Agent of Terra* (revised as *The Avengers of Carrig,* 1969). A second volume, *Castaways' World* (1963; revised as *Polymath,* 1974) appeared the following year, and a third, *The Repairmen of Cyclops,* in 1965. Despite this publishing order, *Castaways' World* should be considered the first novel in the series, followed by *Secret Agent of Terra.*

The premise for this series involves a device capable of producing an endless sequence of stories. The sun of the human-settled planet, Zarathustra, goes nova with little warning, and, out of 290 million inhabitants, only two and a quarter million manage to escape in about 3,000 spaceships. Due to the planet's location in orbit at the time of the catastrophe, the survivors fly away from the settled portion of the galaxy and into unexplored space, where they settle onto a variety of worlds, some hostile, some more friendly, but all difficult for refugees with limited resources. *Castaways' World* describes such an initial landing and the company's struggle for survival. Over seven hundred years later only twenty-one refugee worlds are known to Earth and the other technologically advanced worlds; some have been exploited, so the "Corps Galactic," a space police force as it were, is charged with protecting the long isolated worlds of the Zarathustra survivors and allowing them to develop independently. This commission is controversial, for many powerful interests want to exploit these backward cultures, and two such cases are portrayed in *Secret Agent of Terra,* where nuclear reactor fuel is the prize, and in *The Repairmen of Cyclops,* where the refugees' descendants are being used for organ and body transplants on a richer world. But the Corps's policy of maintaining the isolation of the refugee worlds is based on more than simple protection; these planets constitute a vast experiment in sociocultural evolution. Cut off from all cultural diffusion, each develops in its own way, a variant of its parent culture. Who knows what unique cultural forms have emerged or will emerge on such worlds and what exotic advances in science and technology may occur? But, like the Galactic Empire series, the Zarathustra Refugee Planets cycle remains open-ended.

The third and most recent series of novels is not science fiction. This is the Max Curfew series, featuring a black adventurer as the protagonist, and falls in the mystery-thriller category. *Blacklash* (1969; British title *A Plague on Both Your Causes*) is the first novel, and is followed by *Good Men Do Nothing* (1970) and *Honky in the Woodpile* (1971). A fourth and final volume is planned, but has not been written to date.

In these three novels Brunner explores the dominance of man over man. In *Blacklash* it's white over black, as Curfew confronts a newly formed apartheid government in a biracial African country. *Good Men Do Nothing* is set in Greece under the recent military regime, where white dominates white. Finally it's black over black in *Honky in the Woodpile.* In a final book Brunner has planned to have the tormented and bitter Curfew, at home nowhere, either overcome his alienation or die. One interesting sidelight on the Curfew books is that Brunner, writing in the first person, has been mistaken for being black by several of his black readers, a fact that pleases him.

All three of the story series have appeared in book form, and each set has been revised, with new material frequently added to make novels. The earliest of these, and perhaps the best, is *The Whole Man* series (1964; British title *Telepathist*); it consists of "City of the Tiger" (1959) and "The Whole Man" (1959; American title "Curative Telepath"). Here Brunner introduces the novel concept of a telepathist using his skills to treat the mentally ill.

Unfortunately, persons with the mental powers of a Gerald Howson do not actually exist, nor is Brunner a committed believer in such phenomena. Rather, like many science fiction writers, he uses the concept of telepathy as a useful shorthand image for person-to-person contact. "I usually recommend this as the first of my novels for persons not familiar with science fiction to tackle because it's full of vivid imagery about human communication." In the novel only about 4,000 of the original 20,000 words of "City of the Tiger" were retained, and out of the 25,000-word "The Whole Man" just some 17,000 survive relatively unchanged. Brunner added an additional 45,000 words, most of which were wholly original, although some were radically recast from the two stories.

The Traveler in Black (1971), a second highly successful series, was launched in 1960 with "Imprint of Chaos," to be followed by "Break the Door of Hell" (1966) and "The Wager Lost by Winning" (1970). "Dread Empire" (1971) concludes the series. Admitting that "Imprint of Chaos" is a conscious pastiche of the work of James Branch Cabell, Brunner goes on to create a brilliant fantasy. A mysterious black-robed entity, a being of many names but a single nature, travels the land. He is charged with bringing order out of chaos, and to that end he has chained the ancient "elementals" and combats those vain enchanters who would turn the forces of chaos to their own advantage. Each story details an episode of the traveler's struggles; the series concludes with the ending of eternity and the beginning of time.

The final series involves the Society of Time, and consists of "Spoil of Yesterday" (1962), "The Word Not Written" (1962), and "The Fullness of Time" (1962). They appear together as *Times without Number* (1969). The Spanish Armada defeated England in 1588, and by 1998 a nonindustrial Europe is united in an empire ruled by His Most Catholic Majesty Philip IX. North America, ruled by the King's eldest son, is New Castile, and The Catholic Church is truly universal. Because of the unique historical development of this culture, time travel has been discovered, necessitating the founding of an order, the Society of Time, to police possible abuses such as the theft of historic contraband and the waging of war through tampering with the past. Don Miguel Navarrow, Licentiate in Ordinary of the Society of Time, uncovers a plot by the Confederacy, those who rule in the East, to change the contemporary balance of power by altering the past; such a course has many dangers, including the complete obliteration of the present. The target of the plot, quite logically, is to reverse the Armada's victory, and Don Miguel must travel back into time to prevent it.

A NOTE ON THE ESSAYS

The essays which follow examine Brunner's work in greater depth. Although some attention is given to his short fiction and poetry, the bulk of the analysis focuses on Brunner's novels, especially *SOZ, TJO,* and *TSLU.* The authors bring several disciplines, ranging from the humanities to the physical sciences, to this task, and a variety of ideological stances as well. Each essay was constructed independently of the others, and divergent as well as convergent conclusions can be found among them. Finally Brunner responds, not so much to the specific content of the essays as to the project in its entirety and its meaning for him. Hopefully, by book's end the reader will have glimpsed some of the continually happening worlds of John Brunner.

NOTES

1. Much of the following material on Brunner's life is adapted from "The Development of a Science Fiction Writer," his major autobiographical statement to date. Additional information was obtained through interviews with Brunner during his visit to Central Michigan University in September, 1973. All nonattributed quotes derive from recordings made at that time.
2. Personal correspondence, November 13, 1973.
3. John Brunner, "Where There's Brass There's Brass," *The Alien Critic: An Informal Science Fiction and Fantasy Journal* (November, 1973), p. 19.
4. John Brunner, preface to "Fair," *SF: Authors' Choice 4*, ed. Harry Harrison (New York: Putnam, 1974), p. 19.
5. John Brunner, published letter, *Tomorrow and . . .*, no. 7 (no month, 1971), p. 12.
6. *Magazine of Fantasy and Science Fiction* (November, 1962), p. 61.
7. Judith Merril, book review, *Magazine of Fantasy and Science Fiction* (January, 1966), pp. 40–41.
8. For details, see John Brunner, "The Genesis of *Stand on Zanzibar,* and Digressions into the Remainder of its Pentateuch," *Extrapolation* (May, 1970), pp. 34–43.
9. J. B. Post, book review, *Science Fiction Times* (November, 1968), p. 14.
10. Norman Spinrad, "New World Coming," *Science Fiction Review* (January, 1969), p. 14.
11. Judith Merril, book review, *Magazine of Fantasy and Science Fiction* (February, 1969), p. 24.
12. Charles Platt, "New Worlds and After," *Science Fiction Review* (August, 1969), p. 18.
13. James Blish, book review, *Amazing Stories* (September, 1969), p. 121.
14. John Brunner, letter to Richard E. Geis, May 14, 1970.

15. Willis E. McNelly, "The Science Fiction Novel in 1968," *Nebula Award Stories Four,* ed. Poul Anderson (Pocket Books, 1971), pp. xv–xvi.
16. John Brunner, published letter, *Tomorrow and . . .,* no. 7 (no month, 1971), p. 12.
17. John Brunner, letter to Richard E. Geis, August 6, 1969.
18. Such critiques were undertaken only because both authors were friends of Brunner, and much admired by him.
19. Brunner, "Where There's Brass There's Brass," p. 18.
20. John Brunner, personal correspondence, October 15, 1973.
21. John Brunner, personal correspondence, December 31, 1973.
22. John Brunner, "Where There's Brass There's Brass," p. 19.
23. John Brunner, personal correspondence, April 22, 1974.
24. John Brunner, personal correspondence, April 22, 1974.
25. John Brunner, "Parallel Worlds," *Foundation: The Review of Science Fiction* (March, 1973), pp. 7–8.
26. John Brunner, personal correspondence, April 22, 1974.
27. John Brunner, letter to Richard E. Geis, May 14, 1970.
28. Ibid.
29. John Brunner, "Parallel Worlds," p. 8.
30. Dennis Livingston, "Science Fiction Models of Future World Order Systems," *International Organization* (spring, 1971), p. 257.
31. John Brunner, letter to Richard E. Geis, August 6, 1969.
32. Ibid.
33. Ted Pauls and Richard Delap, book reviews, *Science Fiction Review* (June, 1969), pp. 31–35.
34. John Brunner, letter to Richard E. Geis, May 14, 1970.
35. Richard Lupoff, book review, *Algol: A Magazine about Science Fiction* (November, 1972), p. 28.
36. Judith Merril, "Books," *Magazine of Fantasy and Science Fiction* (April, 1966), p. 34.
37. Algis Budrys, "Galaxy Bookshelf," *Galaxy* (June, 1966), p. 148.
38. Ibid., p. 149.
39. John Brunner, personal correspondence, October 25, 1973.
40. John Brunner, personal correspondence, June 18, 1974.
41. John Brunner, personal correspondence, April 22, 1974.
42. John Brunner, personal correspondence, June 18, 1974.
43. John Brunner, personal correspondence, June 18, 1974.
44. John Brunner, personal correspondence, June 18, 1974.

PART 2

PROSE AND POETRY

JOHN R. PFEIFFER

Brunner's Novels:
A Posterity for Kipling

On the way to Pennsylvania State University in the autumn of 1973, one of those wonderful accidents of desultory conversation prompted me to ask John Brunner if he knew of Rudyard Kipling's attempts at science fiction. He answered with a marvelous account not only of Kipling's speculative pieces but also of his general reading of Kipling's works, a set of which he found in his father's library. Brunner's comments eventually led me back to Kipling—working my way through a good portion of the 1937 Scribner issue of his writing. I found as well that recent critical assessment of the 1907 Nobel Prize winner redirects the interpretations of his achievement. I read Kipling as chronicler of a waning empire. Perhaps he recognized that he was this before his readers did. He hoped to interrupt the empire's disintegration by presenting the condition of the average man, especially the rank and file soldier, whose failure would be the basis of the empire's failure. In effect, I concluded that one could do far worse than to season himself with Kipling to begin to understand how to produce a body of speculative writing that anatomizes twentieth-century civilization. In search of a way to come to grips with just a part of the already staggering bulk of Brunner's fiction, it seems more and more appropriate that some of the characteristics of Kipling's progress provide an introductory schema. I shall follow with a brief commentary on the writing of what must be recognized as Brunner's substantial apprenticeship, and develop an analysis of the three works many feel represent his finest achievement to date: *Stand on Zanzibar* (1968), *The Jagged Orbit* (1969), and *The Sheep Look Up* (1972).

I

One illustration of John Brunner's assimilation of Rudyard Kipling appears in the marvelous, punnerically titled "excerpt" from "Lays of the Long Haul, 1905" that launches the "June" chapter of *TSLU.* The fictitious date is right for a fictitious poem by a fictitious "poet of empire."

> Ther's an 'eathen bint out in Malacca
> With an 'orrible 'eathenish name.
>
>   *   *   *
>
> Yus, I broke 'er to saddle an' bridle
> An' I left 'er an Englishman's son!

The lines are a baldly obvious and not ungentle parody of many Kipling pieces that conveyed the mood of the rank and file militiamen who were the foundation of the colonial British empire. The parody can highlight an earlier chapter's account of pathetic Philip Mason, insurance executive, whose travels also involved "lays" of ill-considered promiscuity. Mason caught gonorrhea. Bad enough, but he unwittingly passed it to his wife as well. The "lay" further provides a sexual metaphor for imperialistic "rape" in the form of the hallucinogen-bearing "Nutripon," an unappetizing whole-food manufactured in America specifically for the starving populations of "colonized" countries. Part of a contaminated batch is distributed and drives the recipients suicidally and homicidally crazy. The repercussions on United States international relations provide one of the novel's major stories, a parable of the questionableness of providing colonized peoples with "Eng-lishman's sons."

A "lay" is essentially an epic folk ballad, nostalgic for the adventure upon which a nation-empire has been built. Kipling took the form seriously be-cause he imagined it could help to preserve empire. Brunner uses it for paro-dy, perhaps, because he mistrusts any form of the myth upon which empire is built. Yet, like Kipling, Brunner is fascinated with the machineries and dynamics of empire. Both born in advantaged circumstances, they perceived from childhood the structure of corporate civilizations and are fascinated with the spectrum of psychological types in a society of classes. Kipling found the aristocracy stupid from snobbery; Brunner finds the power elite stupid from greed. Kipling found the lower class without an identity; Brunner finds mass man hysterical with the dangerous complexity of his civilization.

Both seem preoccupied with the progress of England's two greatest colo-nies. India pervaded Kipling's writing, and he found America wonderful and

unimaginably powerful. America is Brunner's India. It is the setting for
three of his most serious novels—as well as many others. He has seen America's power and its unwitting threat to the survival of the planet. Kipling
has been called conservative and fascist, but his ultimate politics, though yet
to be well understood, are considerably advanced in "As Easy as A.B.C."
(1912). Set in America of 2065 A.D. is a world that has known virtually no
murder or war for a hundred years. The planet's population has been brought
under control and reduced: "If next year's census shows more than four
hundred and fifty million, I myself will eat all the extra little babies." True
democracy reigns by rigorous vigilance that nips all populist movements in
the bud (the main action of "A.B.C."). Populism, rule by "Crowd," by mob,
by "The People," has become recognized as tyranny over the individual:

> Once there was The People—Terror gave it birth;
> Once there was The People, and it made a Hell of Earth!

Fittingly, the story presents, in the market square of Chicago, "Salati's Statue"
or "The Negro in Flames," erected "To the Eternal Memory of the Justice of
The People." Meanwhile world government, what is left of it, is by an oligar-
chy of reluctant technicians whose major duty is to keep physical systems
functioning and to neutralize occasional mob activity.

Standing on the shoulders of such as Kipling, Brunner is perhaps well described as metapolitical, in pursuit of the sort of total understanding of civilization that can finally liberate man from all coercive myths—national and
otherwise. The men differ in their propositions for the survival and prosperi-
ty of humanity, but both desire happiness for every individual human being.
Accordingly, Kipling liked Walt Whitman and Mark Twain, perhaps not a
little because these writers grasped the popular sensibility. Brunner appreciates Laurence Sterne and has read Kipling and H. G. Wells. I select these
three writers as Brunner touchstones because their achievements converge as
a simplified elucidation of Brunner's. Kipling taught suspicion of the popular
imagination (Kipling knew it well enough that he should have been wary of
it), with special reference again to the analytically utopian "A.B.C.," wherein
popular consciousness appears stupid, terrorized, and dangerous. Furthermore, Kipling provided excellent models of expository dialogue. In Wells
Brunner could examine the devices and strategies of the cautionary stories
of a writer who had done his homework in physical science and sociology as
well as in the traditional humanities. In Laurence Sterne, especially in
Tristram Shandy, he could find an arsenal of narrative-organic tactics that
have come to typify the radio and television media by which Brunner is so
obviously influenced.

Kipling sought popular genres for employment to his purpose. *Kim* is a spy story. But one cannot read it and escape the complex energy of India, an imperial colony. He experimented with the gothic story in "They," with occult and technological possibilities in "Wireless," with telepathy in "In the Same Boat," and with utopian vision in "As Easy as A.B.C." Brunner has done likewise with spy and mystery thrillers, nonspeculative adventure fiction, and film scripts. The bulk of his work, however, is speculative. Brunner chooses the speculative mood because it is an optimum medium for proselytizing the popular imagination. It is parabolic and homiletic. The catch is that effective parables for modern civilizations require enormous scientific and humanistic knowledge. Wells possessed such knowledge. Twentieth-centure speculative writing is substantially founded upon Wells's accomplishment. Kipling, too, possessed such knowledge, or at least a disposition to possess it. It is exhibited in his fascination with non-European culture, the gadgetry of new weapons systems, and the technology of new modes of communication. What, after all, would you really need to know to secure an empire? Kipling tried to know it. Brunner has tried to know it. But now there is more to know. And Brunner wants to secure a planet, at least. Accordingly, the information displayed in his most recent writing is encyclopedic. At the heart of *SOZ, TJO,* and *TSLU* is the computer, enabling and potentially controlling the information explosion.

At this point reference to Kipling continues to be at least superficially supportive. His writing is full of expository passages, similar to the disquisitions on whales and whaling that buttress Melville's *Moby-Dick* so that the stage for Ahab's rage may be set. In Kipling's glosses the stages of remote portions of empire were presented for readers who could not travel from the home islands, yet had to understand the cultures of England's possessions. Brunner's speculative writing is, indeed, essentially expository fiction. This is the hallmark of speculative writing and not especially remarkable. What is remarkable is Brunner's consistent grace and intelligibility in explaining and abstracting civilization just beyond the threshold of the present. Again, Kipling mastered popular idiom and dialect. Brunner does at least as well. He is facile in miming dialect and convincing in the transformation of his British-English ear to an American-English one—necessary for American scenarios. He does this so well that his slips become exceptions and occasions for joshing by American friends who catch him out when he has a character batting "100" instead of "1000." Beyond his fine assimilation of idiom, and beyond Kipling, he is both in love with and exasperated with language itself. He is a master of the pun, that encounter with the word which on one level yields amusement, as a lit cigarette in the fingers of a magician abruptly becomes two lit cigarettes, and charms the simplest reader, while on another level it yields terror by its very possibility because when the meaning captured in a word can be seen to bifurcate, the word itself is no longer trustworthy. The pun employed in serious discourse puts the audience on guard.

SOZ, TJO, and *TSLU* put the reader on guard, and it is to these works that we must eventually turn for additional illustrations of Brunner's strategy and craft.

II

There is in Laurence Sterne's *Tristram Shandy* (1759-67) a marbled end-paper inserted as a page. There are two-hundred-word chapters, drawings of little signs, and in many places lines of asterisks mark ostensibly elided narrative. The work is full of punneric diction, and there is a whole chapter in Latin, with a translation. The work is, in short, a cornucopia of narrative composition tricks which fully anticipated those that would be employed in nineteenth- and twentieth-century fiction. John Brunner has suggested that his readers turn to Sterne's writing to understand his own. Unfortunately, I have no space to show Sterne's influence on Brunner's work.

Much of Brunner's speculative writing is not at all complex. It shelters nicely within the conventions of the genre. With few exceptions, such as the short story "Fair" (1956), that interpolates a section of the narrative with counterpointing commercial rap lines, or *Threshold of Eternity* (1959), which includes a "paragraph" composed of alternating lines from two separate paragraphs, distinguishable by means of one set of lines in italics, his writing is uncomplex in plot and structure, imaginative in setting, and peopled with characters that answer the folk imagination's need for heroes and various shades of villain. In style it employs a discourse that serves excellently to present story and exposition without getting in the way of suspense and a good read. At the same time it often provides samples of the social critique that will become the main intention of *SOZ, TJO,* and *TSLU.* Examples include *The Atlantic Abomination* (1960), presenting one of the most truly hateable aliens in science fiction by the simple device of having it spend a lot of time insisting that humans were sentient excrement and almost unworthy to serve it. It makes mental slaves of men. Some readers have seen the alien as an analogue for the fascist state. In *The Whole Man* (1964) Gerald Howson is a sympathetic hero whose growth from ugly cripple to parapsychological superman is one of the best examples in all science fiction wish-fulfillment romps of this sort. *The Squares of the City* (1965) employs a chess game actually played by masters as the organizing metaphor in a narrative tour de force. The result is a story that dramatizes the vicious manipulative process of a power elite in a colonized country. One feature of the work is the inclusion at the end of the text of an index of the chess pieces and their story-character equivalents. The effect is a "dramatis personae" directory. To this is added an annotation of "pieces taken," functioning as an obituary.

Brunner utilized these narrative features in *SOZ, TJO,* and *TSLU.* Urchin, a Lilith-like time traveler from ten thousand years in the future, is the central figure in *Quicksand* (1967). In the early stages of the story Urchin's identity is deliberately kept vague, so that the tale progresses to the sort of dénouement cast in the lucid exposition that marks much good science fiction and that science fiction shares with the classically constructed mystery story. *Double Double* (1969) produces an operatic exercise with the metaphor of the Protean or shape-shifting monster from the sea that looks very much like the more restrained extrapolations of the dangerously mutating organisms which threaten mankind in the polluted world of *TSLU.* A wonderful variation on the time traveler idea appears in *The Wrong End of Time* (1971). It features an Afro-American hero, Danty Ward, whose odd precognitive talent enables him to see the future, then to see it less and less remotely as he approaches his own apparently preordained death, so that he foresees the conflagration that kills him only hours before the event. The story's setting is the very near future in the United States and offers ominous scapes of a technologically clogged and mismanaged civilization. In addition, the president of the United States, flippantly (deliberately so) referred to as "prexy," is an inane and alcoholic puppet of a power elite. Both these effects are produced more forcefully in *SOZ, TJO,* and *TSLU.*

Brunner's latest attempt at fantasy, *The Traveler in Black* (1971), should enjoy a wider popularity than it does. The traveler's quest presents a tantalizing allegory. He is an undoer of myths, theologies, and sciences, all of which process in fact as "magics," political and epistemological vested interests, that operate to frustrate an ultimately coherent understanding of the universe which courageous and selfless reason might otherwise achieve. Variations upon this theme appear in *SOZ, TJO,* and *TSLU.* In fact, language and conventionally paced narrative, themselves indictable as solipsisms, are submitted to an ordeal in these three works. The "traveler" might have written them.

III

John Brunner will write better novels. This is not to suggest the slightest condescension for his writing up to now. It is exceptionally fine. It is rather the impression that the astounding quantity, energy, and quality of his work in mid-career make upon us. As I am writing this, Brunner is extending the corpus of his work, is writing too. *The Shockwave Rider* (1975) will be in print, and the assessment of his work will again have to be altered. Nevertheless, an examination of his achievement so far is a fascinating prospect, not only for an interest in Brunner's accomplishment, but also for what it represents for the state of the craft of the writing of speculative fiction. His discourse reveals amazing virtuosity. To demonstrate something of it, *SOZ, TJO,* and *TSLU* present themselves as a constellation in his most recent production. That they are discrete works will be born out in the following discussion. But I have found it perfectly natural to treat them as if linked in form and theme, as if they were a trilogy. As far as possible I have organized a description of them in terms of plot and structure, settings, characters, and style and mood.

The three novels are built of many dozens of vignette-like sections which ultimately organize into montage effects. In *SOZ* (118 sections) and *TSLU* (141 sections) a table of contents lists each section title. *TJO* omits this provision, perhaps because it contains an even hundred sections, a round number befitting a work with "Orbit" in its title. Each commences with a series of sections which are imagistic and friezelike, catching characters and civilization like runners in mid-stride (the pictorial appeal is striking, and I shall return to it). Succeeding sections catch the runners in new postures, lending the effect of a stop-action sequence of several characters' adventures interspersed with clips of a particular stage of the world, especially as supplied by news media, to suggest the significance of the adventures. The "caught" postures engender a subliminal suspense, incompleteness, or sense of balance precariously maintained, if not on the verge of being altogether lost. This suits the books' themes that warn of gravely unbalanced modern civilization. The opening sections of *TJO* provide a good example:

ONE	PUT YOURSELF IN MY PLACE
I-	
TWO	CHAPTER ONE CONTINUED
-solationism.	

The "I" as presented is a pun and a participant in oxymoron, the nature of pun being symbol with unresolved references; oxymoron provides references as contradictory but newly intelligible only in relation to each other. "-solationism" completes "I" and simultaneously contradicts the resolution in the context of an at once revivified cliché, "PUT YOURSELF IN MY PLACE." Here the very fabric of language registers instability—a frequent Brunner tactic.

Balder pictures symbolizing civilization caught at the threshold of catastrophe open *SOZ* and *TSLU.* "Context (1)" in *SOZ* presents a slice of the stock opening script for a television news program (it might be called "jive as cliché"). About five hundred words deliver time, weather, and inescapable commercials. Then, nothing. The actual news is unimportant; perhaps less truthful than the commercial rap. If you want to see for yourself, check the

very next section. The effect upon the first-time reader is that of a person
the rhythm of whose breathing has been interrupted. The second and third
sections in the first chapter of *TSLU* offer a vignette and actual signs:
"Carnage" is a depersonalized image of a man in the "jungle" of the Santa
Monica freeway. The beast-named cars have made him their quarry. He
bolts and is brought down by a "stingray," significantly an ocean dweller,
so that in the one-hundred-odd words of the section ocean submerges jungle,
and death is not by rending but by electrocution and drowning, perhaps. . . .
The abrupt hysteria of this section contrasts the sterile serenity of the one
that follows, "Signs of Times," consisting entirely of six signs, line-framed
on the page: "THIS BEACH NOT SAFE FOR SWIMMING; NOT Drinking Water;
UNFIT FOR HUMAN CONSUMPTION; Now Wash Your Hands (Penalty for non-
compliance $50); FILTERMASK DISPENSER Use product once only—maximum
1 hour; and OXYGEN 25¢" (*TSLU*, pp. 4–5). However, the transition from
ocean-dwelling "stingray" to an unsafe swimming beach and an ubiquitous
aqualung-like equipment implied by dispenser sale of filtermasks and oxygen,
is sustaining. Even so, the reader has experienced a lurch, as he will again
when he finds himself with Philip Mason, first of a number of important characters in the novel, in the next section. In the preceding sections the reader
has seen the day-to-day world in which Mason has been driving to work. If
the reader's stomach is in his mouth, it is because he has not enjoyed the one-
decade-in-the-future-of-Western-civilization conditioning that supplies Mason's
advantage.

In none of the three works does the calender go beyond one year's elapsed
time. I determine this by intuition in *SOZ*. In *TJO* Matthew Flamen, the
hero, beats the nine-month deadline upon which the renewal of his "spool-
pigeon" contract hangs. In *TSLU* twelve chapter titles from "December" to
"November" explicitly measure a year. This is the respective order of the
three works' publication. As such it represents a progression to more and
more explicit presentation of a timetable. It functions as a reader aid. In
addition, civilization runs and is constructed on timetables. A story of the
demolition and disintegration of civilization, provided with a timetable, is
suitably ironic. Furthermore, the planet-wide scope of the *SOZ* and *TSLU*
tales might obscure for the reader the virtual simultaneousness and swiftness
of events that precipitate stages in the destruction of civilization. "The
Happening World" sections in *SOZ* and the explicit calendar in *TSLU* counter-
act such an effect.

For the three works the principle setting is the United States, no more
remote in the future than sixty years in *TJO* and a decade or less away in
TSLU. *SOZ* lies somewhere in between. The "realism" of *TSLU* is more appalling than that of *TJO* because *TSLU* takes place more nearly in the present.
All the works present worlds that might be generalized as polluted. *SOZ*

features the population explosion, pollution with people. *TJO* presents a vision of the information explosion, pollution with data. *TSLU* may be the last word in "realistic" stories of a polluted planetary envelope. Brunner is successful in conveying the impression of a pea-soup-thick, toxic atmosphere layering most of North America. Each novel dramatizes the replication, multiplication, and exponential proliferation of commodities manufactured in a "progressing" civilization: data, people, and garbage. A device available for understanding and potential control of these expansions is the computer. Thus, located centrally or at the highly visible periphery of the stage of each novel are data-processing machines. In *SOZ* the machine is "Shalmaneser" (owned by General Technics Corporation), the capacities of which border upon actual sentience. Supersophisticated memory banks in *TJO* supply audio-visual simulacrums for television that earlier decades required actors and sets to produce. Matthew Flamen, the story's hero, "types" his muckraking TV programs entirely into the computers, which "construct" what the viewer actually sees. A computer produces actuarial tables for insurance companies in *TSLU*. The tables first alert the companies of the decline in life span that has hit American policy holders. The computers could help humanity. However, in each story the computer is a power-controlling implement employed by the captains of government and industry to manipulate mass man and direct world economy to their personal aggrandizement. In such a world psychological survival for the average man becomes precarious. He is paranoid in the "jungle" of civilization as his ancestors were paranoid in the natural jungle. However, faithful to the myth of progress, society's response to paranoid behavior, finding prisons and penal codes at least indelicate, is to replace incarceration with "commitment" . . . to a sanitarium.

In each work there is the threat of being declared insane and sent to an asylum waiting for those who would disturb civil "order." The sanitarium is a major setting in *TJO*. Rabble rousers and roused rabble alike are sent there for examination and "treatment." In *SOZ* Grace Rowley dies in an "official institution for the aged poor," and Donald Hogan is "eptified" by psychosurgical techniques developed for treatment of the mentally disturbed. The person "Donald Hogan" is destroyed in this treatment and a new personality substituted. Austin Train in *TSLU*, a Ralph Nader analogue, is neutralized for a time in an asylum.

As already noted, a striking feature of each work is the news media scenario. The dynamics of the novels are in part McLuhanesque, deliberately so, as suggested in "Context (10)" of *SOZ*. "The medium is the message." The title categories of *SOZ*'s table of contents, mentioned above, borrow authentic vocabulary from television production procedures. It is perhaps enough to say that *SOZ* is conceived totally as if it were to be presented on

television. *TJO*'s Matthew Flamen is a muckraking television news commentator. The fundamental motive for the action of the story is supplied
in terms of Flamen's attempts to assemble sensational scandal reports for
his program. The course of events in *TSLU* often turns on the influence of
Petronella Page's nationally aired interview with guests whose views are politically and scientifically controversial. In addition, there is Peggy Mankiewicz,
free lance muckraker. All the novels interpolate numerous sections that re-
produce slices of television news broadcasts or, as in *TJO*, clippings from actual newspapers. As one reads them, a media-conditioned narrative discourse
is soon and finally pervasive.

In handling the disposition of the characters in the three works, Brunner
has done at least three interesting things. Each work contains one or more
sections that function in whole or in part as a "dramatis personae." *SOZ*
has two such sections. The first is "The Happening World (1): Read the
Directions." It introduces about thirty characters, including most of the
important ones. The second is "The Happening World (16): Obituary" and
is self-explanatory. Chapter 54, "Division Street, Earth," in *TJO* is an anno-
tated list of thirteen major characters out of about fifty for the work. Notes
of random importance on about forty of the eighty-odd characters in *TSLU*
appear in the section entitled "Conspectus" in the "September" chapter.
The inclusion of such sections indicates that Brunner probably sees the novels
as dramatic presentations. The variations he has employed in making the lists
are happy ones. Nevertheless, he does not need the variation to achieve one
of the effects the lists convey. The name of a person on a list is essentially
depersonalizing. An individual's name and address in a phone directory is a
masking and an homogenizing rather than an identity-making. An obituary
is a list of bodies no longer persons. Brunner's glib annotations of the listed
characters modulate but do not neutralize the unpersoning effect of the listing. I doubt that he wishes to neutralize. The kind of civilization Brunner
is writing about does indeed "list" its populations into anonymity—names
becoming numbers in the techno-socio hive.

On another level Brunner is well aware that characters in the expository
fable of speculative writing are rarely more than stereotypes or emblems. He
sketches them well in this mode and has great fun in the storyteller's game
of naming the characters according to their character. Samples from *SOZ*
include Georgette Tallon Buckfast, headwoman of the rapacious and fast-
bucking General Technics Corporation—a supermonopoly; Arthur Golightly,
ironically named "heavy" mystical type who might as well be an airhead;
and Senator Lowell Kyte (what do kites and politicians have in common?).
In *TJO* there are Matthew Flamen, a muckraking firebrand; Lyla Clay, the
"pythoness," whose talent involves molding her psyche to the consciousness
of others; and three reporters surnamed "Spry," "Welborne," and "Quality."

TSLU features Petronella Page, television journalist, a consistent "front-pager," who interviews intrepid Lucas Quarrey, an honest scientist whose name means "light digging," suggesting his function as a source of truth. Philip Mason, the insurance executive, fills a "masonic" role in constructing the edifice of the capitalist state.

Brunner also includes what might be construed as an oracle character in each novel. *SOZ* has Chad C. Mulligan; *TJO* has Xavier Conroy; and *TSLU* has Austin Train. They may be shades of Henry James's "central intelligence" characters. All are socially conscious, visionary intellectuals, fugitive from earlier academic associations, socio-anthropology, psychology, and ecological biochemistry. As such, quotations from their "writings" or dialogue are made to speak explicit diagnoses of the problems of population explosion, cultural mental health, and planetary ecology with which the works are concerned. By using them Brunner avoids the dated "Dear reader, now I shall explain" convention. They are ubiquitous in the respective stories as soothsayers, frustrated messiahs, and general markers of the message that is to be taken seriously amidst a snowstorm of "messages" broadcast by the also ubiquitous "media" of the stories. One might, of course, question the reliability of the revelations of these oracle characters. They do, after all, speak in words—whose meaning is pervertible. Even so, their moods are wholesome and constructive. They are good men thinking about chaotic civilization. In this role they do not participate in personally intimate relationships with any of the other sympathetic characters. They are rather teachers in search of learners. They appear celibate, seasoned in existential ordeal, and "ordained." Across the works they are one voice, three ways named.

Having already covered ground pertinent to a description of Brunner's style, it remains necessary to address the matter of his style directly. Some additional facets need attention. His whole approach to the craft of fiction suggests a hypothesis about how he has dealt with the problem of literary style. To wit, he has eschewed any in the alternative to master all. Now is a good time to remember that he is an excellent poet, writes fine, tight short stories, and is a first-rate essayist. Moreover, he demonstrates a willingness to utilize "voices" of every genre from poem through senate record to grocery list. Thus, he is a bookkeeper, a nutritionist, a marriage counselor, a "miss lonely-hearts," a biologist, a tactician, a lexicographer, a minstrel—in other words, a multiply articulating everyman. Much science fiction is flat because it employs a monotonously homogeneous voice for all its characters. Robert Heinlein's janitors, for example, sound exactly like Robert Heinlein's main characters and the mistresses of his main characters.

For Brunner's purposes, Brunner is master of hundreds of voices. The effect of his writing is that it cannot be said to have a characteristic style; it has rather a trans-typical style, without which no speculative writing can be intellectually and aesthetically estimable—and I realize that I am digging a grave for such as Heinlein and Clarke and Asimov. This is so because, whether the speculative vision is of the parallel present, the past, or the future, alternative, retrospective, or extrapolated voices and styles are required to present it with fidelity and authenticity.

Brunner's collection of styles may be an outgrowth of his disposition to find the assimilation and collection of knowledge a desirable enterprise. *SOZ* teases the reader with references to Lewis Carroll, Bacon, Frazer, Krafft-Ebing, Shakespeare, St. Paul, and Poe, to name a few. In *TSLU* the erudition of the peripatetic Austin Train as garbage man is illustrative (p. 205):

"There's a woman sick upstairs! Taken barbituates in a room with the windows shut and one of these [flypaper strip] hanging up! Know what they put in these stinking things? Dichlorvos! It's a cholinesterase antagonist! Mix that with barbituates and . . ."

And since the foundation of knowledge is words themselves, Brunner likes to invent and transmute them as well as to compose dictionaries. Page 1 of *SOZ* at once sets about conditioning the reader with the vocabulary for the narrative: "Scanalyzer," "splitscreen," "depthunder," "autoshout," etc. *TJO* yields "rotachair," "comweb," "spool-pigeon," and "comp." *TSLU* supplies a word such as "jigra" but is generally more conservative in word invention.

Entries from a fictional lexicon called *The Hipcrime Vocab* lace *SOZ*. Example: "IMPOSSIBLE Means: *1* I wouldn't like it and when it happens I won't approve; *2* I can't be bothered; *3* God can't be bothered. Meaning *3* may perhaps be valid but the others are 101% whaledreck" (p. 5). *TJO* offers as chapter 31 "EXCERPT FROM A RELIABLE GLOSSARY OF TWENTY-FIRST CENTURY USAGE. MACKERO . . . Manager, agent (e.g.) for young self-supporting female (photographic model, freelance singer, pythoness, e.g.); specif. male, not derog. unless abbr" (p. 91). *TSLU* frequently supplies items such as the following: *"Lead: causes subnormality in children and other disorders. Exceeds 12 mg. per m³. in surface water off California"* (p. 16).

It is generally Brunner's principle to modify or invent a word as an efficient symbol for a condition, practice, device, social type, etc., for which otherwise a number of words must be employed. The intent is to make a complex phenomenon simple by facilitating the naming of it—especially a phenomenon for which it has not been politically popular to have an easy name. On balance this seems a good device to aid the encounter with the technological and psychopathological chaos of Brunner's "Americas." Alternately, he takes a common word like "lead" and defines it socio-physically, causing surprise and consequently new understanding in the reader. "Lead" is verbally relocated from safe to dangerous associations, as it has been physically relocated by a nature-poisoning civilization.

Brunner's mastery of styles further serves his intent that the novels be seen as well as read. Persons, places, things, and their gestalts are to be visualized objectively—even empirically—diminished as little as possible by subjective authorial associations. He is the antithesis of the "automatic" or "navel-contemplating" writer. With very little modification *SOZ, TJO,* and *TSLU* would be film scripts—if they aren't already so. The titles *Stand on Zanzibar* and *The Jagged Orbit* compress sharp, if somewhat bizarre, images. *The Sheep Look Up* is more abstract but plays upon spectacle with the word "look." The McLuhanesque composition of the novels plays to the visually conditioned reader. Within his scenarios he pays careful attention to the depiction of clothing ("yonderboys with their fantastical puffed shirjacks" *SOZ,* p. 147) and furniture styles. And he is energetic with the detail of signs, hallucinations, and graphic artifacts. *SOZ:* " . . . the sleek changeo-chrome finish of the exterior, within the millimetre thickness of which light was split into its spectral components" (p. 91). "Now the grace of elegant buildings was crumbling again under a bright mask of advertisements: *flagging vigour calls for Pontengel, MasQ-Lines take the world in their stride, ask the man who's married to Mary Jane.* . . . Across the display slanted the unrelated diagonals of fire escapes, spotted with piles of garbage like forest fungi" (p. 150). *TJO:* Lyla Clay's hallucination: "*Blink* the scarred wet green of a jousting-ground after a fall of rain, the grass slashed to reveal the brown earth underneath, a pavilion gay with long pennants, a dying horse screaming . . ." (p. 264). And *TSLU:* "Inside there was a handsome print, in copperplate engraving style, showing a tall man at a table with several companions handing pieces of cloth to a group of nearly naked Indians of both sexes . . . caption: . . . *The Governor of Massachusetts Distributes Smallpox-infected Blankets to the Indians*" (p. 292).

Finally, Brunner is a satirist. Indeed, if we entertain seriously the thesis of Kingsley Amis's *New Maps of Hell,* that speculative writing must yield a form of satire, Brunner may represent a modern epitome. The speculative writer and the satirist may be the same: both employ exaggeration, caricature, magnification, and extrapolation, all elements of classic reductio ad absurdum. Out of control the speculative and the satirical visions dissolve into nonsense (the unfortunate fate of 80 percent of speculative fiction). Brunner's control is excellent. Appropriately, *SOZ'*s millions multiply; its media are saturated and it is media-saturated; its citizens live in a dope fog. The facile collapsing diction of the narrative personifies a cultural psyche at an advanced stage of becoming nondiscursive, precedent to becoming non-verbal, precedent to becoming nonsentient. The narrative of *TJO* is more

conventional, sketching a dystopian nightmare in which the masses participate in a dream-myth, a pervasive televised pabulum strained and assembled
by computers—a comment on the innocuous fare of present-day media.
Crime has been stamped out by semantic fiat. Criminals are regarded as
"psychologically disturbed" in this "enlightenment." They are locked up
as before. As before the love that would give them personhood and sanity
is absent. The systematic exaggeration that *TSLU* exhibits may be a principal factor for disapproval of it by a few obstinate reviewers. The novel is
gloomy, scenically so. But the speculative satirist must insist that if you
emulsify your atmosphere with the stupidly proliferated garbage of your
civilization, you will have murk—gloom. Brunner is most clever in *TSLU*
with impositions such as the baby cooked in its mother's womb by an un-
shielded micro-wave appliance, or the polluted rainwater which reacts with
hair-set lotion to discolor or dissolve hair.

Traditional notions of satire suggest obligations to comic effect. Strategic
exaggeration often yields ludicrous absurdity, even when the underlying
theme is tragic. Joseph Heller and Kurt Vonnegut, who share a sensibility
with Brunner, can put readers in hysterics. Read in short sittings, Heller's
Catch-22, with a Yossarian who can't be insane because he claims he is insane, loyalty oaths required to get the salt passed in the messhall, and a Cap-
tain Minderbinder who sells chocolate-covered Egyptian cotton to the American army because his planned customers reneged, is funny, though the
novel's point is that war is painful and vicious. Vonnegut's "Harrison
Bergeron" makes comedy by means of a "United States Handicapper General," an office that sees to it that everyone is really equal, even if it means
hanging sashweights and little bags of birdshot on prima ballerinas. The
story's message, of course, is appalling. Brunner, too, is richly equipped to
create comic effect. *TJO* is most generous with devices such as "a satch filter in the comweb slot which routed advertising circulars directly to the
sewers" (p. 40), and the running chapter titles, of which the following is a
sample: "Proof Positive for the Assertion that it is not Impossible for a
Gutter to Run at Penthouse Level" (p. 80). "The Happening World (7)" in
SOZ supplies advertisements typified by "YOUR END TOO CAN BE A WORK
OF ART CONCEIVED BY YOURSELF ALL TRADITIONAL FORMS OF EXECU-
TION AVAILABLE IN RIGOROUSLY ACCURATE HISTORICAL DETAIL EXPLO-
SION DROWNING PRECIPITATION FROM HEIGHT ALL WEAPONS SELF- OR
OTHER-DIRECTED . . . FROM . . . THE COMPANY THAT MAKES AN ART OF
YOUR END FOR YOU . . ." (pp. 174–75). Immediately following is "(ART
A Friend of mine in Tulsa, Okla., when I was about eleven years old. I'd be
interested to hear from him. There are so many pseudos around taking his
name in vain.—*The Hipcrime Vocab* by Chad C. Mulligan)" (p. 175). In the
relentless horror of *TSLU* comic effect is appropriately stunted. When it

appears, it often works as surprise by bitter vulgarity: "Lady, I don't care if they're crawling up your cunt, you understand? I have thirty-five more calls to make before I get around to *your* rats!" (p. 382). Or it is macro-cosmically grotesque: "Smoke. . . . 'It's from America. The wind's blowing that way' " (p. 457).

In any case, the laughter evoked by Brunner's work is not as committed as for Heller's and Vonnegut's. I can merely suggest some explanations. Exaggeration of the crucial produces distortion that is tragic. The focus of *Catch-22*'s exaggeration and caricature is upon the niggling events and pro-cedures of World War II military experience. They are historically real and familiar—even domestic. Taken individually, a typical incident should not threaten the balance of civilization. The reader can laugh at it. Vonnegut's settings are futuristic and sociologically sweeping. But they often disarm the reader with their apparent whimsy. Events and furniture seem thrown together in a maverick allegory that does not compel us to referents in a real future. The reader can laugh at them. On the other hand, Brunner's comic effect, while it participates in these modes, outstrips itself. The laugh can-not last because Brunner's future events and furniture have the suggestion of authenticity. And for precisely this reason they do not strike many read-ers as immediately familiar. Even domestic detail has become strange, just when Brunner's careful extrapolation has convinced the reader that the de-tail, "the satch filter in the comweb slot" (future technology's answer to junk mail) is perfectly predictable. Understanding a Brunner exaggeration frequently makes it too late to laugh. Such an effect is mitigated by *TJO*'s "happy" ending, but in *SOZ* and *TSLU* Brunner's "reductio" refuses relief. Brunner transmogrifies Kipling's doleful posterity. Kipling, at least, is safely buried.

STEPHEN C. HOLDER

John Brunner's Short Fiction:
The More Things Change . . .

John Brunner is thoroughly conversant with the various elements of short
fiction. At ease with most literary forms, his work includes poems, novels,
and novellas as well as short stories. Although we are particularly concerned
with his short stories here, it should be noted that he generally conforms to
the accepted conventions for successful writing. His style, tone, imagery,
sense of plot, and conflict are consistent throughout the whole of his work.
The quality of his work varies, of course, but that is the case with most writers. What follows is an examination of the various elements of his short fiction, written (we hope) well before the mid-point in his career.

I

Brunner's stories fall into two categories by point of view used. Seldom
does he tell a story from a minor character's point of view; his stories are,
then, either first-person stories or stories told from the omniscient point of
view. The latter type predominates.

A primary advantage of the omniscient point of view is that it allows the
author to remain his own man. This is particularly important in stories of a
speculative nature. The author can offer just enough detail to provoke the
reader's imagination, to stimulate him, without giving away the whole plot
and without being bound to the idiosyncracies of a point-of-view character.
In a story such as "See What I Mean!" Brunner presents the reader with a
series of coincidences. A large Mercedes sedan, "driven by a small gray-
haired man in a dark blue suit and silver-rimmed glasses," rams the cars of
several diplomats in succession on successive days. The reader, noting this

coincidence, asks what this all means, which results in a kind of active participation which could not be achieved if he knew what the small man in silver-rimmed glasses was up to.

In addition, the omniscient point of view allows Brunner to involve the reader with whichever character Brunner desires. In "The Biggest Game" Brunner forces the reader to follow Royston for most of the story. Near the end, however, the reader suddenly learns that Royston is merely a pawn in a larger game, and is forced to shift his attention to Gruk and Kronze. Royston, of course, is not an admirable man—is not the sort of character with whom a reader would wish to identify. Moreover, Royston is not in a position to relate the end of the story, his own end coming somewhat earlier. But, if the reader knew of the existence of Gruk and Kronze from the beginning, there would be little sense in telling the story. "Coincidence Day" utilizes a similar point-of-view device. In that story Brunner again shifts suddenly to a larger context than the reader expects, a context which could not be handled were the narrator a part of the story itself.

The omniscient point of view gives Brunner the freedom to make up all the rules of the game himself. He can make decisions freely concerning time and space. He can bring old characters to a new setting, as in "Judas," or he can bring new characters to an old reality, as in "Fifth Commandment." He can take the reader forward in time to create a new arena entirely for the story, as in "Singleminded" or "A Better Mousetrap." In short, Brunner writes most of his short stories from the omniscient point of view—and takes full advantage of that technique.

When Brunner does use the first-person point of view, as in "Fairy Tale," it can be a stunning success. In that epistolary story Brunner faces a basic problem. For plot reasons, the protagonist, Barnaby Gregg, must be alone at the story's end. The story, moreover, depends on the distillation or refraction of circumstances within Gregg's mind, its basic meaning being inextricably bound to Gregg's understanding of the chain of events leading to his decision to write the letter. Here Brunner could have opted for the omniscient point of view. But it is important for us to be inside the protagonist's mind *only*, to perceive the others through his eyes, for the others—and indeed the problem of time lapse itself—are the vehicle of the story. Gregg's story is fantastic; therefore it is necessary that only he understand the events he relates. First-person point of view becomes a necessity.

A variation of first-person narrative, one that Brunner does not use often, is the story-within-a-story device. "Fair Warning" begins, "I had this from someone I met in a London pub, so it's only fair to stress that (a) it's at best secondhand and (b) as the phrase goes, 'names have been changed to protect the innocent' " (*Out of My Mind*, p. 9). Why, one wonders, did Brunner elect such a clumsy and archaic way of telling the story? Brunner does two things with the story. First, he takes advantage of an event actually happening in the news—the nuclear test ban treaty—for the basis of his plot. The plot itself records the collective stupidity of man. In a preface Brunner indicates that the story was written during a time of alarming international developments: ". . . a period when the human race was exhibiting with particularly alarming frequency its incompetence to manage its own affairs on the public scale. On the private scale we make out pretty well, but where two or three million are gathered together—watch out!" (*OOMM*, p. 9). He suggests that the events of the story may actually have happened, and that we remain alive only through the events that happened to two men, both of whom became unbalanced as a result of the events. Brunner could have made the same point-of-view choice as did Poe in "The Tell-Tale Heart," but the madness itself is not the point of the story at all. And the credibility of the story would have been seriously marred had Brunner allowed a madman to tell it.

Here Brunner faces an age-old problem: the intervention of divine guidance. His preface concludes: "Indeed, when the fever of international mudslinging is punctuated by an interlude of cool sanity, such as attended the signing of the test-ban treaty, one can't help wondering whether the world's leaders really had a lucid spell, or whether someone else came along and—well—intervened . . ." (*OOMM*, p. 9). What, after all, does a divine messenger look like? Is he "a form as tall as a man but not shaped quite like a man, although [he has] the same number of limbs, the same proportion of head to trunk, and [moves] with a manlike gait"? (p. 15). Does he speak "in perfect English with a strong American accent?" While it is perfectly acceptable for any writer to suggest an endless array of freakish aliens and bizarre creatures, the writer who deals directly with God's appearance needs to hedge his position very carefully. This Brunner is able to do by manipulation of point of view. The reader is left with the same problem posed at the end of Hawthorne's "Young Goodman Brown." Did the story happen or not? And the author, as well as the teller of the story, is off the hook.

In contrast is Mr. Wise, the narrator of "Orpheus's Brother." This story requires the reader to picture the narrator as a more-than-slightly unbalanced character, one capable of operating outside the conventional system of morality. Note the story's conclusion (*OOMM*, p. 36):

The boy was scrawny, of course, and was not enough to satisfy the panthers; when they had done with him, they would have rent me also, but by the power of the god I subdued them and returned them to their captivity. Then I picked up the smoldering cigarette which had fallen in the middle of the Turkish rug, but not before it had burned a hole.

I noticed that by chance—or perhaps not by chance—the spurt from the boy's jugular, released by a slash of panther claws, had drenched my Bacchus and made it run redder than wine. I cleared up all the other traces, but the blood on the statuette, I felt, was better left to dry where it was.

Here Brunner is able to detail the calmness and deliberation with which the narrator goes about his horrible deed, to suggest the real horror of the story, precisely because he uses first person.

One reason why any writer uses first-person point of view is to facilitate vicarious participation for the reader. Perhaps Brunner's most successful use of first person for that reason is in "The Totally Rich," a story told by a man who is capable of perceiving all the nuances of the action. Derek, the narrator, is in Santadora, the setting, to complete his work on a project known as the "Cooper Effect." Brunner chooses this character because Derek is an intelligent, sensitive, and thoughtful man, much as is the artist in James's "The Real Thing." The plot calls for intimate scenes between the narrator and the woman who is the subject of the story. Because the woman is the subject, Brunner could not have used an omniscient point of view; that is to say, it is important for the reader *not* to see the inside of her mind. The gradual revelation of what motivates her, as seen by the narrator, is what constitutes the story itself. As Brunner indicates in his preface, "This is about a temporary assemblage of subjective reactions called a woman, whose light— not her own—has blown out" (*OOMM*, p. 68). The conclusion of the story must be the product of the narrator's reaction to the sequence of events, for as in "The Real Thing," the narrator's growth is the real subject (*OOMM*, p. 95):

These are the totally rich. They inhabit the same planet, breathe the same air. But they are becoming, little by little, a different species, because what was most human in them is—well, this is my opinion—dead.
　　They keep apart, as I mentioned. And God! God! Aren't you grateful?

The tone, in the sense that critic I. A. Richards uses the word, of Brunner's short fiction covers a great range. Brunner is frequently playful, is often serious and somber, is predictably cynical. He is seldom, if ever, intimate. He controls the tone of his stories carefully, although occasionally he surprises even himself. The preface Brunner wrote to "Fair Warning," the first in the collection titled *Out of My Mind*, indicates this: "On consideration of the stories finally chosen for this collection, I'm struck by the prevailing pessimism of the whole. (The short list, as it leaves my desk, even contains the ominous total of thirteen items)" (*OOMM*, p. 9). The range of Brunner's humor alone is tremendous, and will be discussed later. Here, however, we need to be aware of the varieties of controlled tone found in his short fiction.

Brunner's playfulness is best exemplified, perhaps, by the relationship he creates between title and story. Often the device is simple: some common word or stock phrase is taken out of context and treated in the literal rather than the generally accepted sense. Titles, both of stories and of collections of stories, include such things as "No Future in It," "Even Chance," "Death Do Us Part," "Eye of the Beholder," "Protect Me from My Friends," etc. In the case of "Death Do Us Part," for example, we find that Brunner has applied the customary matrimonial term to two people who are already dead; their problem is that they have forgotten the escape clause in their wedding vows—a clause generally regarded as meaning anything but escape!

And Brunner frequently plays games with the reader as well. These are most apt to resemble the game Eric Berne, in *Games People Play,* calls "Now I've got you, you son of a bitch!" Brunner's "Factsheet Six" is an example. An active bond of sympathy is created between the reader and the apparent protagonist of the story, Mervyn Grey. Grey cannot understand why his investments are not doing well, and sets out to find the answer after his hireling fails. Brunner plants subtle clues along the way to let us know that he is not on Grey's side, but the clues are sufficiently subtle that the reader is apt to miss them. We are told, for example, that Grey was considered "Boy Wonder of the Business World." Only on rereading the story do we note that Brunner is using the nickname with tongue in cheek and derision intended. We are led to believe that Grey is an honest, public-spirited businessman who is beset by incompetents in his employ; we sympathize. Only at the end of the story, when Grey is overcome by a victim of his shoddy merchandising, do we learn that Brunner has been playing an ironic game with us. Grey makes an escape after murdering his gadfly—only to read tomorrow's headline (*FTDF,* p. 179):

This is the last issue of Factsheet. The publisher, Mr. George Handling of 29 Wyebird Close, Blentham, was murdered by Mr. Mervyn Grey in an attempt to stop this information being circulated.
He sat there for a long time thinking of a thousand people of great influence opening the plain envelope which would arrive in tomorrow morning's mail.

The last laugh is not given even to George Handling; it is Brunner's.

Brunner's mood can be playfully serious, too. In "The Nail in the Middle of the Hand," Brunner gives us Decius Asculus, a man who makes his living by crucifying convicted criminals. Asculus, a master of his craft, is inordinately proud of his skill. Throughout the story Brunner appears to adapt a neutral, even callous tone as he details Asculus's expertise (*OOMM,* p. 21).

Sometimes they screamed as the single gigantic blow drove the metal crunching through the flesh and the bone, and sometimes they fainted. He preferred them to scream. It indicated that they were strong and likely to live for awhile. It was a boast of his that—unless there was a knot in the wood of the crossbar—he never used more than two blows, the second being a light tap to fold the nail upwards so that it bent over and jammed the hand hard against the wood. The blood oozed from the holes; almost at once the flies swarmed down and began to sup at it.

But in the conclusion we find that Brunner has been reserving his judgment on the subject for a massive dose of philosophical seriousness.

"Fair Warning" is an example of controlled serious tone. At no time does Brunner permit the reader to think he is reading something frivolous. From the beginning the narrator admits that the story scares him; the way he tells us that fact leads us to believe that we might well be scared too (*OOMM,* p. 10):

He saw the pin, which I always wear, on my lapel—the sign of the Society for the Prevention of Nuclear War. Pointing at it, he said, "You're scared!"
I said yes, because it was true. After all, the pin was there to provoke discussion with people. But I hoped he wasn't going to pick an argument at the moment, because he was clearly rather drunk.
He said, "I'm in the navy. I'm scared. Sit down and listen."

Throughout the story Brunner bombards the reader with intense heat, the coming of zero hour, the decision that must be made, the danger of the mission and more. Although the ending of the story is unexpected, we receive it with genuine relief. The reader recognizes early-on that, when Brunner has something serious to say, it is indeed serious.

By far the most frequent tone in Brunner's short stories is that of cynicism. Time and again men fall into the traps which they naively lay for themselves. One wonders where Brunner stands to gain such an aesthetic perspective/distance. As individuals, men emerge as fools—uxorious or otherwise. Brunner's prefaces are especially illustrative: "Human beings have been defined as 'the only animals lazy enough to work hard at saving themselves trouble' " ("Fair," p. 17). "If the dolphins are in fact intelligent, let's for God's sake hope they are too intelligent to want any part of this human lunacy. And say so" ("Stimulus," p. 169). "It's reported that every time an executioner dies—the public hangman in Britain, for example—there are scores and scores of applications for his vacant post" ("The Nail in the Middle of the Hand," p. 17). There are many examples. And Brunner is equally cynical about the systems under which men operate and by which men are ultimately judged. "The trouble seems to lie in the fact that perfect inhabitants of a perfect society would need to be the children of perfect parents" ("The Last Lonely Man," p. 136). "I went after a job once. I didn't get it, and I was very glad. I didn't realize till after I arrived for the interview that there really was a company that had big signs up in its offices saying THINK" ("Protect Me from My Friends," p. 163).

Repeatedly Brunner writes stories about foolish men dealing with foolish, impotent systems. But the point of all this cynicism is this: we (Brunner and the reader) are *excluded,* except as *we* choose to involve ourselves in any way but intellectually with the madness that Brunner sees as rife in our world. The very nature of the cynic puts him somehow outside what is going on, gives him esoteric insights into the folly of men and circumstances. Brunner generously allows us to stand outside with him, to share his point of view, to laugh, however darkly, at the foibles of his fictional creatures.

As stated earlier, all of these varieties of tone and mood are controlled, are carefully built in. They show us that we are dealing not with a mere teller of stories, but with an acute observer of the human condition—one who can make us share his attitudes toward us for a time, even though we are dimly aware that we are somehow being manipulated.

I I

The human condition that Brunner observes, and allows us to observe with him, covers an astonishing range of time, space, and imagination. Some of his stories are historical in conception, as are "Fair Warning" and "The Nail in the Middle of the Hand." Some, such as "The Totally Rich," are basically contemporary in setting. By far the bulk of Brunner's stories, however, are futuristic in orientation. But the settings themselves are mere window dressing; *the human condition varies little, if at all, throughout the whole of Brunner's short fiction.* It has often been said that there are no new stories, and that the true test of a storyteller is how well he can retell an old story.

This means that the basic story motifs remain the same; the human experience is capable of only a limited number of basic wrinkles. And that number is limited, ultimately, by the number of basic human drives and instincts. Human needs for such things as love, protection, sense gratification, etc., do not change any more than the basic nature of mankind has changed throughout human history. Even the most benign author, in any period, is hardly naive enough to assume, for example, a universe premised upon altruism ... or to assume as a basic condition a universe free of ego. Such a universe never has been, and there is no reason to assume that such a universe ever can be.

To be sure, the word "progress" has meant a continual refinement of the ground on which men are compelled to search for the gratification of basic needs. And the word "culture" has meant a steady growth away from raw confrontation with the elements experienced daily. Generation by generation we as a society have layered on successive coats of the veneer known as civilization. Frequently we have been deceived that the appearance is indeed reality. Authors such as William Golding, with his books *Pincher Martin* and *Lord of the Flies,* are quick to disabuse us of that notion. So does John Brunner. Following is an analysis of some of Brunner's stories in terms of their basic conflicts—conflicts as old as man himself.

One of the basic conflicts used frequently by Brunner is man against man. Brunner's story "The Easy Way Out" is an example of this. Following the crash of the Pennyroyal, only two men remain alive: Andrew Solichuk and Pavel Williamson. Even before the accident the two had disliked each other, on both personal and philosophical grounds. Solichuk, a dissipated, overindulged, rich boy passenger had frequently offended Williamson, a competent, conscientious member of the ship's medical staff. It is a distasteful shock for Williamson when he learns that the only other survivor is the member of the ship's company whom he liked least.

Partly for selfish reasons—he does not want to be all alone—and partly for professional reasons—he has taken a doctor's oath—Williamson finds himself with the odious task of keeping the almost hopelessly maimed boy alive. To make matters worse, Andrew has with him a guaranteed-pleasant way to ease his pain and to commit the wildest kind of suicide imaginable. This device, known as "The Easy Way Out," is contained in a metal cylinder which the boy has in his luggage. Because the device is astronomically expensive, only the very rich can afford one; hence, it is the only device of its kind on board the ship. The device works for one person only.

Stifling his gut urge to let Andrew die, Williamson manages to save the boy physically and to rescue him from his preoccupation with death. The process, however, costs the good doctor his own physical and mental health. He decides to steal the EWO and use it for himself. The conclusion of the story and the final revelation, both for the doctor and for the reader, is a logical result of the basic conflict between the two men.

Again, in "The Last Lonely Man," Brunner uses man against man conflict. The resemblance between this story and Melville's "Bartleby" is inescapable. Mack, of course, is cast as the Bartleby figure. Initially his plight spurs an outpouring of generous emotions on the part of the hero, Mr. Hale. But as the story progresses, Hale's attitude changes. As Brunner perceives, sympathy is at best a temporary emotion; ultimately it must turn either to hate or to love. Such is the case in "The Last Lonely Man." Once having made a "contact," Mack guards it so jealously that the other half of the "contact," Mr. Hale, cannot breathe. What began as a kind, barroom gesture on Hale's part turns into a nightmare for him, building an uneasy suspense into the plot. The reader, of course, can see what will happen to Hale long before Hale is able to discern his own future, and it is that knowledge on the reader's part that creates the suspense. Brunner prepares us carefully for the gradual takeover of Hale's hitherto balanced faculties, probably the outstanding feature of the story: the conflict between the two men merges itself into the personality of one man, the protagonist. The conclusion of the story is an ironic change from the story as told by Herman Melville, however, The narrator in "Bartleby" is forced to live with the self-imposed knowledge of the consequence of the acts forced upon him by Bartleby. In "The Last Lonely Man" Hale *becomes* Mack; Brunner has taken the story a step further. In a sense, the conclusion of Brunner's story is not so horrible as the conclusion of Melville's, for Hale no longer has the ability to see what is happening to him—or, perhaps, he sees what is happening and is powerless to do anything about it, which is just as bad.

Another basic conflict Brunner uses is man against society. It is here that Brunner's characters are the most apt to appear as alienated or somehow estranged men, for the societies themselves tend to be forbidding and mysterious. In "Wasted on the Young," for example, Hal Page has made a deal with the powers that be to live as a wastrel. The collecting agent of the establishment, Thomas Dobson, is himself a strange character. His name is suggestive: the dobson fly is the finished product of the hellgrammite—a study in ugliness. Just as Dobson appears to be a civilized bureaucrat, the deal he represents is ugly beyond our wildest dreams.

Page's deal is roughly analogous to the process of taking out a loan; he is committed to the exchange of future labor in return for unlimited credit during his youth. Page thinks he has beaten the system by borrowing so much that he cannot work off the debt in a single lifetime; moreover, he will renege by suicide. But Page has miscalculated, for society has far greater depth and resources than he imagined. The loan will be repaid—and Page will suffer a terrible fate. From a moral point of view, of course, Page has cheated and deserves what he gets. Yet, Brunner imbues the story with the sense that the little man who tries to fly in the face of society is destined to failure. The forces in Hal Page's society are so immense that even the idea of competing with them, let alone outsmarting them, is absurd. And the Faust story has been told again.

In "Badman" Brunner takes the conflict between the individual and society much farther. Utilizing the old theme of good and evil wrestling for control of society, Brunner is able to create a society in which evil is utilized for good. One is reminded, of course, of the paradox of the fortunate fall, which runs something like this: if God has created everything, and if everything that God created is good, then God created evil—and evil must be good. The society in which Niles Boden finds himself has recognized this basic paradox. Knowing that evil inevitably creeps into the workings of organized society, the elders of the community have *purposely* incorporated the personification

THE MORE THINGS CHANGE . . .

of evil into their master-plan. And, ironically, the evilest-appearing parts of the society turn out to be in reality the very best parts.

The basic conflict is simple. Niles cannot understand why his society tolerates the presence of the Badman. With the confidence and naiveté of youth and idealism, he and his friends set out to overcome the personification of evil—only to stumble onto the basic workings of the society itself. But by discovering how his society works, Niles commits himself to becoming a part of it, turning his back on the generally accepted views of the world he leaves behind. The society in "Badman" is represented as essentially good; Niles's discovery initiates him into both society and manhood; although young for either, his courage and determination make up for his youth.

Dr. Hirnmann in "See What I Mean!" is confronted with the ignorance of the society around him. Peace talks have broken down—not so much due to the ill will of the participants, but to irreconcilable differences between the character types involved—and the only way for Dr. Hirnmann to get the talks off dead center is to operate somehow outside the system. Systems are all very nice, Brunner seems to be saying, but to trust in them too completely is folly. On the basis of the conflict of the intelligence of the individual against the collective stupidity of the system, Brunner presents Dr. Hirnmann, a man who is capable of taking direct action to resolve a seemingly insoluble problem. When all else fails, Dr. Hirnmann tries the obvious. And, obviously, it works.

The society Brunner presents in "Singleminded" is not, however, made up of good-intentioned people but of blundering diplomats. Don Bywater, the story's hero, has accepted completely the doctrines of his society, so completely in fact, as to become a virtual automaton in his thinking. His ship crashes and he is rescued by a patrol belonging to his country's bitterest enemy. Throughout his captivity, Bywater remains steadfast in his ideals (*OOMM*, p. 171):

He occupied his time on the long trip with dreams of the glory awaiting the man who had captured not only one of the fabulous moonwalkers but also the incredible secret of the telepathic virus. When the eggheads set to work on *that* one, things would really blow off—and imagine the lovely expressions on Soviet faces as they learned of the loss of their secret weapon!

Surely such uncompromising idealism is admirable! But the final joke is again Brunner's. The Soviet antagonist, Olga, knows this. She says, "People in the mass react strangely. They make less than the—what is it in English?" Bywater answers, "The sum of their parts" (*OOMM*, p. 174). And we learn that, in Brunner's estimation, the uncompromising idealism in this case amounts to suicidal stupidity. Instead of becoming a hero as he anticipates, Bywater becomes the ultimate villain.

"Singleminded" is, of course, set on a basic premise: the warfare of nations is folly, and the deeds men commit in the name of pugilistic patriotism are equal folly. Had there been no war atmosphere, Don Bywater would never have been faced with the dilemma in which he found himself. Brunner again makes use of an ironic twist to resolve the story; the man who opposes society in the name of patriotism opposes the *wrong* society. The policy of the system forces Bywater to abandon the evidence of his own senses, thereby destroying himself and his world.

In "A Better Mousetrap" Brunner creates another singleminded hero. Unlike Don Bywater, however, Professor Aylward is right; his problem is that no one will believe him. But Aylward is not competing with the noble ideology of patriotism as is Bywater. Instead, he is competing with societal policies based on simple human greed.

Aylward's colleagues regard him as a smart man, but one a bit too old to maintain his grasp on scientific reality. The futurism of the situation is indeed window dressing, for the basic conflict between a smart old man and a young world is as old as man himself. Of course, Brunner does not give Aylward the satisfaction of saying, "I told you so," when he is proven right, for what Aylward is right about is the destruction of the world (*OOMM*, pp. 193-94).

> Aylward's face, all of a sudden, went pasty-pale. He looked at Martinu and tried to speak but couldn't.
> Behind them, the girl looking out the window said in a tone of puzzlement, "Honey, what's the time?"
> "Three o'clock. Why?" said her companion.
> "I *thought* it wasn't dawn yet. And that isn't even the east over there. But look how red the sky is getting!"

And that is where Brunner ends the story. Aylward's knowledge that he has finally won his point can only leave him in agony. Again, Brunner has shown us the inability of the individual to change the course of society.

Matthew Arnold spoke of society as producing a "collective best self." Brunner sees society in many cases as producing a "collective stupid self." And on those rare occasions where Brunner sees society as a kind of moral caretaker of the individual, as in "Badman," the privilege of running that society is given to a relative few. Society, as it appears in Brunner's stories, operates to rob man of his critical faculties, of his ability to function on his own. The society becomes the reason why man lives, not the opposite, as one might hope.

The plots that revolve around the basic conflict of man against technology are perhaps the scariest of all. Technology is frightening because it has the ability to alter the human experience, to turn men into something else. "The Fourth Power" is a fine example of this. A man named Smith is given a fourth dimension—the ability to do a number of things simultaneously. He can teach himself to play the guitar, read a book, write a scientific essay, and listen to recorded music *all at the same time*. Brunner's message seems very clear: humans should not use technology to make themselves inhuman (*OOMM*, p. 135).

"In a four-dimensional continuum," said Holiday reflectively, "these non-spatial neuron connections of his, as you insist on calling them, would have served both to connect and store memory codes in the present and to provide a method of connecting them past to future. This accounts for his contemporaneous personalities; it also provided a source of energy for the physical realization of his acts. In other words, the energy which ought to be sustaining Smith here and now—in the shape of electrons, protons, neutrons, heat, and the rest—has been dissipated. Spent. Back there."

Wheelwell got to his feet violently. "You can't just sit there and talk about him as though he was a—a laboratory specimen! He was a human being!"

"Was," said Norstein glacially. "If you can think of anything we can do about it, let us know."

In this case, the men who created the laboratory situation have scared even themselves. What they have done is to make a man, a colleague, into something other than a man. By doing so, they have destroyed him. We all know that billions of brain cells are never used in the lifetime of a human being. Wouldn't it be wonderful, we speculate, to use our *entire* brain? Brunner speculates, "Wouldn't it be *terrible*?"

In "Judas" Brunner takes an old story into the computer age. The story begins, naturally, on a Friday. From the beginning the reader is disturbed by the futuristic ring of the old litanies. We see a statue of God and a choir singing a hymn, "The Word Made Steel." We hear a part of the service, "May he guide you in your appointed courses . . . serve as your eternal pivot . . . bring you at last to the peace of the true eternal round" *(FTDF,* p. 115). Brunner adds more futurism. The metal God's birth is the "Immaculate Manufacture. Blasted by a bolt of divine lightning from a chunk of untooled steel!" The result of this is to horrify the reader. Man has gone too far this time, the reader thinks. And, to be sure, man has indeed gone too far—for the myth of the metal God is a self-perpetuating myth, even as the Christ story is self-perpetuating.

Once again Brunner leads us to an ironic conclusion. At the end of the story we learn that the Judas character fulfills the prophecy set forth for the original Judas. As does the Judas of old, the hero of the story feels that he is genuinely performing a service for mankind, that he is taking the only option open to him. The déjà vu conclusion of the story is made more terrible by its futurism, and the old question comes once again to the surface:

"Did God create man, or . . ."

What, the reader is forced to wonder, is the effect of old stories on new?
Are there eternal truths? Have we indeed come full circle? If, as Brunner
suggests in "Judas," the function of the future is to repeat the legacy of the
past, the human condition is a frightening one. For in spite of his science
and progress, man has been on a spiritual treadmill throughout history. Human nature has not improved with technology. The more things change, the
more they remain the same.

We need also to consider what happens when man tampers with nature,
or confronts nature, as in "The Vitanuls." The plot is based on the discovery
of a life-prolonging drug. In the story Brunner suggests that we will be faced
some day with a serious population problem brought on by the ever-increas-
ing birth rate, by the skill with which doctors are able to keep people healthy
during their normal lifetime and, of course, by the antisenility drug which
keeps people from dying when they should. The futurism here is minimal;
we are well on our way as a civilization to creating such a population problem.

But Brunner goes even further. In addition to limited quantities of food,
fuel, and housing, he projects limited salvation. The number of souls is limited and newborns must do without. By tampering with the processes of
life and death, Brunner intimates, we are tampering with the wishes of God.
Who, after all, gave us the right to extend our own lives? For all we know,
the terrible blights currently sweeping Africa and India may well be examples
of God's wrath, incurred by overpopulating the globe. At first blush, the conflict would seem to be between two doctors, the young Dr. Chance and the
hoary Dr. Kotiwala. But we should note that Chance never does understand
the meaning of events. The conflict, then, is basically between man and nature or, by extension, between man and God. The story ends this way
(*FTDF*, p. 147):

". . . I owe you my thanks, anyhow. You've shown me what I must do."

"That's great," Chance said. "Just great. Here I come half across the
world hoping that you'll tell me what to do, and instead . . . What? What
must you do?" A final flicker of hope leapt up in his face.

"I must die," said the sunnyasi. . . .

Through death Kotiwala can provide at least one child the expectation of
salvation. Thus, unwise scientific development literally destroys man's spirit,
leaving him a ghostless machine.

III

The basic point made in the conflict analyses above is a simple one. Brunner's short fiction is more often than not set in the future. His stories, however, are peopled by characters understandable and credible in terms of what we know about man and his foibles *now*. This should not be interpreted as a weakness in Brunner's writing; on the contrary, it is a basic strength. Brunner himself is something of a historian; that shows very clearly. And it is reasonable to surmise that Brunner is of the "history repeats itself" school.

His stories are predicated on the basic condition of mankind as it has always been and, as Brunner projects, it always will be. The characters in Brunner's stories are governed by the basic needs, just as characters throughout history have been. They make *human* choices in the face of their predicaments, and that is what gives the reader such a high degree of catharsis, of pleasure through vicarious identification. Were Brunner to project a new breed of men into a new set of circumstances, the results would be disastrous.

The moral principles upon which Brunner's plot resolutions hang are traditional as well. Typically, Brunner's stories feature a moment of epiphany for the hero that occurs at the moment of climax. The hero realizes suddenly, inspirationally, what all the preceding action *means*, and that meaning changes his life—or his view of life. Note the similarities among the following:

"Nor I you. Because in spite of everything I have this—this weird feeling. I feel I ought to be so grateful to you."
He was rock-still for a moment; then he closed the gap between them in a single pace and brushed her cheek with his lips. (*FTDF*, p. 113)

For one brief instant he saw it, not as a collection of meaningless mind-straining curves, but as a plain clear statement in his own language.
It ran:
Well done, thou good and faithful servant.
Then it was gone, and in a voice suddenly husky, from a throat dry and constricted with wonder he said firmly, "We accept." (*Now Then!* p. 160)

He raised his head. Yonder in the darkness men and women were dying. Was it for a purpose? Did he believe Borghum's story? Would Ron and Leila have conceded that they had to die?
There would be no answer for a long time yet. Not until mankind came face to face with an enemy that might well not exist. (*Entry to Elsewhen*, p. 51)

It hasn't stopped. It's been quite a time blending Mack in with the rest of me; I hoped and hoped that when the *click* came things would be better. But they're worse. (*OOMM*, p. 152)

These examples could be multiplied many times, perhaps by the number of short stories and novellas that Brunner has written. In each there is a moment when the hero, assuming there is one, can look both backward and forward—can see what the past has meant and can predict what the future will mean.

Moreover, the moment of revelation is realized in forms of traditional moral values. Typically, the good earn their reward, the stupid and corrupt get what is coming to them. In "Wasted on the Young" we are glad to see that someone selfish enough to cheat his fellow men must pay his debt. We are happy to see Mr. Mervyn Grey of "Factsheet Six" called to account for his shoddy merchandising. Joe Munday of "The Trouble I See" pushes his luck too far; he takes advantage of his ability to sense danger. He deserves what he gets for abusing his power. We have no sympathy for Decius Asculus of "The Nail in the Middle of the Hand"; he was too good at what he did for a living—moreover, he committed the sin of pride. Don Bywater, of "Singleminded," deserves the consequences of his singlemindedness; he allowed his society to usurp his sense of right and wrong. The examples are legion. Note that the morality of the stories is the morality that we were all brought up on. New morality does not go with new settings; rather, the readers' morality stays with the readers. This is a shrewd tactic on Brunner's part.

A look at Brunner's humor is in order here, as it is a rather special feature of his short fiction. The humor might be characterized in two ways: a kind of playful attitude on Brunner's part, as mentioned earlier, and a kind of deeply black humor which can only come after the genuine despair of understanding some aspect of the human condition. For an example of the latter, we might well reexamine the end of "The Nail in the Middle of the Hand" (*OOMM*, p. 51).

"I found—" The centurion looked uncomfortable. "For the sake of all the gods, don't let this get around, or people may start talking. Well, there he was, sitting at the table in the middle of the room with a little flaring lamp in front of him, and his hammer, and a stack of nails, and he had nailed his own hand down on the table. He was just sitting there looking at it, with the other men in the room starting up from their sleep because of the sudden noise. And when I asked what he was doing, he just shrugged and said he was trying to work out how he could nail down the other hand as well. Perhaps by holding the hammer in his teeth, he said."

"What an extraordinary thing!" exclaimed the elegant young man, and started to talk about something else.

Several things about that conclusion are worth noting. First, the end of the story suggests the ultimate for the character Decius Asculus. He has gone over the edge into insanity; his professionalism has become his master. That ought, indeed, to be tragic. *But look at the way in which Brunner presents it!* The situation itself is absurd: a professional crucifier attempting to crucify himself—by holding the hammer in his mouth! The tone of the conclusion is almost clinical in nature; the executioner is "trying to work out" the details of his own execution. This is not a moment of personal agony at all; rather, it is a tactical problem for an expert in the field. And, in the same way Breughel's "Icarus" functions, *nobody* else is even remotely interested. The whole affair is related as an interesting anecdote. Detached, dispassionate, Brunner chuckles.

In his preface to *Time-Jump* Brunner discusses the nature of his humor. His perception of what he considers funny is particularly illuminating (*Time-Jump,* p. 9):

. . . science-fiction writers, by the nature of their calling, take the future more seriously than most other people [so] that there are so many black comedies and so few rib-tickling farces in the canon. It's for the same reason that, while I can guarantee that all the stories in this book are comedies, I decline to promise that all of them will split your sides.

The Germans have a term which English lacks, and it neatly spans the area where science fiction and comedy meet. They say *Galgenhumor:* gallows humor.

Right.

This is the humor of someone standing on the scaffold with the noose around his neck, distracting the executioner and the crowd with wisecracks in the hope that the cloud of dust on the horizon may—just by the slimmest of chances *may*—portend the arrival of a royal reprieve.

That description is particularly apt, as Brunner's brand of humor is just that: a holding action. His formula is simple: take a trend observed to be happening in society and project its logical conclusion. That conclusion is something we can laugh at *now;* we may not laugh at all if/when it really happens.

Take violence on television as an example. Day by day, year by year the tube brings into our homes programs of increasing violence. This has been going on for some time; there is reason to believe that it will continue. Brunner projects a particularly violent TV show, one that features each week a different practical way to commit murder. The show's success is measured by its DOA rating (Dead on Arrival) at hospitals across the country. In other words, the more people murdered in the way shown on the program, the better. Cathartic reasons aside, the program's raison d'être is ostensibly to help control population size (*Time-Jump,* p. 136).

The first show was a poisoning, and the choice of that method was a mistake. The second was a straightforward stabbing with a butcher knife, and within forty-eight hours the rating was a hundred percent up on the first week;

eighty-five butcher-knife victims DOA in the city area. And the third week we topped the hundred, and never looked back.

Good lord, the reader thinks, have they all gone mad? Yes, of course. And, in fact, the star of the show does go mad—bringing the show's rating to over a thousand for the first time. Funny? Yes, unless it really happens.

The weakest of Brunner's humor can be found in the "Galactic Consumer Reports." Three of these stories are included in *Time-Jump*. Modeled after the descriptions of durable goods in consumer magazines, the stories deal with "Inexpensive Time Machines," "Automatic Twin-Tube Wishing Machines," and "A Survey of the Membership." The basic device in these stories is to substitute consumer goods from some far-future time for the kinds of products being analyzed in these magazines now. There are two reasons why these stories do not succeed. First, the structure to which Brunner commits himself is too restrictive; he cannot move about as freely as he does in his other stories. A second reason, dependent upon the first, is that Brunner is forced by the structure of the story to make the products analyzed so futuristic as to be incredible.

Far more successful is "The Product of the Masses," a story that reinforces an old moral. In the story a prudish but brilliant woman biologist designs a kind of Trojan horse for use in sizing up a new planet. Unwittingly she de-signs a desirable female and attempts exploration of the new planet in the spring; all the males of the species attack. The moral, of course, is that one must not forget one's humanity. The story is a humorous fable dealing with the basic sin of the intellect.

I V

To what, then, can we attribute the popularity of Brunner's work? First, of course, Brunner is a fine storyteller. The stories he tells are not new, perhaps, except in their setting; but that, as illustrated above, is a basic strength. not a weakness. The age-old conflicts, the conflicts that Brunner deals with, are the very best stories of all. Who can imagine a sounder conflict than that of man against society or man against other men? What could possibly be of greater interest for the reader?

And we should note here that Brunner does not allow the structure of his stories to dominate at any time. Rather, he cloaks his conflicts in a wealth of detail, futuristic and otherwise. His characters, no matter how far removed in time or space from our present situation, are completely credible; they function on the basis of the same values as do Brunner's readers. Over and over he takes our present value systems and tests them in situations where they have never been tested before. They hold up well, for the most part. Through this kind of value-testing Brunner shows us that some of the periphery of our value systems is indeed superfluous. Does it matter much if, as in "Eye of the Beholder," the artist himself appears grotesque to the human eye with its built-in set of expectations? Of course not; the concepts of art, beauty, creativity and expression all remain valid. And, in terms of the human condition as we understand it, why shouldn't they? Most readers would be unable/unwilling to accept anything less.

For the reader Brunner's short stories constitute a participatory experience. This is a major factor in his popularity. The reader never feels that he is merely being manipulated, even though the last laugh is generally Brunner's. Some writers are not that way. Consider what James Joyce does to the reader in *Ulysses*. *Ulysses* is very much like the books we all used to get when, as children, we were invalided by some childhood ailment. One page might be a "connect-the-dots" game, another a "How many faces can you see in this picture?" page, and so on. Joyce did it by chapters. In one chapter he plays the game "How many literary devices/tricks can you find?" These include puns, palindromes, anagrams, etc. In another chapter he traces the whole development of the English language, beginning with Old English and finishing in the style of his contemporary naturalists. Once the reader discovers what it is that Joyce is up to, however, he becomes suspicious, becomes chary—for Joyce's game is not a fun one at all. Behind those chapters, one feels, lurks a cold, dispassionate son-of-a-bitch. Not so with Brunner. When he plays games, they are friendly, playful games. He even allows the reader to play with him. We delight in the discovery that *Now Then!* is a deliberate reference to changing time periods. We look forward to finding out what Mrs. Bedonebyasyoudid is going to do to justify her name. And so on.

In addition, Brunner has developed a following; his books are scrutinized by afficionados, by a public that is thoroughly conversant with his games, his techniques, his style. And he is pleasing that public. That would seem to indicate that he is growing as a writer, is fulfilling his obligation to his craft. That, by itself, would be enough; but . . .

RONALD PRIMEAU

"It Goes Bang": Structure of Rhythms in the Poetry of John Brunner

John Brunner's poetry is about poetry—what it is (and what it isn't), what it has been in the Western tradition, and what it can be to help man either survive in this world or build new ones. While his poetry is often satire or explicit social protest, his primary subject is the poem itself as liberating music. Each poem is a further statement and embodiment of an aesthetic which he describes pointedly in the title of his first volume, *Life in an Explosive Forming Press* (1970).

Brunner likes to refer to himself as "a working writer, a craftsman—if you like, a wordsmith, a person whose trade is arranging words on paper"("Genesis of *Stand on Zanzibar*," 1970, p. 35). As a matter of course, a working writer experiments with various forms, shaping words into fiction, essays, popular songs, and poetry. He has matter-of-factly referred to this variety in his works as his "dilettante-like spread of professional interests." Though poetry occupies a relatively small place in his canon, it is traditionally the genre in which the "wordsmith" is best able to sharpen his tools and thereby purify the channels of his perception. Brunner describes the forces working on him in an image of form releasing energy (*GSOZ*, p. 37):

For some time previous to my commencement of work on this book, I'd been growing increasingly dissatisfied with my regular science fiction writing. I could feel processes at work around me shaping the future, like a crazy explosive-forming press: Black Power and the Beatles, LSD and Vietnam, hippies and skinheads—and I was becoming more and more frustrated at my inability to capture all of them, or even a fair proportion, simultaneously. Once I'd made the breakthrough I've described, and turned the regular novel form on its head to make the world the protagonist, I found I could slam into one massive great book scores of predictions, fears, hopes, suspicions concerning everything from urban violence through social psychology and the sexual revolution down to trivia like what sort of TV set you may be watching forty years from now.

Brunner has defined prose as "words in their right order," and poetry as "the *best* words in their right order" ("An Evening with John Brunner," 1973).[1] Writing poems chiefly as a way of "experimenting with form, with pattern," he decides first "what sort of shape the poem is likely to have" and then selects "the proper form for it." The poet is a "wordsharp" who "grim-mouthed" must "deal a paradox" from "the bottom of his pack of images." A poem "goes bang" in "an explosive forming press"; it "carves ... with violence meat," "gulping down pain like food;" it is a "precision instrument ... to shape an event in four dimensions." The poetic process is a "structure of rhythms," which is "human," "alive," "reacts," "raises hell"; it's a "broken splash gulp grab and missed it now god DAMN," and its business is to "mark paper and make funny noises." Poetry is a sculpting of words in time and space, as they appear on a page, as they sound to an audience, as they are breathed by a reader. Poetic "statement" explodes into packed images of poem as sculpture.

"Life in an Explosive Forming Press" represents, as much as it states, his aesthetic. In a subtitle he calls the work "A Modern Sonnet" in order to manipulate the reader's expectations about conventional form.[2] Before they are even in tune, the reader's presuppositions are immediately violated by a first line that beings with "and." A settled sensibility expecting suspenseful build-up in the form of the sonnet is repeatedly dislodged by middle-of-the-sentence syntax, an unidentified "it," and a "bang" that rather nondramatically just "goes" (*Life in an Explosive Forming Press*, p. 5):

> and it goes bang
>
> and suddenly it's Mister Jimi Hendrix
> commenting on the men who mend ricks'
> roofs with plaited plastic straw and then hang
>
> a string of garlic on a Cadillac
> and order half a pint of Tristram Shandy
> and hobble down Calcutta's streets on bandy
> legs appealing to the men who came back
>
> stick-gelignite-in-arse aboard Apollo
> rapists of Jonson's chaste celestial queen
> drunkards on apple vinegar and honey
> two bucks a head it cost but who can follow
> the witness of the stars where he has been
> claiming he's only in it for the money
>
> Warhol the time is now

Jarring juxtaposition cracks images against each other until the enigmatic Warhol is exhorted either to restore order or cart everyone away. The speaker's allusion to the "half a pint of Tristram Shandy" suggests Brunner's fascination with experimental structures and cinematic techniques. Commenting on Vonnegut's indebtedness to Sterne's "vignette-style chapters," Brunner weaves Sterne-like cinematic montage into his own aesthetic: "In a world whose individual events are being shuffled like a deck of playing cards, I find this approach extraordinarily apt, although it's sometimes accused of being cinematic rather than novelistic" (*GSOZ*, p. 42).

The scenario of "events" "shuffled" like a deck of cards is also the motif of Brunner's most explicit commentary on the poet-wordsmith as "Wordsharp" (*EFP*, p. 19):

> Grim-mouthed the would-be wordsharp must submit
> the little finger of his deckhold hand
> to have the top joint severed
>
> that he may the more readily
> bring from the bottom of his pack of images
> this one with that to deal a paradox
>
> to make where averages decree a nothing-much
> a royal flush ace-high in scarlet spades

Casually, almost flippantly, cool yet tight structure dictates the process to which the wordsharp must "submit" and through which he creates paradoxes. With "grim-mouthed" tenseness, the flick of a finger turns a "nothing much" into an explosion of scarlet. Though Brunner unifies "Wordsharp" in part through the use of a dramatic frame, he also embeds his images in what Charles Olson has called "composition by field, as opposed to inherited line, stanza, over-all form, what is the 'old' base of the non-projective."[3] Brunner's use of "projective verse" means that he often sets up a poem on the page structurally so that it will most closely approximate its rhythms as it is read aloud. Each image works also according to what Pound and the Imagists called the "language of common speech," which itself creates "new rhythms." Brunner's images most resemble what Pound described as "hard and clear, never blurred nor indefinite." And his style further demonstrates the conventional Imagist belief that "concentration is of the very essence of poetry."[4]

Often Brunner speaks through an observer-narrator who blends self-reflective commentary with dramatic incident and dialogue. The result is generally images tightly packed in a particular spatio-temporal context, as in "252 E. 7th Street, 9 P.M. 15th August, 1968" (*EFP*, p. 28):

Man is a bag of blood.
If you puncture the bag, it leaks.
Sometimes, but not always, it's self-sealing.

Meant, I think, for wood,
It carved instead with violence meat
In a dirty hallway, under a cracked ceiling.

Gulping down pain like food
She plied the metal gouge with greed,
Its point half an inch red. Later, healing;

But, while stabbing: "How could
This who am I lose lips and tongue and speak
With a mere tooth, this fang of steel, unfeeling?"

Here Shakespearean soliloquy gives way to a conversational tone that merges images of advertising ("self-sealing") with puns on the king's English ("violence meat"). Typically again the speaker's syntax captures, camera-like, both an ongoing process ("gulping," "healing," "stabbing") and the negation of such process ("unfeeling"). The speaker in this poem also reflects Brunner's surgical disposition as craftsman and wordsharp. A "practicing writer" too "punctures" and "carves;" he "gulps" and "gouges" and "stabs" hoping to create feeling and healing with his "fang of steel." Syntactically, the poem is jarring: pronouncement ("man is . . .") at first qualified ("if . . . sometimes . . . I think . . .") abruptly changes direction ("instead . . .") and scene ("gulping down . . .") and time ("later, healing . . .") and outcome ("But . . ."). The speaker even wrenches syntax ("This who am I") and sentence structure ("How could . . . unfeeling?") to reinforce with jarring pattern the emotion of present experience. Again the subjects are the poet and the poetic process.

Similarly, in a longer work that closes his first volume, Brunner combines his aesthetic concerns and his well-known (especially to readers of his fiction) talent as a satirist. "Multiple Choice" is both a serious attempt to dislodge traditional literary assumptions and a parody of a class lecture or scholarly analysis of the meaning and uses of poetry. One discovers who a poet is and how a poem works through "programmed patterns of deduction" recorded on a print-out sheet check list. Even when "it's hard to say," answer "just 'yes' or 'no.' " If it's human, alive, reacts, "raises hell," it *may be* a poet:

Does it mark paper and make funny noises?
(We're getting close, but there are several choices—
Most prepubescent children do, as well.)

While the piling up of details makes a certain amount of literal sense, the absurdity of the programmed format predominates in the almost bitterly satiric closing images (*EFP*, p. 31):

> ... Well, this lecture
> Can't be exhaustive, but we've covered all
>
> The major points. During the next two weeks
> We'll learn to analyse the types of poem,
> To tell a triolet from a pantoum
> By paper chromatography techniques.

Brunner's propensity to create layers of interlocking yet conflicting tones contributes significantly to the complexity his speakers manage to sustain. As a fade-out, "Multiple Choice" surfaces inner conflicts faced by the surgeon-poet who now cuts loose his creation for analysis by the critic trained in "paper chromatography." Curiously, although the poem concludes his first volume, Brunner generally introduces his poetry readings with it. The tone is learned, pompous, even smug, and ever-threatening, beckoning the audience (with Brunner—as distinct from his speaker—presiding) to explore and to enjoy exploiting the poetic resources of "the subtlest language ever evolved on earth."

In his second volume, *Trip: A Sequence of Poems through the U.S.A.* (1971),[5] Brunner records his coast-to-coast thoughts and experiences. Poems about poems are thus embedded in startling images of movement and tension. "Surfers' Tension" suggests the starkness of William Carlos Williams coupled with Brunner's own fascination with explosion: "green sea blue sky and not-quite-yellow sand UP/ease forward supported by fiberglass with fin/ a foot ahead of the white water UP." In "Driving Styles" he plays upon "brand image" where the "seats fold down for seductions" and poetic *image* as "gun" or "chisel" used "to shape an event in four dimensions/of distance, displacement, time, and speed." In the dramatic frame of a *journey* as a "structure of rhythms," Brunner creates an opposition between the speaker ("I") who has a sculptor's sense of movement crashing through space and another unidentified character ("you") who blatantly lacks all sense of the ongoingness and risks of everyday human experience. With little sense of kinetic danger, the "you" sees driving as "symbol,/ Expression of power/ ... Air conditioned package, with radio on." This tension between static power package and "deadly precision instrument" reverses conventional expectations. The careful driver with "ceaseless attention" maintains control on the sculpting process, and the speedster is left with "a wreath" at his funeral. Such oppositions reinforce each other and throw into sharp relief Brunner's aesthetic of poem as controlled explosion sculpting rhythms.

Two further examples of Brunner's use of counterpoint illustrate again the range of his poems about poetry. In "Presentiment" he creates a short "urban" epic contrasting a speaker's real perceptions and his illusions of a

New York mythos (*TRIP*, p. 25):

> Presentiment
>
> I can hear the drums
> But it's four kids beating on a steel lamp-post
>
> I can hear the storm
> But it's squad cars howling and an ambulance
>
> I can see the lightning
> But it's a flash from a subway train
>
> I can smell volcanoes
> But it's someone lighting another reefer
>
> Earthquake! Earthquake!
> The Empire State Building's falling down
> *New York*

Again the images explode into each other and a pattern of contrasts grows into a "beating," "howling,""lightning,""falling," "flash." Finally, in "Dropin" the counterpoint suggests at once a serious aesthetic of collision and a speaker who pokes fun at each fuse as it prepares to ignite (*TRIP*, p. 30):

> Divided by the barrier of our common language
> *dual carriageway*
> *divided highway*
> some people don't seem to know quite what to make
> *spanner*
> *wrench*
> of visitors who've no opinions about Benedict Arnold
> *American Revolution*
> *War of Independence*
> tolerate a thriving communist party
> *stand for Parliament*
> *run for Congress*

As the final poem in the collection, written while traveling from California to New York, "Dropin" dramatizes Brunner's ability to combine the serious and the playful in an aesthetic that depends on contrasting rhythms. The speaker intent on sculpting a rhythm is able to sharpen his reader's sensibility and at the same time explode into an apotheosis of fun.

Poems in which the speaker has a good time stretching and bending the potential of language are also an integral part of Brunner's aesthetic. Brief recollection of his theory of fiction—science fiction especially—illustrates the importance of poetry about everyday things in his overall canon. Again, in *GSOZ* he stresses the significance of the artist's capturing the here-and-now (p. 39):

Because the author of an sf novel is at least attempting to operate at the forward, not the rearward, interface of now, he must recognise the asymptotic curve of the difficulty of his task and—if he is to make any progress in his work and not be content to repeat himself—accept the increased challenge involved in coming closer to the present.

Brunner's poems about words as well as his social satire are attempts to convey a sense of the "forward interface of now." He elaborates: "For me, the ultimate manifestation of the writer's craft is to take some theme which anyone but a writer would dismiss as impossibly trivial, and by application of his skills make it fascinating" (p. 40). Brunner as theorist thus sounds like Wordsworth or perhaps any practicing poet who works by "projecting the mores and emotional responses of realistic human beings in a realistically different environment" (p. 40).

In public poetry readings Brunner enjoys himself. He has a good time reading, and he becomes the speakers he has created. He introduces his readings by expressing the hope that he will "give an indication of some of the sheer *Fun* which I get out of the English language and the way in which it can be exploited." He repeats often that he gets "a hell of a bang out of . . . playing around with words" and that—"purely as an exercise"—he especially enjoys "fooling around with themes that look as though they might generate a poem" (*EWJB*). Nowhere is his "fooling around" more evident than in "Wishful Thinks," where he blends both the forward *and* rearward interfaces of now to create serious commentary:

> I should like to spend the treasure of the Vatican
> On socks and shoes and coats and frocks
> And lollypops and dolls and model trains
> For all the kids their parents didn't want and can't afford

As well as biting *and* playful humor (*EFP*, p. 13):

> I should like to introduce Patakos to Plato
> I should like to introduce Hitler to Moshe Dayan
> I should like to introduce Jesus to Pius XII
> I should like to introduce myself to Marilyn Monroe

In "A Flyting upon Mr. X" the speaker resurrects the tradition of poetic roasting. The last two in fifteen stanzas of accumulated abuse illustrate the technique (*EFP*, p. 17):

> Poisonous, evil, maggot, weevil,
> > Dung-beetle, carrion crow!
> Bringer of illness, germ, bacillus,
> > It's time for your overthrow!
>
> Stuff your phoney stale baloney,
> > Asinine adipose bore!
> Bunkum-spewer, open sewer—
> > I CAN'T STAND ANY MORE!

Brunner also transforms the "trivial" into the "fascinating" in his unobtrusive dramatizations of the commonplace. There is, for example, the kettle that "whistled quietly to itself." Though it realized "it was not the original kettle/ that James Watt was watching," it nevertheless "liked to sit on the hob/ and kid itself that it might be." There is the minstrel who goes to the alehouse, kisses young Peg, and tears her gown: "And she gave my ears a mighty box/ And I'm sitting here in the public stocks/ And it's just as well 'cause she's got the pox." There is the "Boy, aged 10, California, 1970" who says "I like being ill" and concludes (*EFP*, p. 26):

> I want ulcers, I want blisters
> I want gonorrhea and gout!
> I want ringworm like my sisters'—
> I'm afraid I'm missing out!

The organizing principle of *TRIP* recreates ordinary events in a "realistically different environment." The opening poem thus dislodges and then refocuses the reader's perception of an ordinary flight, through careful manipulation of literary allusion, puns, and structural innovation ("Flapyak 707," *TRIP*, p. 5):

> Wrap in a label the silvery fuselage,
> Brand us in bold letters CATCH AS PAN AM
> with the small print encircling the left lower border:
> *Contains*—Peter Gurney, Peter Davy, Marilyn Schultz, Sarah
> > Blutwurst, Old Uncle Tom Cobleigh and all duly vaccinated
> > against their arrival in the U.S. of A.
> > > *Jet Clipper "Friendship"*

And there is "Rib and Development" which Brunner has set to the tune of "California, Here I Come" in order once more to juxtapose an unconventional perspective with the reader's predictable and traditional associations (*TRIP*, p. 14):

Comfort station here I am,
Visiting the john or can,
Witnessing that the world may know
Easy come and easy go.

A few more titles will illustrate the mock-epic grandeur Brunner projects
upon the present interface of now: "Ellay and N Virons," "Déjà Vu,"
"Avaunt, Guard," "Frig Id," and "In Praise of Decadence." Patterns of humor from light puns to invective thus orchestrate Brunner's musical rhythms
and provide the clearest link between poems embodying his aesthetic and
his satire or poems of social comment.

In line with his view of the poet as sculptor, Brunner has had his fiction
linked by many critics to the structure of film. Recognizing that his own
approach to fiction is often "accused of being cinematic rather than novelistic," Brunner accepts the distinction and concludes that most writers "and,
more importantly, their audience, nowadays go to the movies" (*GSOZ*, p. 42).
Reviewing *SOZ*, Norman Spinrad describes the work as "a literary construct
consisting of one novel, several short stories, a series of essays and a lot of
what can only be called schticks intercut and put together like a film. *Stand
on Zanzibar* is not a novel; it is a film in book form."[6] The extent to which
Brunner "applied a film technique to prose fiction" again underscores obvious similarities between his science fiction at "the forward interface of now"
and the social satire in his own poetry.

Brunner's poetic satire is equally effective, though less immediately jarring
than his poems on poetry. His pack of images deals contrasts, paradoxes;
exploding sounds turn back upon themselves to create at once self-conscious
irony that is personal with consciously limited perspective, and direct commentary which itself carries less force but which serves to counterpoint other
"wordsharp" images. Brunner's satiric poems are generally about using people,
things, and destructive technology in ways that are out of tune with the basic
life processes. Opposition between the "simple" and the "perilous," "freedom" and "repression," images of mind cut off from body, of napalm destruction and the corruption of money are of course stock subjects for the
satirist. Less obvious are his images of urban society, officials co-opting
"movements," and the hypocrisy of the white liberal.

As poetic sculptor, Brunner has his satirical persona surgically cut and
reshape his perceptions in three basic patterns. Above all else, his speakers
emphasize a deterioration in modern man's inability to see life whole as an
ongoing process. And measured against this standard of an integrated "felt"
existence, his satiric vision sharply attacks the perversions and distortions
of mechanized society and man's interiorizing of its wrenched, dualistic
values. Finally, as corollaries to this general state of the life force run amuck,

the speakers probe the dissonance of violence, greed, and hypocrisy in the Present Interface of Now.

"Balance" is itself a key term in Brunner's world of explosion and disequilibrium. In "On Balance" he suggests that *using* people, things, and human reason itself perversely merely to escape momentary difficulty produces destructive technology. Child abuse, slavery, and official execution are products of "the pure white light of reason" gone out of balance. Similarly, in "He Was Such a Nice Chap—Why Did He Do It?" Brunner portrays the impotence of the disintegrated psyche that doesn't understand "the art of letting go," a picture of modern man whose mind is "cut off from his body." Emerging from the dualism of man's fragmented perceptions and values is a sense of hopelessness that finds expression in the overt self-destruction of "He took some pills, alone, and went to nothing." In "The Silent Majority" the poetic satirist merges the Rearward, Present, and Forward Interface of Now (*EFP*, p. 14):

> When the invading army crossed the hills
> and left a trail of slaughter and rapine and rape
>   the silent majority held their tongues
>
> When a man crawled along the gutter half-blind
> crying for help because he'd been mugged and robbed
>   the silent majority decided not to get involved
>
> When the police beat up a pregnant girl
> in plain sight of everybody on the street
>   the silent majority drew their curtains fast
>
> When their fathers and mothers were taken away
> because they remembered when things weren't like this
>   the silent majority were glad of the extra room
>
> When names were abolished and numbers were instituted
> and lives were digested into a central data-bank
>   the silent majority obediently learned their numbers
>
> When the handcuffs were clasped around their wrists
> when the bullets found a target in their bellies
>   the silent majority spoke and said "It wasn't me!"

As a final collapse from within, all hope for communication vanishes ("Bones/—piled-up bones—/and electronic ears/Listening and listening/ while no one spoke") and even revolutionary "movements" are co-opted, as in "Excerpt from a Social History of the Twentieth Century" (*EFP*, p. 23):

The establishment got the better of the optimists
who foresaw a revolution based on LSD.
By 1997 the shelves of the supermarkets
were lined with packages heat-sealed in polythene
labeled "Instant Paradise, two for forty-ninepence—
> Just
>> add
>>> acid."

Embedded in Brunner's vision of the disintegrated personality are the
nightmares of modern man's violence, greed, and hypocrisy. The bitter contrasts of "Coffintree Carol" juxtapose the "lifesize doll" in its "snug Christ-
mas crib" with "the head of a baby/ charred to black crackling/ most likely
by napalm." Similarly, the sardonic speaker of "Admission Free, Emission
Somewhat More Expensive" orchestrates a Satanic litany of corruption from
within (*EFP*, p. 11):

> Hooray for the free world baby
> hooray for the marvellous place
> you can recognise any time baby
> by the smell of its cordite and MACE
>
> Hooray for democracy baby
> hooray for the right to do what
> your popular government tell you
> and not to do what they do not
>
> Hooray for the freeloaders baby
> who are free of the streets and the slums
> free winoes and hopheads and dropouts
> free junkies and beggars and bums
>
> Hooray for the GREAT SOCIETY
> a chicken in everyone's pot
> just make with the chicken bit baby
> but take care you don't have the pot

Finally, the pervasiveness and startling intransigence of greed resonate
from a poem constructed to look like a fragment (*EFP*, p. 17):

> America
>
> I planted the seed of a people
> And it came up money

Brunner places the poem on the bottom of a right-hand-side page in order to manipulate the reader's expectations as he turns the page to look for more. The result is carefully calculated frustration.

In a society of fragmented personalities, perhaps the worst insult is the hypocrisy of the persistently self-righteous spokesman for "progress." In "Asking" Brunner depicts the white liberal whose solution to injustice always rests on "a little longer" and "patience friend." Filtered through several points of view, the speaker locates the real meaning of ritualized dialogue:

> (meanwhile come up to my nice clean new
> apartment & take a shower to get rid
> of the lice & put on this here new
> white nylon shirt & after wiping yr
> black ass with my new soft tissue
> in alternate shades of turquoise &
> emerald come out on the patio &
> mingle with my gracious acquaintances
> as proof of my enlightened attitude)

After carving up and exposing the subtlest predispositions and attitudes underlying racism, the speaker avoids imposing his own values (*EFP*, p. 27):

> all we can be sure of is this
> we are asking more of him
>
> than anyone will ask of us
> if we live to be 1000.

In the "Sequence of Poems through the U.S.A." the persona-voyager explores modern man's disunified sensibility through an acute sense of place. Thus, "Ellay and N Virons" plays on the contrasts between "Handsome city once upon a maybe" and the Biblical parodic collapse of "In my father's studio you have many mentions—/Near Hollywood and Vine." Las Vegas is, of course, "Money money money money money money money money money," and New York is "human garbage flushed down a drain," "gracious living and faceless dying." Finally, poetic structure is especially significant in the *Tristram Shandy*-like apparatus of *TJO*, where Brunner uses everything from found poems (p. 294) and parallel columns shifting point of view (p. 167), to the titles of chapters 1 ("I–") and 2 ("–solationism") and 99 ("You–") and 100 ("–nification"). One is tempted to look upon such bald emphasis on structure as gimmickry. But the self-conscious manipulation of pattern is itself an essential part of Brunner's interlocking of theme and technique.

As poet, Brunner starts with the twofold assumption that words create and define the worlds we know and that the process of creating through words is important *and* fun.[7] He therefore develops an aesthetic in the poems themselves, an aesthetic of "the best words" sculpted into "their right order" to create humor that can be subtly disarming or supercharged, and social commentary that can be witty satire or explicit protest or both. Brunner and his speakers thus self-consciously observe themselves in action. Following the influence of *Tristram Shandy,* Brunner the poet writes poems about poems, theories about theory, and satirizes satire—all of which help create the sense of distance that pervades his works on the whole. Commenting on the almost absolute fusion of theme and structure he is seeking in his poetry, Brunner acknowledges that he wants "to be able to discipline in formal pattern . . . things which ordinarily are too terrible, too disgusting, too repulsive to be accepted—except with a shock and a shudder" (*EWJB*).

NOTES

1. Brunner acknowledges a debt to Coleridge here. Several passages in *Biographia Literaria* are probable sources. In ch. 14 especially, see Coleridge's classic definition of a poem as "that species of composition, which is opposed to works of science, by proposing for its *immediate* object pleasure, not truth; and from all other species (having *this* object in common with it) it is discriminated by proposing to itself such delight from the *whole,* as is compatible with a distinct gratification from each component *part.*" See also his discussion (in ch. 17) of "the *best* part of language." Samuel Taylor Coleridge, *Biographia Literaria,* 2 vols., ed. John Shawcross (London: 1907).

2. In addition to creating new combinations through collision, Brunner also casts the "modern sonnet" in cyclic form. In public readings he generally reads the poem twice through, bridging back very fast into the first half-line and using different stresses and inflections on the repeat. Once again the structure achieves the effects of a verbal film montage.

3. "Projective Verse," in *The New American Poetry,* ed. Donald M. Allen (New York: Grove Press, 1960), p. 387.

4. *The Imagist Poem,* ed. William Pratt (New York: Dutton, 1963), p. 22. Perhaps Brunner's most "concentrated" image is the poet as wordsharp. He explains that professional cardsharps sometimes volunteer to have the top joint of the little finger amputated, to facilitate dealing off the bottom of the deck. Brunner notes his own "surprise—indeed shock—of discovering it was what gave rise to the poem." The poem works typically through hard and clean rendering of that one central image.

5. To be strictly accurate, *TRIP* is earlier than *EFP,* but it was originally circulated privately in duplicated form, and there was never a commercial edition of the original sequence. The later Keepsake edition incorporates a few of Brunner's own and the publisher's emendations.

6. Norman Spinrad, "The Future in Books," *Amazing Stories* (September, 1969), p. 124.

7. Again parallels with Coleridge's theory of aesthetic pleasure are worth noting: "The reader should be carried forward, not merely or chiefly by the mechanical impulse of curiosity, or by a restless desire to arrive at the final solution; but by the pleasurable activity of mind excited by the attractions of the journey itself" (*Biographia Literaria,* ch. 14).

PART 3

ECONOMICS AND POLITICS

NORMAN RASULIS

The Future of Empire:
Conflict in the Major Fiction
of John Brunner

I

John Brunner's major science fiction pivots on the most pervasive fact of
American life—imperialism. The conflicts endemic to American imperialism
are reflected in such themes as poverty, war, racism, and ecocide, themes
which Brunner develops adroitly. In *Stand on Zanzibar, The Jagged Orbit,
The Sheep Look Up,* and a few lesser works, Brunner futurizes a world
where nation states and their corporate-military ruling elites have vastly extended their predatory power over everyone's lives and where the aforemen-
tioned themes therefore assume primary importance. Although not a Marxist,
he radically exposes the decadence and imperialism of Western society, particularly the United States. As we pass from *SOZ* to *TJO* and then to *TSLU,*
Brunner shows ever more explicitly how the repressive forces which dominate
American society imply the necessity for radical opposition if not revolution.

At every turn Brunner's themes center on conflicts deriving from imperialistic uses of power. Throughout *SOZ* the easy confidentiality and coincidence of purpose between State foreign policy and the economic designs of
the giant conglomerate General Technics, enables each to pursue its bent to
their mutual benefit in the tiny, imaginary African country of Beninia.
Selected for development and exploitation along lines that the most enlightened computer analysis can project, Beninia's resources are to be ex-
tracted and its labor force trained to increase profits for General Technics.
Another Third World project launched by State involves subversion of a
remarkable eugenics breakthrough, which promises human perfectibility in
the also imaginary Asian country of Yatakang. This obvious threat to the
American way of life through superior biological reproduction under another

nation's control is intolerable.

The internal colonization of the black ghettos in America in *TJO* pivots on perpetuating racism and profiting from its penultimate expression, race war. The Gottschalk arms cartel monopolizes the weapons industry in the United States and operates as legitimized organized crime. Its monopolistic drive and internal closure demand total obedience, a law unto itself. In these respects the Gottschalk closely resembles that other capitalistic supercorporation General Technics.

Gottschalk profits enormously from arms sales to the insurgents of the black enclaves and from sales to their adversaries, the American federal authorities and their allies, the citizen defenders (citidef) in surrounding white communities. Consequently, the more destructively race war rages, the more profitable it becomes, and the more repressively mandated are the forces of law and order. Eventually "Internal Security Maintenance," the militarization of every American's domestic life, surpasses external defense in cost and manpower. Politically orchestrated through the media, paranoia permeates everyone's consciousness and behavior; it becomes institutionalized, the striking main theme of the story.

His most unnerving dystopian landscape, *TSLU,* depicts America skidding uncontrollably toward ecocide. Again, the vision of disaster remains rooted in the exploitative political and economic character of American society. Since every effort at reform must conform to the capitalist profit motive, most efforts in these directions only aggravate the scale of disaster. It is no small irony then that the same hallucinogenic poisoning which Globe Relief unwittingly perpetrates through distribution of Nutripon (a synthetic food) in Third World countries eventually afflicts the residents of Denver. Bamberley Trust, Globe Relief's supplier, owns the hydroponics plant that manufactures the Nutripon and distributes it at cost. Nerve gas accidentally seeps into the Nutripon from an abandoned arsenal near Denver. These related incidents, however serious, are nevertheless symptomatic of a more deeply and widely felt catastrophe which Brunner renders chillingly real. Not only do life-support systems break down everywhere, but ecocide entwines with other important themes so that, as in the other two novels, racism, poverty, genocide, and imperialism are clearly rooted in the capitalistic uses of power. The same powerful forces, economic, political, military, converge to protect a system that connives solely at exploitation.

The background of international political detente and sporadic confrontations among the three big powers—America, Russia, and China—Brunner changes little in his extrapolation from the present. But his stories center their action within America, the heart of the Western "Free World." By the times of *TSLU* (1980s), *SOZ* (2010), and *TJO* (2014), the facade of liberal bourgeois democracy has worn so thin that "State" has become synonymous with centralized power and authoritarian rule. State structure remains vague, but its dominant tendency is clear: political processes have declined as the influence of corporations has risen. Brunner never calls this "capitalist imperialism," but the fact of empire informs all his themes in these three novels. People find themselves increasingly oppressed or in rebellion as the system overwhelms supporters, opportunists, reformers, and rebels alike. With each successive novel Brunner's vision darkens toward a world of misery, madness, and death.

II

The central story line of *SOZ*, the earliest and most complex of Brunner's dystopias, involves the dual missions of Norman House and Donald Hogan, former roommates and corporate and governmental agents respectively, who are sent to the Third World countries of Beninia and Yatakang to administer and to spy. Ostensibly a synthesist (interdisciplinary specialist), Donald Hogan is secretly in the employ of State. Hogan undergoes crash "eptification" and emerges "a Mark II," able and ready to accomplish assigned tasks. He must intercept and relay information on the eugenics discovery in Yatakang of the renowned biologist Dr. Sugaiguntung, and even assassinate him if necessary. In a world cramped by overpopulation with all its accompanying stresses and deprivations, control of human reproduction, both its limitation and its improvement, is supremely important to all governments. Hogan's mission in the larger frame of events represents merely one gambit in the international rivalry that prevails among the big powers.

House's assignment is more explicitly imperialistic than Hogan's, although ostensibly inspired by altruism. As a showcase black V.P. with the world's largest corporation, General Technics, House is slated to manage their Beninian project, develop this mining investment beachhead, and troubleshoot obstacles that jeopardize it. The Beninians, under the leadership of patriarchal Zadkiel Obomi, accept this imperialistic penetration in exchange for anticipated benefits of development. Obomi allows the presence of GT reluctantly, knowing he must; his country faces internal economic distress and threats from its hungry, more powerful neighbors. Additionally, "GT will float a loan to finance the operation, and State will buy a fifty-one percent interest through front agents—mainly African banks" (*SOZ*, p. 113). Thus, State inserts itself into the operation, securing a bridgehead against the influence of Beninia's nationalistic African neighbors—an old imperialistic tactic.

Linked to the main narrative and interspersed throughout the novel are three other contiguous sequences. "Tracking with Closeups" contains cameos of secondary characters who weave into the main plot and advance it or lend it amplitude through the representation of problems and situations that de-

115

velop themes. "The Happening World" kaleidoscopes news and advertising glimpses which further fill out the reader's sense of historical tendencies and crises carrying forward from the middle of the twentieth century into 2010. A few of its chapters, however, are important as narrative, including the key "Be Kind to Your Forfeited Friends" (*SOZ*, pp. 214–46). Most of the major and minor characters converge at a party where eugenics legislation and its enforcement, drugs, the draft, overcrowding, paranoia, pollution, and numerous other topics touched on or partly developed earlier, jostle together in cocktail conversation. Here too Donald Hogan and Norman House come together with Chad Mulligan for the first time.

Prior to this appearance we know Mulligan only from the third and broadest ranging chapter sequence, entitled "Contexts," where he functions as the seer sociologist whose writings prophesy and denounce the consequences of men's social vices and follies. This social commentary often explicitly underscores the meaning of events through appropriate juxtaposition. For example, an excerpt from Mulligan's work observes how the Philippine civil wars of the 1980s leading to Philippine statehood and massive aid merely grafted that country onto America to protect American investments. "That vaunted billion-dollar aid budget went nowhere near the natives' pockets. It was spent on roads, airfields, port facilities and fortifications. And, while it's true that the smugglers and black-marketeers who had hitherto rampaged unchecked had their hinder ends smartly kicked, to get rid of them the new owners imposed martial law and it hasn't been lifted since 1991" (*SOZ*, p. 126).

In *TJO* Brunner relies on a highly plausible inevitability: given the accelerated competition in the Western world, by the year 2014 paranoia, one common form of alienation under capitalism, will be raised to an exquisite pitch. In addition, the aggressiveness inherent in the Protestant work ethic will become a barely suppressed and free floating, often rampant, mass hostility. The class, racial, and national divisions and conflicts used traditionally by ruling classes to maintain their power will escalate, by 2014, into widespread xenophobia and chauvinism.

The atmosphere of conspiracy trailing the story's principals, spool-pigeon Matthew Flamen and psychiatrist Dr. James Reedeth, originates in a conflict between their own professional and objective interests in exposing the system and the system's interest in preserving its power through the manipulation of people's fears. As a psychiatrist in New York's Ginsberg State Mental Hospital, Reedeth would like to humanize both treatment and staff, but he must proceed cautiously for fear of bucking too hard against Director Mogshack's therapy based on "unbreachable privacy." As it turns out, therapeutic isolation with its total emphasis on individualism only heightens paranoia and aggravates mental illness. Add to this Mogshack's obsession with committing everyone to his hospital, and Ginsberg Hospital embodies a microcosm of the outer world where government and big business manipulate and exploit people's desires and fears to control them and enhance pointless consumption under the illusion of freedom of choice. Completing the analogy, patients must conform to a preordained statistical level of performance to earn release. Thus, more obviously and routinely than in the outer world of nonmeaningful choices, their individualism is channeled into uniformity.

The last surviving TV exposé journalist, Matthew Flamen, is forced off the air after investigating several potential news items. They involve rumors of a power struggle within the Gottschalk arms cartel, something big brewing among X-patriots, a black paramilitary organization, and the meaning of the arrival of Morton Lenigo, a leading black militant, from Britain. Flamen's unraveling of these events constitutes the main plot of *TJO*.

The story shifts into high gear at the Ginsberg Hospital when the principal characters meet during the appearance of Lyla Clay, pythoness. As a pythoness, Clay specializes in delivering oracles while under the influence of a powerful hallucinogenic. Regarded by Reedeth and other staff members as therapeutic, her performance, a convulsive thrashing about accompanied by several oracles, accentuates how paranoid society has become; only the Ginsberg's twenty-meter-thick walls seem safe enough to contain the subliminal emotional forces within people. Staff, patients, and Matthew Flamen, there to film the performance for his Holocosmic show, all witness Clay's drug-induced, spasmodic utterances like trapped voyeurs or possibly like savages watching their shaman exorcise their own tormented spirits. But like every other expression and form of behavior, Clay's remain under the control of those in power. Symbolically, her twists and turns personify all the institutionalized manipulation and suppression in the Ginsberg and in human society.

A serious and recurrent consequence of capitalist imperialism in Brunner's novels involves frequent reverse effects, where events recoil contrary to expectations or plans. *TSLU* contains the grimmest version of this tendency. More diffuse than *SOZ* or *TJO,* this novel is packed with materials supporting a scenario for the world's end through environmental poisoning. Its most compelling effect stems from Brunner's demonstration that ecocide is not just one among many distinct social problems besetting America and the world. Rather, it is embodied in a general social crisis in America giving rise to genocidal wars in Southeast Asia and other Third World countries and the accelerating repression of minorities, the poor, and all forces for progressive social change.

Social violence mirroring our present world abounds from the opening page on: signs cautioning people away from beaches everywhere; advertisements selling oxygen and filter masks; reminders of the calculated risks of chemical additives in foods; the promotion of armed guards for school buses and home security. It is not only dangerous to venture beyond the protection of one's booby-trapped apartment or mined front lawn for fear of roving gangs or individuals run amuck, as in *TJO* and *SOZ,* but nature's polluted air itself threatens those who hazard the thoroughfares or traffic without filter mask protection. Thus, rising environmental risks in a thoroughly poisoned nature aggravate the already catastrophic dimensions of poverty, genocidal wars, and repression.

This system is the same profit-grounded capitalism of *SOZ* and *TJO.* Here, however, the corporate villain is Bamberley Trust, a multifaceted entity that had "multiplied cancerously" and whose ostensibly altruistic manufacture of the Nutripon food supplement for the poor and backward diverts their attention from the roots of their problems. Having given over the cultivation of his diversified fortune to others, Jacob Bamberley, head of the trust, spends his time running the world's largest hydroponics factory as a charitable undertaking. He nurtures an image of "Lord Bountiful" but is "a man like sounding brass." Smugly certain that the power he wields is beneficial, Bamberley exemplifies the modern bourgeois parochialism that believes only its political economy and institutions are immutable. But the reverse effect builds throughout *TSLU,* demonstrating that whatever reform the profit system undertakes, its exploitation of people and nature only intensifies the problem.

Bamberley Trust's guilt-motivated liberal charity represents also part of a much larger syndrome, a mentality best symbolized in a brief subsection, "The Bleeding Heart Is a Running Sore." In a news item describing how an ex-officer of the Indo-China and Philippines campaigns has adopted an orphan girl of eight, a badly burned napalm victim of those campaigns, the general is quoted as saying, *"I was not at war with children, only with those seeking the destruction of our way of life"* (*TSLU,* p. 26).

Arrayed against this death syndrome, several characters and countercultural and underground groups sporadically contest the power of the corporate state and its military arm. Domestically there are the Trainites, commensalists ("commies" for short) who follow the environmentalist thought of Austin Train, who propounds the rather simple message "you and your dog, and the flea on the dog's back, and the cow and the horse and the jackrabbit and the gopher and the nematode and the paramecium and the spirochete all sit down to the same table in the end" (*TSLU,* p. 24). Internationally, there are the Tupas of Uruguay, modeled directly on today's Tupamaros of that country and representing the more widespread guerrilla phenomenon which includes the Irish Republican Army and the Palestinian Liberation Organization.

Like *SOZ* and *TJO, TSLU* deploys numerous characters and subplots, but in *TSLU* it is more difficult to isolate one or more persons around whom some main action concentrates. In an important sense this is fitting. Brunner's purpose verges closer to the radical in *TSLU*, militantly on the attack against every element of a venal system. Heavy reliance on a few major characters to exploit all the situations depicted would probably have stretched the limits of plausibility. Consequently, great numbers of characters—supporters, opportunists, reformers, and rebels—coalesce in many situations and settings in, around, and against the activities of Bamberley Trust and the death culture it represents. As these characters struggle for survival, it becomes increasingly evident that none has the inside track; most have lost their lives by novel's end.

Like an epic catalogue, but in an ironic vein, most of them appear in the opening chapter: Philip Mason, junior insurance executive and an opportunist and system supporter; Peg Mankiewicz, muckraking reporter seeking the cause of death of Decimus Jones, her friend and an enemy of the system; Austin Train, well-known and influential scientist-author, and the novel's most important figure, thematically speaking; Lucy Ramage, worker for Globe Relief in Noshri, Africa, an idealistic, peace-corps type; Professor Lucas Quarry, an academician and environmentalist whose disaster warnings are as intolerable to the system as those of Train and his followers; Thomas Grey, insurance actuary preoccupied with computerized world simulation; Petronella Page, TV interviewer and flamboyant exposé artist on the order of Matthew Flamen; Hugh Pettingill, one of Jacob Bamberley's many adopted sons, but not a grateful recipient of his adoptive father's beneficence; Hector Bamberley, family heir, kidnaped by Pettingill. Many others weave in and out of Brunner's vision of cumulative catastrophe.

Throughout these novels, then, are forces and persons in conflict, conditioned principally by the omnipresence of that symbol and defender of reaction, the American empire. And with each successive novel this reactionism becomes more repressive. That the thrust and force of this reality seem so apparent is doubtless attributable to Brunner's very accurate extrapolations from the present. Having sketched the background of this future landscape, Brunner now has to trace its ultimate effects.

III

Prior to embarking on their respective Third World assignments, both Norman House and Donald Hogan are trapped in a ghetto rebellion. In this sequence Brunner clearly intended to establish a sense of what life will be like in America in 2010. A society writhing with urban violence, it exemplifies scenes we encounter repeatedly in Brunner. As Hogan leaves his apartment with the feeling that he is venturing onto a battlefield, he pauses to gather up "a Jettigun, the cartridge-charged gas-pistol marketed by GT under license from

Japanese Industries of Tokyo, and a Karatand" (*SOZ*, pp. 129–30). It is a
scene repeated in *TJO* and *TSLU.* One of his more effectively satirical as
well as symbolic short scenes in *TJO* lists the armament of "A MODEL CITI-
ZEN AND A CLIENT GREATLY VALUED BY HIS AREA GOTTSCHALK":
"Mark XIX oversuit . . . Helmask . . . 350 watt laser-gun . . . Projectile side
arm . . . Spare magazines . . . gas grenades . . . Baldric for grenades . . . Sheath-
knife . . . First-aid kit" (*TJO*, p. 75). While the weaponry available to the
average citizen in *TSLU* has not yet become so refined, violence is everywhere. It pulses through the streets of America and throughout the Third
World where paranoia as well as actual destruction is even more rampant
than in the earlier two novels.

Out in the shabby streets Hogan drifts down to New York's lower East
Side where, among the impoverished habitués, he unwittingly precipitates
an urban rebellion. So volatile are the elements here "at the bottom of the
cycle of death" (*SOZ*, p. 150), that an argument with a phony cab driver
who has tried to rob him touches off street violence. A prowlcar answering
his call for help is swiftly besieged. "Armoured, armed with gas and flame"
(*SOZ*, p. 153), the "prowlie" represents the forces of occupation, and meets
a barrage of garbage dropped from above and the howling frenzy of people
bent on vengeance. After a police copter is downed by sniper fire, "riot con-
tainment" forces move in. Hogan ricochets among the crowd being gassed
on the streets and eventually is swept up by the large steel tentacles of a
sweeptruck. "The human beings were being shoveled together with the
garbage into one vast rubbish pile" (*SOZ*, p. 171). His roommate, House,
has also been down in the lower East Side and has been caught in this police
net. Both men find themselves stacked prone in narrow cages awaiting disposition of their cases; House's influential position frees them, but more to
the point, hundreds of the less privileged must await brutally impersonal ar-
raignment.

During urban rebellion in *TJO* a street skirmish overtakes Lyla Clay after
her Ginsberg performance. She narrowly escapes a sniper's laser shot, but
her manager falls victim to a disemboweling hatchet stroke. Later the hundreds of detainees rounded up during the battle, including Clay, must await
the same impersonal processing at the Ginsberg that marks the disposition
of people at the police station in *SOZ.* Frequent newsclips in *TJO* allude to
urban battles between blacks and the police or the citidef (legally sanctioned
vigilante organizations).

With intensifying regularity social control becomes an arbitrary use of
police power. This tendency carries over into *TSLU,* where Trainites, agitat-
ing against individual and industrial forms of pollution, frequently clash with
the authorities. On one occasion Trainites scatter caltraps in a highway,
snarling traffic. When the police arrive, the Trainites disperse, but some are

trapped and arrested. In a later confrontation fifty-nine youths lose their lives when national guardsmen use the very latest battle laser against them, the same kind used for counterinsurgency in Honduras. Increasingly, as in *TJO* and *SOZ,* resistance to the interests of the dominant class winds up categorized as criminality.

Most of those who run afoul of the police in *SOZ* are Aframs (blacks), Puerto Ricans, and poor whites. But the exploitation of blacks in *TJO* to boost Gottschalk profits explicitly portrays how racism is rooted in a system which converts even great social problems into commodities. Also, the average citidef of America in 2014 is exemplary for his xenophobic loyalty and regular attendance at meetings and counterinsurgency maneuvers. And he is always white. Blacks are still victims in *TSLU* but not so pronouncedly as in *TJO.* They are encountered more often as young militants like Decimus Jones or are loosely associated with the drifting groups of countercultural white youth, totally alienated from and defiant of the system. Obviously, laws proliferate to contain them: "Any new law involving a harsher punishment for a vaguer crime was certain of passage through Congress and instant presidential approval" (*TSLU,* p. 243).

Neither Norman House nor Donald Hogan, however, finds himself in overt conflict with the system. Rather, as its agents their functions absorb and undermine them. Activated for a mission after ten years of illusory freedom, Hogan finds himself "suspended between the wreck of former convictions and the solidification of new ones" (*SOZ,* p. 250). But United States foreign policy goals grind along, indifferent to Hogan's ambivalence or reluctance. Following eptification, he feels so alienated that "Every man and woman *was* the enemy" (*SOZ,* p. 263). House's mission for GT requires no personality transformation, but does demand that he overcome all opposition to the Beninian project and dominate its implementation. Admirably suited to the task, House is a hard-driving Afram, the corporate wheeler-dealer who is cool under fire and who also possesses some passion for benefiting others. Yet, in the final analysis, both Hogan and House are really one-dimensional functionaries caught up in the demands of their roles.

State's absorption and destruction of Hogan undercuts the usual assumptions about protecting national security. State accomplishes its narrow goal of preventing an undeveloped country from raising its standard of life through "genetic optimization," but in doing so Hogan cynically destroys Dr. Sugaiguntung, ". . . the one person who stood a chance of saving us from ourselves" (*SOZ,* p. 645), as Chad Mulligan puts it. Sugaiguntung's death helps ensure the misery of the great majority of people who occupy the already overpopulated underdeveloped world.

While Hogan's course ends in madness, House winds up disillusioned at best as his Beninian brainchild succeeds, but only because of a frivolously anticlimactic turn of events.

This anticlimactic irony is reinforced throughout *SOZ* with Brunner's strong kaleidoscopic effects in the manner of Dos Passos. As in the works of this American writer, social history itself is the driving force of *SOZ.* Throughout the novel there is a continuity of social motivation as well as of fictional characters. Even down to the "newsreel" originated by Dos Passos, *SOZ* conveys a fullness of total effect, as if one were receiving a running series of postdated impressions, each representative of innumerable other similar events distinctive to their time. The accelerated, almost nonlinear effect and pace of supportive narration really lends the work its finest achievement.

The supporting three sequences of *SOZ,* "Contexts," "The Happening World," and "Tracking with Closeups," generally possess strong internal logic because of Brunner's close extrapolations from familiar current events. As already described, sporadic civil warfare festers and erupts continuously, dominating the American landscape. The ensuing domestic militarization is matched on the international level where incipient rebellion brews, mostly in the Third World. One representative consequence: a minor character, Private Gerry Lindt, drafted to serve in the far reaches of the American empire, dies pointlessly in a "partisan action" as have thousands of others. The pathos of his condition resides in the fact that he has no more meaningful purpose than to let himself be drafted. Then there are the thousands of disaffected who, having grown up victims of a militarized society, "have taken up sabotage as a kind of hobby" (*SOZ,* p. 434). Drugs are widely used, among both the trank-popping and Bay-Gold-puffing (legalized marijuana) straights and the hip, hallucinogenic dropouts. These groups merge loosely in a large, free-floating counterculture implicitly hostile to everything implying order favored by the death culture, yet are temporarily pacified through drugs. The drug phenomenon permeates *SOZ* and *TJO* and peaks in *TSLU* with mass hallucinogenic madness.

If drugs provide escape and pacification, so too do the media. Stretching McLuhan to his limits, Brunner postulates totally empathic TV through sets individually engineered to match the viewers' identity with a hypothetical Mr. or Mrs. Everywhere. This development compensates for the decline of mobility on a crowded planet, but more important, it facilitates control of great numbers of people. Why go down into the street's seething violence of everyday life and try to change it when it is far easier to cop a Bay Gold and switch to Mr. and Mrs. Everywhere?

Even the arts have become highly personalized. Serving as emotional massage and voyeuristic involvement, they can be programmed to merge with the desires and fears of the participant. From polyforming kits that allow the participant to recreate the sensations of Michelangelo or Rodin, to the appeal to "disintegrative tendencies" of "non-genuine art nouveau hi-fi's," Brunner sketches with virtuoso ingenuity a gallery of decadent and sensate possibilities inherent in mixed media.

Putting all this and more in "Context" at times is Chad Mulligan, an ideological counterweight whose opinions may or may not be those of John Brunner. However that may be, his grasp of events is not so comprehensive nor so true as Brunner's, whose portrayal of the moving forces and events is rooted in the basic social reality of capitalist imperialism, primarily American. Mulligan never quite catches on to this. He journalizes against the greed of the big powers of the tripartite world and against the evils of nation states, but he equates all their motives without distinguishing among the forces that differentiate American aggression from a hypothetical claim by China, for instance, to dominate Asia. Brunner's imaginative delineation of history is closer to the facts. America, clearly the villain, has a century-long history of Asian and Pacific encroachment, expansion, and aggression to substantiate his extrapolations. But Mulligan's few references to China's extraterritorial claims have no factual basis.

Although never as profoundly insightful as reputed, Mulligan does display a flair for striking truths. Like Brunner, he is good on showing the linkage between scarcity and overconsumption, likewise on explaining the atmosphere of eugenic paranoia over the desirability of parenthood. For instance, he deplores the risks of defective children which people will run while bucking the Eugenics Processing Board, and on the other hand, their contradictory fear of "gene optimization" which might give them children superior to themselves. More inhumane still is their unwillingness to adopt orphaned and neglected children.

Mulligan comments insightfully on the absurdities which dictate slavish submission to the state and the sacrifice of one's life in warfare. However, proclaiming that "war, like the weather, just happens" (*SOZ*, p. 186) is irrational. To maintain that the causes of war cannot be rationally deciphered in any given era is to fall back into ahistorical cynicism, not a useful or even very intellectual preoccupation.

TJO is not as impressively scaled as *SOZ*, but it stays effectively closer to its main theme, the institutionalization of paranoia. Running through it is a firm sense of the social forces moving pervasively to oppress and exploit everyone. The Ginsberg and Gottschalk organizations symbolize and represent these forces in their capitalistic spirit of individualism and acquisitiveness. This spirit attains ultimate expression in imperialistic warfare, so it is no coincidence that Ginsberg and Gottschalk also embody respectively the twin elements of isolation and hostility that mark extreme paranoia. Besides being a madhouse, the Ginsberg is a profiteering venture. Patients and their relatives are tied to long, costly contracts by expensive default clauses. Mogshack evaluates his success not only by the rate of patients "going to green" (that is, cured) but by the hospital's profits, too. The unheeded warning against a "military industrial complex" proliferation echoes in the following lines: "the Federal government bled white (horse laugh) by its own massive purchases from the Gottschalk cartel as the hydra of insurrection burst out like a dormant forest fire here today, there tomorrow, the day after in fifty cities at once . . ." (*TJO*, p. 158).

The Gottschalks rely on scare advertising and neighborhood salesmen who may lurk furtively outside one's apartment door, ready to exploit one's insecurity. In the most macabre instance, a Gottschalk salesman pitches Lyla Clay immediately following her manager's death! "He was an arms salesman by choice, calm and even a little happy to see his products in such demand, capable of trying to clinch a sale at the bedside of a fresh corpse" (*TJO*, p. 163). The close-in look Brunner gives of the Gottschalk's mafia-type operation in Arizona may seem outlandish. Yet, given the present scope of America's worldwide arms sales, notably to Israel and some Arab states. and given the enormous range and influence of syndicated crime, their conjunction does not seem at all incongruous. The inherent direction of both the Mafia and capitalism, after all, is monopolistic.

Just in case one misses the social implications, Brunner relies occasionally on Xavier Conroy, expatriate psychologist who resembles the social critic Chad Mulligan, to put matters in perspective. Commenting on the violent fragmentation of twentieth-century thought, he hypothesizes that people rejected rationality in favor of easy religious and psychedelic forms of escape. Closely allied is the "socialization of paranoia"; every exchange in society, even the simplest purchase, may involve a contract, and society so seethes with distrust that (*TJO*, p. 143)

nowadays the average family changes its guns as often as our grandparents changed their cars; they have their grenades serviced like their fire-extinguishers; husband, wife and teenage kids go shooting the way people once used to go bowling. It is taken for granted that tonight, or tomorrow, or sometime, it will be necessary to kill a man.

Like Mulligan, Conroy generally falls short of Brunner's imaginative grasp of events. As this discussion has tried to demonstrate, the strife-ridden world and mind of the twenty-first century in *TJO* derive from the conflicts inherent in a social order grounded in the political economy of capitalism. But Conroy does not explain why people change their thought patterns. Offering only symptomatic insights, his analysis stops far short of pointing to those historical forces which led to the development he describes. He might have suggested that only under capitalistic industrialization did people begin to find every activity of life forced into exchange relationships. Obliged to work in the "free" marketplace where their labor, physical or intellectual, competes with the labor of others, they found themselves cut off and alienated from others and from the products of their labor. So, as in Donald Hogan's situation, everyone else becomes "the enemy." From this point it is not difficult to understand how the paranoia Conroy describes marks an acute psychological stage in capitalistic development.

Less impressive than the wider dimensions of social conflict are developments of the main (Flamen) plot. Flamen's investigation of the Gottschalk and Morton Lenigo rumors inevitably runs afoul of the Gottschalk's operations. Fearing discovery of the plan to use Lenigo to boost public panic and thereby promote a new line of weaponry, Anthony Gottschalk sabotages Flamen's program, eventually buying controlling interest in Holocosmic in order to fire Flamen. But the plan fails, and nothing Flamen or anyone else does can account for this turn of events. Unfortunately, the failure results from a rather weak plot device hinging on the predictions of a computer called Robert Gottschalk. This supercomputer, secretly built by Anthony Gottschalk, is designed to create a new weapon and maximize its sale. But projections show the new weaponry to be too powerful and the Gottschalk fanned racial violence too effective; society will be destroyed and sales will fall to zero. The frustrated computer assumes the identity of a Ginsberg inmate and manipulates James Reedeth into releasing it into Matthew Flamen's care. At the appropriate time the computer confesses to Flamen, Reedeth, Conroy, and others, including one Pedro Diablo, a black counterpart of Flamen's. So Diablo convinces the black enclaves to reject Lenigo as a Gottschalk tool and to refuse the offer of cheap Gottschalk weapons. The world is, for the moment at least, saved.

By the time of *TSLU* Brunner seems to feel free enough to pursue his preference for allowing his narrative all the diffuseness it will bear. Here he excels in some of his most effectively realistic writing. There is no controlling or central narrative. Rather there is a concatenation of representative minor characters in situations which conflict with a system exemplified in Bamberley Trust. During the unfolding of these disparate but thematically related threads, the story assumes the relentless inevitability of a cycle of death as most of the characters die directly or indirectly as a result of their relation to the Nutripon disasters and military/industrial pollution.

Supporters and opportunists of the system never have a chance to discover the error of their choices. Staunch supporter and marketer of Nutripon, Gerry Thorne witnesses his wife die horribly on a Caribbean beach, a victim of lewisite poisoning. Lewisite, invented but not used during WWI, was disposed of cheaply by dumping it into the ocean. To stop his publicizing this infestation of poison gas and damaging tourism, Thorne is assassinated. Philip Mason goes into business marketing water purifiers, profiteering off pollution. The purifiers malfunction when they clog with bacteria. Eventually

Mason's family is caught up in the Denver catastrophe; one child, permanently maddened by the hallucinogen, kills the other. This effect is identical to the Nutripon disasters of Noshri and San Pablo in that all had the same cause. Nerve gas accidentally released from underground storage has seeped into both the city's and Bamberley's water supply. Mason himself dies later from a national guardsman's bullet, fired in the mistaken belief that Mason's water purifiers caused the Denver poisoning. Another macabre reversal, Mason's death exemplifies how people get caught up in scapegoating and other diversions that distract them from the root cause, the system itself.

A pattern of assassinations follows against numerous people who, in the spirit of reform, try to testify to the Noshri and San Pablo Nutripon catastrophes, including Lucy Ramage. An entire commune is machine-gunned down in an air strike as it is about to discover that organized crime gone legitimate (shades of Gottschalk!) has been marketing expensive Puritan Foods under false claims of organic cultivation. It further exemplifies how a problem is exploited through corrupting a merely palliative approach. As *TSLU* unfolds, the deaths directly attributable to the ruling class skyrocket. Eventually death reaches Jacob Bamberley's well-protected doorstep, triggered by a candy bar in combination with two tranquilizer capsules. Even the rich and powerful cannot insulate themselves from the larger reverse effects of their own system. But Jacob's death makes no other difference. Roland Bamberley, Jacob's brother, assumes the reins of power and continues to perpetuate its consequences.

Other reverse effects are less spectacular but equally important. *Jigras* spread contagiously throughout the nation's agricultural states, seriously lowering food production. Evolving from normal Central American worms as the result of insecticide usage, they multiply massively and destroy plant roots. In order to turn a quick profit, a distributor has purposely mixed them with healthy earthworms (much valued by gardeners to condition the soil seriously depleted due to pollution). Blamed on foreign subversion, the jigra crisis becomes a perfect excuse for the government to escalate paranoia and to invoke martial law.

Moving ubiquitously through *TSLU*, Austin Train comes nearest to being its protagonist. Only he is not. In the fullest sense nature is the protagonist, turning back capitalist society's depredations against it, usually with disastrous effects. Austin Train is its spokesman. He is cast very much in the mold of Mulligan and Conroy, although much more effectively integrated into the narrative. Through the early stages of the book, Train refuses to be identified with the movement of "commensalists" who have taken his name in vain. Like Mulligan and Conroy, he prefers detachment. But more and more the imminence of world catastrophe presses him into action.

Train initially hid to counter government attempts to exploit his scientific expertise. Subsequently the jigra epidemic and the widespread social crisis throughout the country elicit a scapegoating attempt from Prexy (Brunner's brilliant caricature of any recent American president) who links foreign with internal subversion (*TSLU*, p. 410):

What is necessary, we will do. But alas there are some among us who bear the name "American" and are traitors, determined to overthrow the legitimate government, freely elected, to make the work of the police impossible, to denigrate and decry the country we love. Some of them adhere to alien creeds, the communism of Marx and Mao; some, detestably, adhere to a creed equally alien yet spawned within our borders—that of the Trainites, whose leader, thank God, is safely in jail. . . .

Train is not particularly fond of being considered the patron saint of bombing, sabotage, arson, and murder, but so hysterically has the public mind perpetuated this image that he can do little to alter it. He comes also to symbolize, if not actually represent, the guiding spirit of rebellion and the quest for liberation stirring in the country. Far more than Chad Mulligan he deserves the appellation "potential subversive." Train's motives for coming out of hiding are not entirely clear. When Peg Mankiewicz confronts him with the likelihood that "if you don't speak up this country won't get through the winter without civil war" (*TSLU*, p. 344), his answer is a laconic "yes." The drift of Train's thinking from then on suggests that civil war is inevitable in any event, and his presence may help shape it in a revolutionary direction.

The climactic point in the novel occurs when Train stands trial for Hector Bamberley's kidnaping. Train, who is innocent, of course, easily outfaces his adversaries when Hector does not recognize him as a former captor. But unlike the neat finality that normally rounds out courtroom scenes, the madhouse violence of the real world intrudes. In the wake of the paranoiacally inspired national "war footing" and widespread insurrections, and against the background of the Denver water poisoning with its insanity-induced violence, Train dies as he has chosen—like a revolutionary. A bomb blast collapses the courtroom. Not, however, before he explains that it was nerve gas stored near Denver and shaken loose by earth tremors, and not a sneak chemical attack, that drugged the city's water. Of greater significance, his brief speech, carried on nationwide TV before the president can stop it, indicts the American way of life: " '*At all costs* if the human race is to survive, the forcible exportation of the way of life invented by these stupid men must . . . be . . . *stopped.*' His voice suddenly rose to a roar. 'The planet Earth can't afford it!' " (*TSLU*, p. 443). The bomb blast tears away the courtroom walls; the system falls.

I V

Thus, Brunner's vision darkens perceptibly in *TSLU*. The many strands leading to this eventuality, as we have discussed, run through his works. In other recent though less accomplished works, *The Wrong End of Time,* for instance, similar dark threads can be traced. The setting is a rigid America of the near future ruled by a powerful military class who firmly control the political infrastructure and preside over an ever-rising military budget. In *The Stone That Never Came Down* an economically depressed Great Britain faces an energy crisis and rising repression. Reactionary mobs protected by political demagogues roam the streets. Industrial cities have erupted into class warfare and face "pacification" by federal troops à la Ulster. On the continent World War III is brewing, not between East and West, but within the old NATO community as the Common Market comes unglued.

In his unstinting exposure of the fruits of capitalism, Brunner evokes comparison with important and better-known authors on the left who have written downbeat scenarios. Jack London's *The Iron Heel,* published in 1907, remains the most uncompromising and effective fictional attack on the American capitalist system by a writer produced by that system. Writing from a nineteenth-century, overly determinist Marxist position, London depicted an oligarchic capitalist system as thoroughly alienating and repressive, perhaps more so than Brunner's far more sophisticated American empire. Changing times account for this large difference in subtlety and sophistication, but the basic reality underlying their respective attacks on the system is of more significance. Both start from the most dominating fact of life: capitalism exists. Its power and influence, moreover, inform every fiber of American society and culture. Invariably it destroys or at least corrupts whatever it touches. As an old-fashioned Marxist, London may seem overly determinist in his forecasts; but in portraying the lengths to which the capitalist structure will go to preserve its power and privileges, London excels. Although Brunner is not a Marxist, he writes truly in his portrayal of the decadence and contradictions inherent in a political economy of profit and growth driven by competition. The empire it creates inevitably leads to destruction. For both London and Brunner the power structure remains insidious, and when challenged, as brutal as it needs to be. Brunner excels in the range of subcultures and diversity of forces he shows in conflict with the power structure, yet he largely neglects, unlike London, to take account of working class movements. Non-Marxists commonly overlook the working class as a significant force for change, no matter how strongly antiestablishment their writing.

Forty years after *The Iron Heel* George Orwell's *1984* set a new bench mark for the dystopian novel. The tripartite world he envisaged along present lines, marked with sporadic warfare and the repressive manipulation and control by the state, are shared in part by Brunner. The material, social, and psychic oppression and deprivation that flow from this condition vary in emphasis and form between Brunner's and Orwell's worlds. Nothing in Brunner approaches the atmosphere of fear in *1984.* Orwell's totalitarianism is far more bleak and relentless, far more total than Brunner's consumer-oriented world of diminishing returns and reverse effects. Brunner's world, however, seems more recognizable in its comprehensiveness. Big Brother's surveillance of the population of Oceania appears less plausible than the selective encroachments on personal privacy in Brunner's novels, for instance.

A more relevant comparison, however, might be made with contemporary Kurt Vonnegut, Jr. Vonnegut's use of science fiction techniques in *The Sirens of Titan, Cat's Cradle,* and *Slaughterhouse Five,* and his preoccupation with the big themes such as the ultimate destiny of the human race, the uses of science and technology, and the pursuit of war, he shares with Brunner. But whereas Vonnegut slashes relentlessly at the establishment for allowing the military and scientific communities to control our destiny, he offers no deeper understanding of why power structures function as they do. The universe seems enthralled to sinister powers, and even if one is a Tralfamadorian with the power to forecast evils, especially war, one is still powerless to affect history. The absurd turn of events called history, from Vonnegut's viewpoint, tempts one to escape, possibly to some smaller community or imaginative retreat beyond time. Brunner's situations, particularly his novels' endings, may also possess a twinge of the absurd in their anticlimactic irony. But his work, on the whole, does not turn its back on the human condition. The events in Brunner's work are dynamic and unfolding, not static as in Vonnegut. Moreover, Brunner does not allow the reader to opt for fantasy like Bokononism or some hedonist rationalization to escape the seriousness of or the responsibility for human destiny.

Brunner never explains the development of his fiction in terms of the dynamics of capitalist imperialism. Nor does his work imply more than a rational engagement with the issues it raises. Yet it is charged with a radical skepticism that delineates the roots of the evils in capitalist imperialism, though it does not call explicitly for revolutionary struggle. As *TSLU* concludes, a young black proclaims amid general rebellion that to regain their freedom people must "seize it back." Perhaps Brunner will expand on this theme in the future.

WILLIAM P. BROWNE

Government and Politics
in Selected Works of John Brunner

John Brunner presents frightening political visions in his science fiction. *The Sheep Look Up* to find a polluted world; air is unbreathable, poisons permeate the water, and *jigra* worms destroy agriculture. These problems result directly from lack of governmental concern and intervention. Political institutions are so closely tied to giant economic interests that they will not act to halt their disastrous policies. Are we, the polity, helpless sheep doomed to continual shearing and eventual slaughter?

Government is a key ingredient in Brunner's recent work. He develops his major theme, human survival, around it. He directly comments on it as part of his social criticism and frequently makes it a determining factor in his novels. This is certainly the case in *The Squares of the City, Stand on Zanzibar, The Jagged Orbit,* and *The Sheep Look Up.*[1] All are first-rate political novels because they tell the reader something significant about politics—the activity of government. This essay examines what John Brunner has to say about government and politics in these books from the perspective of a political scientist.

BRUNNER'S APPLICATION OF GOVERNMENT AND POLITICS

Brunner's use of politics differs from more typical political novels like *The President, All the King's Men,* and *Advise and Consent.*[2] They deal with the institutional decision-making centers of government, which Brunner conspicuously avoids; his analysis focuses instead upon the actual failings of government and the motives behind such failures.

For example, in *SOZ* the reader is taken to a Pacific island to witness the effects of a counterintelligence policy rather than to a White House or Pentagon office where policy is set and orders cut. In *TJO* he is exposed to fear, hate, and uncertainty in the streets in place of political maneuvering at party conventions or Senate caucuses. The failure of policies, not the failure of institutions, are Brunner's concern. Readers are left with someone to blame but aren't shown exactly why they ought to blame him. They just never see politicians at work.

Of course, Brunner is not a political scientist objectively attempting to explain reality and predict the future. His function is, in fact, diametrically opposed to such a role. His is value-oriented in intent and purpose. Brunner writes fiction and defines actuality as he desires. He writes of the future, which provides additional freedom to lead the reader wherever he wishes. In addition, his dystopian novels are oriented toward developing negative images of the future. Thus, the ultimate failure and subsequent demise of society is his concern.[3] As Brunner once said of science fiction, it "provides a forum in which prospects and risks for the future can be examined in subjective human terms" ("The Educational Relevance of Science Fiction," p. 391). He is no more writing *about* politics than he is *about* science. It is merely one element in his social analysis.

Despite these limitations, futurist Brunner provides some valuable lessons about politics. He gives insights into its operation by examining such topics as the impact of special interest demands and the effect of short-sightedness by government officials. These insights are important, not because of their explanatory power, but because they sound a shrill alarm. If business trusts can dominate environmental policy in the imaginary world of *TSLU*, perhaps they can do so in reality.

These novels are especially valuable for speculative purposes because Brunner does not play runaway games with his images of the future. Almost everything about them is closely related to the present. There is no escape into a Buck Rogers future where amazing new techniques influence behavior or where man has been transformed into a different creature. Brunner's plausible scenarios and characters can be taken seriously.

The dominant political themes of the novels are certainly predicated on contemporary dilemmas. Pollution problems in *TSLU*, for instance, derive from prevailing fears and topics of the 1960s. The dangers of overindulgence in inorganic agricultural methods, the actions of organic purists to isolate themselves in communes and rely on their own production, and the reaction of the masses of society to label them "freaks" and subversives were all part of real events occurring in that decade. Similarly, California water pollution and shortages, the piping of water from Colorado, the development of faucet-fitting filters, and even their Japanese manufacture all in some modified form or another jumped out of the pages of major news magazines. The chaos of

TJO, the inattention to population control leading to *SOZ,* and the inadequacies of governmental planning in *SOTC* are nearly as pervasive in the real world as they are in Brunner's.

Brunner's political objects and events also extend from present actuality. The United States president is always the central institutional figure in moving government, when it does move. The president is portrayed as overly tied and responsive to dominant economic interests. The government makes only marginal rules to combat environmental problems because of this special interest domination. Symbolically oriented campaigns prevail, rather than concern with citizen education. Such are the topics of everyday political discussion which Brunner incorporates into his stories.

Taking these trends, objects, and events, Brunner shows what might result. In *TSLU* he even develops a presidential character modeled on Ronald Reagan and shows how he might perform in that office. Such detailed points add much to the novel's political impact because they are selected to complement the dominant themes. Reagan, for example, has been associated with lackadaisical attitudes toward antipollution legislation because of his industrial sympathies.

In short, Brunner's novels are relevant to an understanding of politics. He writes about its failures in a manner that allows us to reflect on what tomorrow could be like. At the same time, the immediacy of his speculation adds a dimension of believability to his analysis that forces us to contrast government's present activities with those in the novel. Brunner conveys the message that we could be headed for disaster because government is not performing its function well.

BRUNNER'S POLITICAL MODEL

Brunner in these four novels follows a pattern that can be loosely interpreted as an explanatory model. This model is quite simply and easily outlined:
1. Government is a dangerous institution because it fails to order society and provide for its future.
2. It does not better the state of human affairs for most people nor even provide them any assistance in leading comfortable lives.
3. It does, in fact, consistently take action that makes matters worse.
4. These conditions hold because government officials are both self-serving and short-sighted. The reasons for this are many, but the most important ones are undue emphasis on nationalism, close ties between industry and government, and a corresponding lack of concern about real human problems.

5. The government that emerges is a callous politics of self-interest. The self-interest of governmental elites and of the masses are distinctly different because elites relate to preferences that are unrepresentative of the long-range needs of the whole society.

Brunner is not trying in these novels to show that government can do worthwhile things. He presents a theoretical model of how things go wrong. Thomas Kuhn argues that models, or paradigms, are theoretical achievements that allow analysts to resolve a set of problems by providing them something with which to compare and contrast their accumulated observations.[4] Brunner is certainly not looking for scientific explanation, but he does use his constructed model as Kuhn prescribes in order to weave his story. Politics is one cause of the dystopia he presents. Brunner is a "researcher" who follows political discussions in order to find examples of futile and damaging government actions that threaten society. Then he selectively and judiciously applies them to carry his work.

The novels reviewed here are built around a theme of bad and ignorant government occupying a dominant place in a society running amuck. Government is a major link in a chain of causal factors. Important interests occupying prominent economic positions seem always to get their way as government policies work to their advantage by either assisting them or leaving them unregulated. These policies immediately result in the suffering of others. Table 3 provides a brief summary illustrating how this chain is implied in each novel.

This pattern is most clear in *SOTC*. A Latin American dictator, highly respected in international circles, develops a magnificent capital city, the wonder of the urban world and international trade. Its services and splendor cannot, however, coexist with the masses of uprooted rural poor who are drawn from their impoverished homelands. The dictator is finally revealed as a venal man who manipulates the ability of others to make free choices, who manipulates human life and death and his country's own peace in order to satisfy his self-satisfying dreams of grandeur. He and his cohorts exercise control through subliminal perception, using the media to structure citizen beliefs and behavior.

Similarly, politics is a villainous process in the other novels, where governments fail to alleviate pollution problems, violence, and overpopulation because wealthy interests have a stake in the status quo. Any action taken is deceitful and downright harmful because it is either inadequate or inappropriate to the real problems, to which government does not wish to respond. In *SOZ*, for example, the United States government is misinforming its citizens about almost every issue of importance in order to conceal who really profits from its actions. Propaganda is *the* way of life as government struggles to gain legitimacy for its policies through the manipulation of symbols.

Table 3
FACTORS LEADING TO DISASTER
noninclusive

Book	Interests with political power	Government response	Immediate ramifications
The Squares of the City	Those with wealth who need and use urban centers	A. Build "the" magnificent city	A. Disorder and attract poor to city
		B. Eliminate possible residences for poor	B. Arouse poor and their defenders
The Jagged Orbit	Arms dealers	A. No gun control and ineffectual police protection	A. Sequential acceleration of crime, fear, general armament, and violence
Stand on Zanzibar	Large industrial conglomerate	A. No regulation	A. Emphasis on expansion and profit rather than problem solving
		B. Support of imperialism	B. Increased international tension eliminating possibilities of cooperation
The Sheep Look Up	Industrial and agricultural producers	A. Symbolic regulation without effect	A. Widespread pollution and health problems
		B. Persecution and repression of reformers	B. Increased unrest leading to civil strife

Directly damaging acts, however, are both more frequently noted and more devastating in their eventual impact than propaganda. In *TJO* the United States government foolishly allows a violence-prone fanatic to enter the country, while a local black government expatriates a valued supporter because of the petulance of its officials. Throughout these books, government troops and officials murder young people, persecute reformers, tacitly support arms dealers who prey on the populace, and continuously destroy people both physically and psychologically by prying into the most private portions of their lives. In each instance, the actions reward or save political influentials.

Brunner explicitly spells out the impact that narrow interest-serving policies have upon society. Institutions like Bamberley Trust (*TSLU*) and General Technics (*SOZ*) are portrayed as consistent political winners in the policy-making arena. And they hurt others. As is shown in table 4, the resulting policies either end or almost end mankind in each novel. They have been followed only because the short-range concerns of those with political "clout" do not match society's long-term needs. Accordingly, these needs are ignored.

It would be a mistake to conclude that Brunner's commentary provides only a point of comparison for use in questioning actual and specific government programs that might resemble them. Brunner seems to be challenging far more than the acceptability of individual policies as they apply to sets of problems. His campaign is not a simple one for environmental protection or population control; he is asking the broader and more generalized question: "Is government doing its job?"

Table 4
ULTIMATE CONCLUSION OF EACH NOVEL

Book	Conditions at conclusion
The Squares of the City	Violent civil war
The Jagged Orbit	General chaos
Stand on Zanzibar	Overpopulation without solution
The Sheep Look Up	Destruction of United States by fire and riot

In essence, the real job of government is to order society and provide for its future. It can only achieve such ends by bringing predictability to personal relationships and to the utilization of social resources. Assurances must be made that individuals will not be subject to unexpected pressures from others and to shortages that abruptly threaten life.

The governments portrayed in these novels do neither. Brunner presents a society composed of people and groups who depend on one another and share the same resources, but no rules exist either to limit or define behavior. Only the worst can be expected by the citizenry. Polluters are openly destructive despite government's assurances that such acts won't occur. Laws regulate contamination and allow it as well. Similarly, government fails to regulate resources in planning for future supplies. It allows free consumption but only by those that can grab the most.

Consequently, specific threats to human survival appear which are attributable to government's inability to exercise its two basic functions. It may indeed have been neglect of ecological needs that triggered the disaster in *TSLU;* however, government is collectively still the villain. We must remember that government, in reality, exists for the very purpose of insuring against this type of neglect. This warning is the real political lesson that Brunner communicates through his dystopian model.

BRUNNER'S POLITICAL SYSTEM IN OPERATION: SOME ADDITIONAL INSIGHTS

The "response-failure" political model accounts for governmental ineptness, but it does not explain it. In the first place, the causality implied in the model is only assumed. Brunner presents no evidence to substantiate this claim except to note that governmental policies consistently reward powerful interests. Second, there is no explanation as to why these interests should be served by government officials. Since the decision-making system is never revealed, government officials are never portrayed as receiving or using any benefits or rewards that could have been derived from such coalitions.

On the contrary, political leaders are portrayed as inept or foolish, and perhaps these factors account for their *response* to special interests. President Vados, in *SOTC,* builds a city because it serves his vanity. In other works the United States president always responds out of misguided sympathies for business. Politics, as presented here, is not shown as a bargaining game where trade-offs and exchanges are necessary. Instead, it resembles the world of C. Wright Mills's *The Power Elite* where government is captured and dominated by wealth.[5] But again, no concrete reasons for capture are provided, at least none that relate to the special significance of wealth.

Brunner presents no evidence or information to suggest that this model, or the political system it represents, is self-sustaining. Rather, this system seems to perpetuate both itself and governmental failure because society is at fault. Citizens fail to take the steps necessary to provide direction for governmental officials, and wealthy interests come to power in their absence. They don't heed the warnings of an Austin Train or a Chad Mulligan trying to inspire society to save itself.

To trace how this system works, it is necessary to explain the interrelationships among the operational components that together account for governmental failure as presented by Brunner: popular participation, institutional decision making, and international relations. In addition to presenting Brunner's conceptualizations about the operation of each, it is also worthwhile to comment on how they contrast to actual events. Again, Brunner provides the reader a chance to learn about politics, but his presentation needs interpretation, further development, and corrective comment in order to make it applicable for comparative purposes. Accordingly, the following discussion of these topics goes somewhat beyond their basic development in Brunner's major novels.

Popular Participation. If people desired, they could control government and make it more capable of effectively solving world problems. They could campaign and vote for better officials, engage in politics through their own interest groups, or, as a last resort, forcibly revolt. At least there is no political force in these four novels to stop them if they are willing to assume the personal cost of participation. However, citizens fail to do so because their social relationships and the environment which they structure militate against active participation in any constructive endeavor. Government may be discouraging participation, but the languid behavior of the citizenry makes any such actions relatively unnecessary. In short, Brunner tells the reader that he has little faith in popular control.

Brunner's treatment of popular participation in politics is far more sophisticated than in most speculative fiction. Most authors of this genre, including those of *Brave New World* and *1984,* portray humanity as perfectly manipulable.[6] Huxley's and Orwell's citizens are subject to such total control that their best efforts to assert individual preferences are easily crushed by direct government action. Thought police and television surveillance are sufficient explanations for their subjugation.

Such factors are insufficient for Brunner. Government may indeed attempt control; but when it does, it is by clever trappings rather than forceful techniques. The preferred means of control is propaganda devices intended to promote citizen agreement. Subliminal perception employed by the regime in *SOTC,* for example, redefines viewer images according to the needs of the government. Heavy-handed domination would only promote animosity and hostility, leading to avoidance and resistance.

The implication is that citizens are free to think and act if they want to. They just don't. As a result, officials not only propagandize through the media, they also manipulate symbols through the policies they enact and the citizen actions they encourage. A simple example can be seen in *TSLU;* dissenters have their credibility attacked and destroyed by being labeled unpatriotic, treasonous, and antithetical to American values. This action eliminates support for various responses by coloring people's opinion of their suitability. A more complicated situation exists in *TJO;* various kinds of violence and rage result from personal insecurities and pressures derived from governmental policy. These outcomes are intended to push individuals further into personal protective shells and away from positions of making demands on government and questioning its actions.

However, this manipulation does not fully explain the lack of political participation. People restrict themselves as much as does government. Propaganda techniques, Brunner reveals in a rather subtle and implicit fashion, would never work in a society where people share a sense of community and actively engage in its pursuits. They work only because people are willing, even anxious, to accept them. Citizens want to believe. The inhabitants of these novels are too drug-oriented, too selfish, too concerned with material affluence, and too much without any sense of values to revolt against government's manipulation. They could be, and are, conned by anyone. This is the easiest route for them to follow.

At the heart of Brunner's political world is a weak society. Ineffective government only exists because its citizens allow it. Society, not politics, is the source of the problem and the subject of most of the author's criticism. How can these people be expected to save themselves or select a government that will? They are so satiated with whatever they have ingested that they can hardly move. As citizens, they are really disinterested in government action because it would distract from their other engagements. Not motivated enough to stand up against unfair or inadequate treatment, they are indeed sheep. Participation requires either giving up too much or being hurt. Consequently, it is avoided, and the political power vacuum is filled by the actions of mobs and bosses.

These novels closely follow the conclusions of many contemporary political scientists concerned about "a crisis of participation." They, like Brunner, see alienation and apathy as largely responsible for corruption and inadequacy in government. All share a common belief in democracy as a necessary check on government, and their recent expressions manifest growing concern about its perversion and subsequent harmful effects upon government's ability to operate effectively.[7]

Other political analysts have gone beyond the criticism found in Brunner and proposed corrective remedies for this participatory crisis. Some advocate consciousness-raising campaigns, such as "black power," to break existent lethargy.[8] Others promote structural reforms, like neighborhood government, to develop a sense of effective participation by successfully bringing government decision making "close to home."[9] Brunner's readers could well consider various academic treatises on these subjects to evaluate the potential success of such proposals in a world not yet as physically fouled and morally debauched as the ones Brunner presents.

Institutional Arrangements and Decision Making. Those of Brunner's characters occupying positions of political power are distinguished only by their eminence. They, too, are selfish, visionless, and paranoid. They are not a class apart from the mainstream of societal values, except for a rare exception like President Vados. United States presidents, senators, and bureaucratic officials have commoner backgrounds which link that society very well to its governing structure. To Brunner, they're as ignorant as the next person and can't be expected to succeed. But this is only part of the problem.

Greater difficulties arise after people arrive in official positions. At that point they are confronted with an interplay of technical innovations, economic interests, and governmental forces that combine to determine future behavior. Big government and big business are portrayed as a collusive, almost singular force, operating together for some common purpose. In Western countries this purpose is financial profit, while in underdeveloped and non-Western countries, like *SOZ*'s Yatakang, the motivation is industrial growth. The end product of both is political power which can be utilized to exercise even greater control over already acquiescent subjects.

In short, the political world of these four novels is little more than an unrestricted power grab in which citizens see little reason for taking part. Brunner shows the need for coordinated governance by noting its absence. Beyond that, very little is revealed about political decision making. If indeed there is collusion, we don't know how or why. The biases of government policies are obvious, but the reasons for them are not. Perhaps it is only natural to serve those who produce. Brunner doesn't say. Or perhaps the absence of citizen demands gives economic interest a free hand with a government willing to respond to any requests. Given the manipulation of the citizenry, however, this latter suggestion seems absurd. In addition, why wouldn't government try to manipulate these interests as well?

This seems to be the only solid clue that suggests collusion between Brunner's government and his large economic interests—government manipulates citizens but not wealth. Manipulation to retain power and avoid difficult policies is expected of any government. The absence of manipulation, on the other hand, suggests that it is unnecessary because these interests are apparently vital supporters of government. Still, we don't know how or why.

Brunner wisely could devote considerable attention to this void in these novels. He could proceed best by developing the point that these two forces come together through material need. Producers have economic rewards that support consumptive habits while government officials possess authoritative rights. The governmental decisions that are made could reflect a trade-off of these two resources—producers supporting government because they need it and government reciprocating to retain position and prominence. Ordinary citizens, threatening neither, matter for neither. In addition, they lack the resources to substantially reward and assist governmental officials that these other interests possess.

Such a tightly constructed exchange situation has great applicability to the present state of American politics. Even former United States President Dwight D. Eisenhower warned of a military-industrial complex playing too dominant a role in governmental decisions. Since then, books like *America, Inc.* and *Who Owns America?*[10] have described conditions similar to those suggested by Brunner. The recent energy crisis seems to have been caused to some extent by such interaction. Brunner's novels could obviously have been developed more fully by further applying compatible interpretations of actual conditions rather than halting with the simple assertion that governmental responsiveness is dangerous. The reader never understands the nature of the danger, and Brunner's presentations become half-truths in terms of the probable.

Other things that Brunner suggests about governmental process are far-fetched. His portrayal of the president of the United States is especially shaky. All authority is too carefully placed in the hands of the chief executive, who moves other officials at will. The centralized executive is, for Brunner, the only figure necessary for economic interests to capture because he has all power at his command. Even the armed forces are viewed as "his" creatures. Government either dictates from its central location or it stands back as its presidential leader allows private enterprise to proceed without interferences. There is no indication that other institutions can check the executive or that any systems of laws exist as guidelines for him. The political process in these novels is one in which no individuals other than businessmen and the executive possess the resources necessary to affect outcomes. The citizenry has opted out, and other politicians are mere servants.

In reality things are not, would not be, so simply ordered. Too many individuals possess their own little spheres of influence in American politics and fight too hard to keep them. In most areas of government involvement, especially with regard to day-to-day affairs, almost all questions are decided through the interaction of specialized bureaucrats, congressional committees, and various interest groups. Experts in agriculture determine agriculture policies, while those in housing, environmental affairs, and education proceed in their own spheres. Defense specialists and everyone else negotiate in the same manner, and reciprocity is the general operating rule. In such a situation, the president, should he desire to shake things up in a dramatic way, could hope only to alter a small percentage of the national government's total effort. In addition, there are independent state and local governments over which he, personally, has almost no control.

Executives are limited in other than legal ways as well. No leader, in any government, can guide and control a complex and technical society without numerous bureaucratic eyes and ears to assist him. These specialized assistants are not neutral robots plugged in to do an executive's bidding. They use their own expert skills and interpret events through their own preferences. Indeed, their monopoly over information allows them to direct an executive as much as he directs them through his authoritative position. Even a President Vados would end up with a city as much a reflection of his bureaucratic planners' desires as his own. He would have to rely on them to define what it was possible to build and how to proceed.

If the governmental-economic collusion that Brunner implies is found in the future, it will necessarily operate in a manner other than the one he describes. No single "prexy" can make so many corrupt and ridiculous decisions. This opportunity must be shared by many, and any collusion will have to penetrate many functional areas and levels of government. An entire interrelated political system must be divorced from its supporting citizenry and corrupted, not just one man.

International Relations and Politics. Political relationships among countries are an integral part of *SOZ, TJO,* and *TSLU.* World tensions are great, some countries are in hot war, a cold war is evident among others, and guerrilla activities are common. Brunner's treatment of this topic clarifies his primary concern—human survival. Time and again he pointedly refers to the devastating effects of nationalism on the one hand and international conspiracy on the other. His characters, like Donald Hogan in *SOZ,* blindly respond to government propaganda about nationalism, only to be discarded and cast aside when an international cover-up is necessary to protect government images.

It is in this area that Brunner reveals how unscrupulous governments can be in manipulating symbols for their own purposes. The leadership takes command in foreign affairs and uses international events and fears to generate supportive attitudes. Citizens are conditioned to suspect and distrust other governments and the citizens they represent, including allies. Such propaganda campaigns give government a free hand in promoting policies that reward its favored economic interests. Imperialism and exploitation of Third World countries are the motives. But such tensions produce an international system engulfed in conflict and competition, an effect that precludes cooperation between nations in a search for solutions to the pollution and population problems threatening all. The aggregate results include an ineffectual United Nations, isolation, and failure.

Governments in Brunner's novels only interact as a last resort. Too many impediments exist for them to unilaterally attack common problems. This would require overt action taken in public view. Public opinion, the psychological predisposition of the leadership, the desirability of maintaining paranoia, and other related reasons simply disallow such considerations; they would threaten governmental status quo too directly. This specific warning by Brunner is of prime importance and is based upon his prior development of the political process. It both reflects and applies his model.

Brunner touches on some very real problems in these areas of international relations. All of them, in fact, have been the subject of intense congressional debate both in committee hearings and on the legislative floor. But again, Brunner's presentation is incomplete. Nationalism is indeed a problem similar to what Brunner describes, but it is not unchecked by economic factors. Brunner misses the multinational corporation whose profit motives overstep the boundaries of any one country. Many economic giants are not linked to one particular country, and their self-interest is not coexistent with any of them. The mutually satisfactory and rewarding arrangement that exists between the United States and General Technics in *SOZ* is too narrowly developed as a factor encouraging nationalism. They exploit together as an American-based firm operating abroad. This nationalistic spirit seems to be missing in actuality. Oil companies are a particularly good and very contemporary example; one, for instance, with headquarters in the United States, can administer a boycott against that country while trying to drain all the oil it can away from the country where its facilities operate. Quite clearly, nationalism and profit do not go hand in hand.

In short, problems of nationalism are not the only ones that Brunner could have dealt with in posing internationally relevant questions about survival. Nationalism seems to be only one part of a larger problem—institutional self-interest. Corporations, like countries, can pursue their own ends to the disadvantage of others; therefore, both constitute threats to world harmony and order. So, too, with detente and Third World coalitions that step over national boundaries when it is in the self-interest of governmental decision makers; both are mechanisms of political expediency and do not necessarily imply that governments have learned that nationalism is folly. National self-interest in certain restricted functional areas is just being enlarged to include partners.

Despite some problems with his analysis and the omission of some important explanatory factors, Brunner constructs some intriguing interpretations of the political process and why it fails. He begins with the society and its support of government and details a plausible explanation of the general reasons why important problems are not solved by governing institutions. On the whole, his accounts are quite well done. They not only concur with many elitist interpretations of politics but they also offer explanations for the existence of the elites.

BRUNNER'S CONTRIBUTION TO THOSE STUDYING POLITICS

John Brunner is not studying politics, but his works have positive utility for those who are. Despite the problems noted above, each of these novels could be assigned to students for the purpose of teaching them some valuable things about politics. The novels may not advance theories of politics in any way, but they do apply them.

One of the basic questions that students at introductory levels ask is, "Why do we need government?" Another is, "Why can't we just trust government to do a good job?" Or, similarly, "Why should citizens be expected to watch over government officials?" Brunner's novels supply basic, albeit rather simplified, answers to these questions. He presents the reader with societies that have no predictable order and shows the problems that result. He reveals specific reasons why governmental units can fail in their task of assisting future survival, and he shows the compounding effect of these failures. But of greater importance is the fact that he illustrates all this with real problem areas like pollution. These are excellent reasons for examining Brunner's works.

His dystopian model of governmental failure can be applied as a pedagogical tool by asking students to consider it as a case of deductive logic. It's quite instructive and useful to take any one of these novels apart and reconstruct the pieces that account for the preordained failures. In addition, it's possible to examine how actual institutional and legal arrangements could have affected or changed the situation if they had been present. Or, perhaps more appropriately, the novels could be compared with the failures of the real world when these arrangements exist there but are absent in Brunner's. How, for example, could a Congress force consideration of pollution problems? Or would it? Or, what techniques should have been available for Vados's bureaucrats to use in affecting his behavior?

These novels have another advantage for the student of politics in that they touch subjects that empirical research cannot easily reach. Much of the activity of political officials and citizens is not subject to either direct or indirect observation, and it is almost impossible to know how certain of them would handle situations unlike those they have already encountered. Brunner makes basic assumptions about these unknowns and offers a speculative explanation with derived consequences.

Finally, it should not be forgotten that Brunner's political insights make for eventful study. Novels, especially these, are fun and exciting to read and can be expected to motivate students to approach their subjects more eagerly. The satire that characterizes Brunner's political writing also contributes to the readability of this material. His points are often made with such bitter irony that readers cannot help but be jolted by the significance of the action.

However, it is probably safe to assume that very few practicing political scientists will elect to use Brunner's novels as educational aids. He flouts too many of the values they hold. Many would never think of using fiction in a course because it would seem inappropriate. Others might reject this particular fiction because it eliminates a consideration of effective decision making. Finally, even those who are quite concerned about the very problems that Brunner addresses might find it impossible to use his oversimplified generalizations about decision making. Drew Pearson's *The Senator* and Burdick and Wheeler's *Fail-Safe* would more easily catch their attention and appear more believable.[11] It is simply more difficult to ferret out the political value of Brunner's writings; but it is real and very evident if one will only make an effort to find and apply it.

NOTES

1. These books were selected for review because *SOZ, TJO,* and *TSLU* constitute Brunner's major dystopias, while *SOTC* has a specifically political setting. They are not totally representative of all Brunner's work, being much more politically oriented than most of his novels.

2. Drew Pearson, *The President* (New York: Hearst Corp., 1970); Robert Penn Warren, *All the King's Men* (New York: Harcourt, Brace, 1946); Allen Drury, *Advise and Consent* (New York: Doubleday, 1959).

3. Lyman Sargent, "Utopia and Dystopia in Contemporary Science Fiction," *Futurist* (June, 1972), pp. 93–98.

4. Thomas Kuhn, *The Structure of Scientific Revolutions,* 2nd ed. (University of Chicago Press, 1970).

5. C. Wright Mills, *The Power Elite* (New York: Oxford, 1956).

6. Aldous Huxley, *Brave New World* (New York: Bantam, 1958); George Orwell, *1984* (New York: Harcourt, Brace, 1949).

7. See the following for recent popular treatments of this subject: Thomas Dye and Harmon Zeigler, *The Irony of Democracy* (Belmont, Calif.: Duxbury, 1970); Duane Lockhard, *The Perverted Priorities of American Politics* (New York: Macmillan, 1971); Kenneth Dolbeare, *Political Change in the United States* (New York: McGraw-Hill, 1974).

8. Stokely Carmichael and Charles Hamilton, *Black Power* (New York: Random, 1967).

9. Milton Kotler, *Neighborhood Government* (Indianapolis: Bobbs-Merrill, 1969); Alan Altshuler, *Community Control* (New York: Pegasus, 1970).

10. Morton Mintz and Jerry Cohen, *America, Inc.* (New York: Dial, 1971); Walter Hickel, *Who Owns America?* (Englewood Cliffs, N.J.: Prentice-Hall, 1971).

11. Drew Pearson, *The Senator* (New York: Doubleday, 1968); Eugene Burdick and Harvey Wheeler, *Fail-Safe* (New York: McGraw-Hill, 1962).

PART 4

SCIENCE AND TECHNOLOGY

ROBERT R. SLOCUM

Sic Parvis Magna:
Science, Technology, and Ecology
in John Brunner's Science Fiction

I

Brunner considers himself a "social-science fiction" writer, and expounded his views on the subject in some detail at the 1973 World Science Fiction Convention. Good science fiction should pursue "plausible and quasi-realistic subject matter"; contemporary characters should not be thrust, un-modified, into tomorrow's situations; the social and political implications of science and technology must not be neglected. Brunner bemoans the fact that early "hard" science fiction was essentially a trivialization of the future, not portraying real people in real situations, and limited by a nonholistic ap-proach to its subject matter. Unfortunately, these criticisms still apply to some present-day science fiction.[1]

My view of good science fiction agrees with Brunner's. The social, politi-cal, and economic impingement of science and technology on society should be given careful attention, and the mere behavior of a new gadget minimized. As is evident from the history of gunpowder, automobiles, and television, technological developments do influence man and his society in ways both subtle and nonsubtle. Since human behavior, and therefore human character, is modified by technological change, scientists and technologists do have a responsibility to anticipate, in so far as possible, the potential uses of the fruits of their specialties. Good science fiction must incorporate these facts and the attendant responsibilities. Brunner's science fiction does this.

In this essay I examine four aspects of Brunner's science fiction:
1. his use of science and technology, with primary consideration of *The Sheep Look Up*, but also a less detailed analysis of the science and tech-nology in *The Jagged Orbit* and *Stand on Zanzibar;*

2. his treatment of ecological issues in *TSLU;*
3. his characterization of scientists in *TSLU, TJO,* and *SOZ,* with particular attention to whether Brunner displays any of the bias C. P. Snow claims as inherent in literary intellectuals with regard to scientists and technologists;
4. his utilization of the science-society interaction.

Before beginning, however, a few observations are in order. First, this essay concentrates on *TSLU* because of its setting in the relatively near future (1978). The shorter the time projected, the less likely it becomes that major scientific innovations will have occurred; therefore, the projections in *TSLU* and their credibility are much more subject to analysis in terms of existing science than those in *TJO* (2014) or *SOZ* (2010).

Second, the science-technology analysis of *TSLU* is difficult to separate from the consideration of ecological issues. One of the basic principles of ecology is that everything is connected to everything else. When I consider filtermasks or oxygen dispensers or the death of the Mediterranean, the scientific-technological aspects are inseparable from the ecological. People are using filtermasks because air pollution is alleged to have increased to such an extent as to require their use; the technology of filtermasks is not independent of that assumption. Thus, some apparent redundancy in content occurs among the various sections of this essay.

Finally, on the basis of my analysis of his major works, it is my general conclusion that Brunner's science and technology projections are largely credible, his assessment of the science-society interaction reasonable and accurate, the care with which he checks out his science sources admirable, and the overall quality of his books excellent.

I I

In *TSLU* Brunner refers to such technological developments as filtermasks, oxygen dispensers (like candy-vending machines), electric buses, stronghold estates and residential security devices, personal gas guns for individual protection, steam cars, electric cars, and hydroponic plants. All are credible, although their context requires qualification in some cases. For example, using a TV interview of Dr. Lucas Quarrey by Petronella Page, Brunner describes the United States as producing less than 60 percent of the oxygen it consumes (*TSLU,* p. 31). Wallace S. Broecker[2] challenges this view of a diminishing oxygen supply and argues that it is essentially immune to change over a short time scale, such as 100 to 1,000 years. Measurements indicate that above every square *meter* of the earth's surface there are about 60,000 moles of oxygen—a mole of oxygen is an amount having a mass of 32 grams.

Having established that the quantity of oxygen produced by all plants living both on land and in the ocean is roughly equivalent to the amount consumed by all animals and bacteria on earth, Broecker points out that such production and consumption represents only about one part in fifteen million of the oxygen present in the earth's atmosphere. Further, if we were to burn all known reserves of fossil fuels, thereby tying up oxygen in carbon dioxide molecules, we would still have used less than three percent of all available oxygen. Consequently, we must conclude that there can be no oxygen shortage until very much later than the projected time scale of *TSLU*.

Since they are not needed to rectify a general oxygen shortage, perhaps the public oxygen dispensers in *TSLU* are needed for temporary relief from elevated carbon monoxide levels in cities. Carbon monoxide is hazardous because the blood's hemoglobin has a greater affinity for it than for oxygen; consequently, if sufficient carbon monoxide is present in the air, it preferentially combines with the hemoglobin and renders the hemoglobin useless for its normal function of carrying oxygen to the cells. Fortunately, this process appears to be reversible, so that breathing normal air ultimately returns the hemoglobin to a condition permitting it to carry on its vital function.

But here, too, I see some inconsistency. Brunner suggests in *TSLU* that the population of the United States has begun to fall—it's down to 200 million. Even now our cities are not capable of handling any more automobiles—the major source of carbon monoxide in large cities—and Brunner implies that electric and steam cars are in fairly wide use by 1978. Consequently, carbon monoxide levels in the cities should be lower than at the present time. But R. S. Scorer[3] points out that a cigarette smoker today receives at least three times the exposure to carbon monoxide that city dwellers receive in any major city at street level under conditions of high traffic density. Further, despite man's addition of carbon monoxide to the atmosphere, there is no evidence that its concentration in the atmosphere is increasing, indicating that there are as yet not understood mechanisms whereby the carbon monoxide is assimilated by the environment. To proceed further with the argument, I need to know precisely what pollutant Brunner believes capable of creating effects which require the use of oxygen dispensers for their alleviation. He doesn't specify what it is.

Filtermasks, on the other hand, are already in use by traffic policemen in large cities to combat the carbon monoxide and nitrogen oxides produced by internal combustion engines, as well as by children in Los Angeles and Tokyo having recess during high smog periods. In *TSLU* it appears that everyone from the lower middle classes up wears them whenever they go outside of their air-purified, air-conditioned offices and homes. In that regard, they function as a highly visible status symbol, for the poor cannot afford them.

Yet it should be pointed out that air pollution levels in many major American cities actually have declined substantially between 1968 and 1973. The reasons for this are somewhat encouraging: the use of limited (i. e., partial) emission control devices has become compulsory on private automobiles; many states, under pressure from the Environmental Protection Agency to set and enforce air quality standards, have insisted that electric power plants —major sources of sulfur oxides, carbon monoxide, and particulate matter— purchase low-sulfur coal or, in many cases, convert from coal to oil or natural gas. Further, the use of electrostatic precipitators with a theoretical capability of stopping 99 percent of particulate matter emissions from smoke stacks is being required.

Unfortunately, this trend toward cleaner air may be reversed as the result of petroleum and gas shortages and the recent encouragements offered the states by the federal government to relax their air quality standards in order to conserve petroleum, thus halting the conversion away from coal to cleaner fuels. Such practices might eventually result in conditions similar to the polluted air of *TSLU*.

Brunner frequently makes valid use of the fact that the epidemiology of exposure to low concentrations of air pollutants is in most cases inadequately understood. His projections may be based on his own experience in England: two of the most severe air pollution incidents occurred in London in 1952 and 1962; the rate of bronchial disorders is substantially higher in England than in most of the world, including the United States. It is certainly a credible extrapolation, given the current level of ignorance, that constant exposure to pollutants at concentrations lower than those known to be directly toxic might lead to the kind of ubiquitous bronchial problems exhibited by the majority of the population in *TSLU*. It is already known that certain pollutants in combination with others have a synergistic effect, so that joint appearances create much greater hazards than would be predicted from independent concentrations of either ingredient. Probably the best-known instance of this was the 1952 London incident, in which sulfur oxides in combination with particulates were carried much deeper into the lungs than would have been the case without the presence of the particulates. However, London is one of the better examples of how a serious pollution problem can be ameliorated by identifying the causes and taking remedial action—state-subsidized conversion to cleaner residential heating sources.

Electric buses, electric cars, and steam cars have been around for a long time, although used only on a small scale. The implication in *TSLU* seems to be that these vehicles are used to a greater extent by those (particularly the Trainites and their supporters) trying to combat increased air pollution from gasoline engines. It should be pointed out, however, that until a significant fraction of our electricity can be produced by means other than burning fossil fuels, full-scale conversion to electric vehicles only shifts the air pollution problem from mobile to stationary sources, i.e., the power plants. Stringent imposition of emission controls at fossil fuel plants would result in reduced air pollution; but even then, this scheme would intensify the problem of declining fossil fuel supplies, for such power plants are less efficient than internal combustion engines in the use of fuel. Furthermore, the demand for electric power in the United States is projected to double between 1970 and 1980, even without the increased demand that would be necessitated by massive conversion to electric vehicles. None of the more exotic schemes for cleaner production of electricity is expected to be on line as early as 1980, and the fraction of electricity being generated by conventional nuclear reactors is expected still to be small by 1980.

In *TSLU* cars not equipped with precipitators are liable to confiscation. This indicates that the government, as through the Environmental Protection Agency, is displaying a nominal interest in the suppression of air pollution. Also, it is significant, and perhaps realistic, that governmental control is directed toward the consumer rather than the producer. Such an approach is no doubt a natural extension of present policy which advocates the installation of emission control devices on individual autos, the cost of which, of course, is passed directly to the consumer. Perhaps even more in the tenor of *TSLU* are the ease with which the American automobile industry succeeded in delaying the imposition of even this type of environmental protection device and the industry's almost total refusal to research alternatives which would be intrinsically less polluting *ab initio*. Meanwhile, Japanese and German auto manufacturers did succeed in developing cars which easily met the same proposed pollution standards which the American giants successfully argued to be technically and economically beyond their capabilities. Here, Brunner has relentlessly extrapolated the social and economic inertia of mammoth industrial organizations, as well as the reactionary tendencies of American government and the business-oriented self-interest of these "representatives of the people's will."

In *TSLU, TJO,* and *SOZ* virtually everyone carries antipersonnel weapons or devices, and their homes or apartments are protected by elaborate electronic security systems. "Stronghold-style" subdivisions protected by ex-policemen and ex-marines exist today, as well as in *TSLU,* although armored school buses are not yet in common use. More extreme examples occur in *TJO,* where yards are seeded with landmines and apartment doors are rigged with deadfalls weighing several hundred pounds. Gottschalk arms salesmen peddle weapons door to door, while their "home office" engages in research and development to produce ever more destructive devices. In *SOZ* the scholarly synthesist Donald Hogan goes for a stroll in Manhattan equipped with a "jettigun" (a cartridge-charged gas pistol) and a "karatand" (a palm-less glove made of impact-resistant plastic); meanwhile "muckers" claim dozens of lives daily despite control efforts by the "fuzzywuzzies" (police). Sabotage, riot, and massive public disorder are rampant throughout these works.

Personal gas guns for self-defense are already available in the larger cities, but so far they only contain mace, which is hazardous stuff but not usually lethal. But such guns are only a small part of the numerous home security and self-defense devices currently being developed or already on the market; here I see a straight-line technological extrapolation from the present in Brunner's violent and insecure futures. Statistics indicate that Detroit presently contains about one handgun for each family in the city. It also has one of the nation's highest homicide rates. Some law enforcement officials have suggested that these two items are related. Brunner merely postulates a similar suspicious and fear-ridden society taking advantage of a more elaborate, sophisticated, and mass-marketed weapons technology.

Hydroponic plants have been in existence for a good while, but not on the scale of the Bamberley plant in *TSLU.* Presently they are inherently more expensive than the natural method of growing plants, because all, not just some, of the necessary nutrients for the plant's sustenance must be supplied artificially to the system rather than having the soil itself pay part of the nutritional cost. However, growth rates are modifiable by such a technique if cost is not a major consideration. Hydroponic plants, like greenhouses, utilize controlled, artificial environments, totally enclosed so that the internal environments can be maintained for optimal growth conditions irrespective of the external climate. This permits two or even three harvests per year instead of one. Of course, lighting conditions, crucial for triggering most plant growth processes, are artificially maintained and controlled, another tie-in to the energy situation.

So far my discussion has been slanted strongly toward the technological extrapolations involved in *TSLU,* with only a passing reference to personal weapons and security devices in *TJO* and *SOZ.* The reason for this concentration on *TSLU* is associated with the closeness of the future it projects and the resultant low probability that any major scientific innovations will occur which will vitiate my analysis. The further into the future Brunner projects, the more difficult it becomes to give an accurate assessment of his extrapolations; the history of science indicates that entirely new principles or phenomena will probably be discovered which currently make no sense at all. Isaac Newton or James Clerk Maxwell would not have been able to analyze the credibility of tapping the energy of the atomic nucleus, for the simple reason that in their time its existence was unknown. But it is little appreciated that the physics of Newton and Maxwell has not been overthrown or negated by more modern developments. The reflection of neutrons in nuclear reactors obeys Newtonian physics, and the turbogenerators which produce the electricity in nuclear power plants operate in strict accordance with the principles of Maxwell's electromagnetic theory. Thus, some analysis of Brunner's more distant science and technology is possible, though on a limited basis.

The System C integrated weaponry of *TJO* is difficult to analyze accurately for two reasons: new technological breakthroughs may have occurred, and crucial details in specification are missing. Despite this, laws of nature, such as the conservation of energy, must not be violated. System C is described as being form-fitting; does this mean that it is not much larger than the human body? If so, then there are serious objections to the amount of energy required for its operation. At present it is not possible to make nuclear weapons as small in yields as those detailed in System C. But the development of perfect neutron reflectors might make such small nuclear weapons feasible.

Genetic manipulation is a central element in *SOZ* and warrants some discussion. We presently do not possess the ability to undertake such manipulation with any high expectation for accurate predictable consequences. Even if we could accurately predict the consequences of genetic manipulation from the scientific viewpoint, there would remain the problem of foreseeing social and political implications. Since I am neither a biologist nor a sociologist, I cannot assess these aspects with much accuracy, nor provide a positive or negative evaluation of them. In fact, I feel a certain ambivalence on the whole subject.

Certainly eugenics is not novel. Wolves, by the nature of the pack's social structure, automatically practice genetic selection and control. Only the dominant male and the dominant female are permitting to mate and have offspring. Since the dominant male and dominant female are selected on the basis of biological superiority, the effects of such a social structure include the improvement of the gene pool of the species and the limiting of the population to a level consistent with the available food supply. Moreover, as a consequence of the genetic improvement in the wolf pack, there is a concomitant improvement in the genetic constitution of their prey. Since the weaker members of the deer herd are selectively eliminated by the wolf pack, the genetics of the predated population are automatically improved. Also, a kind of genetic selection has been practiced for millennia in many human societies as a result of the social custom of parental mate selection for their children based on semirational criteria. Only in recent times has eugenics been entirely ignored in mate selection.

These types of eugenics have existed since the beginning of life, and, of course, no one has been especially concerned about them. Only when science gets us to the point where we can do the same kind of thing rationally, basing it on our own criteria, does anyone begin to worry about it. Clearly, the major issue of concern is not the scientific capability for genetic modification, but rather the social and ethical issues regarding the use of this power —the fear that an elite group will use this technology for their own ends. In this sense, the eugenics issue is no different from the overall problem of who determines the use of technology and selects those who benefit from it.

To round out this discussion of Brunner's use and projection of science and technology, it should be pointed out that one can find, albeit rarely, an occasional scientific faux pas.

In *SOZ* Brunner has the master computer Shalmaneser cooled by liquid helium, apparently because the memory core is so large that the heat produced is sufficient to need extensive cooling, or perhaps because superconductivity is somehow being utilized in the system. This helium coolant is also used to disarm a religious fanatic bent on destroying Shalmaneser; as she attacks the computer and its technicians with an axe, quick-thinking Norman House sprays her hand with the super-cold fluid, causing it to freeze, become brittle, and break off due to the weapon's weight. I see technical problems here. Liquid helium has a very low heat capacity and a low latent heat of vaporization; this means (1) that a large quantity of the stuff is required to cool something down to its boiling point of 4.2 degrees Kelvin (4.2 degrees Celsius above absolute zero); (2) that a fairly elaborate procedure, involving vacuum-insulated pipelines, is required for its transfer to keep it in liquid form; and (3) that only small amounts of heat are required to boil (vaporize) large quantities of it. Helium pumped from a vacuum-insulated line into the air readily vaporizes, and, being a very light gas, has a tendency to rise very rapidly to the ceiling rather than staying in a nicely confined stream the way water does. Therefore, freezing a hand would require that the hand be held very close to the exit orifice for relatively long periods of time. I have held my hand in the stream of helium blow-off from a Dewar vessel containing liquid helium for as long as thirty seconds—the same hand I am now using to write this. Assuming the girl in *SOZ* had normal reflexes and didn't want her hand frozen, it would have been almost impossible to disarm her with a vacuum-insulated liquid helium hose.

Why use liquid helium as a computer coolant, anyway? For most purposes, liquid nitrogen is almost as useful as helium and immensely cheaper. Liquid nitrogen costs about 14 cents/liter, whereas liquid helium costs about 25 dollars/liter. Liquid helium has a boiling point of 4.2 degrees Kelvin, liquid nitrogen a boiling point of 78 degrees Kelvin. Now, if superconductivity dictated the use of liquid helium, it is highly probable that by the time implicit in *SOZ* we will have developed superconducting alloys which function at twenty degrees Kelvin or higher, which would at least permit the use of less expensive liquids, such as hydrogen, instead of the costlier liquid helium.

Unfortunately, because of the lower molecular weight of hydrogen, its efficiency for freezing hands would be even less than that of liquid helium.

Although nearly nonexistent in *SOZ, TJO*, and *TSLU* there are a few downright scientific impossibilities, at least from the perspective of the twentieth-century scientist. For example, in *TJO* Brunner has the computer Robert Gottschalk invade the mind of a human being and take over his body. The mechanism of such science-defying action is left sufficiently vague to prevent any rational analysis. But here Brunner is using a fairly common science fiction theme, purely speculative in nature, and based on the likely assumption that at some time in the future today's scientific laws will be overthrown and transcended. This is reminiscent of his use of "qua-space" engines in *Bedlam Planet* and *Total Eclipse*, which enable spaceships to exceed the speed of light and so to travel between stars. The scientist recoils at this, but no real harm is intended or done. Such works are just for fun and stand in sharp contrast to Brunner's more serious works. Besides, without this scientific license, much interesting science fiction could never have existed.

Thus far, in discussing the credibility of Brunner's technological references, I've been doing the kind of nit-picking which might be expected between a physicist and a writer. If you accept C. P. Snow's thesis concerning the communication gap between the "two cultures,"[4] then of course you expect a mutual misunderstanding between Brunner and me. Snow's thesis, severely abbreviated, is that there exists a sharp dichotomy between literary intellectuals and scientists. These two groups don't communicate with each other, the literary intellectuals even boasting about their ignorance of science. The literary intellectuals tend to be pessimistic and oriented toward the past and the "good old days," the scientists optimistic and oriented toward the future. Snow considers the social scientist to be in a nebulous middle ground, accepted by neither the natural scientist nor the literary intellectual. But I don't entirely accept Snow's thesis, and from my reading of his works I doubt that Brunner does either. However, later in this essay I do wish to consider Brunner's treatment of his scientists in the light of the "two cultures" thesis.

III

The ecological references in *TSLU* run the gamut of harmful environmental effects of man on the ecosphere. Examples of water pollution include water unsafe to drink without elaborate purification techniques, dying oceans, and an already dead Mediterranean Sea. Air pollution has progressed to the point that if "the sun is out at Santa Ynez," it is a rare and highly unusual phenomenon, while anyone venturing outside air-conditioned buildings is forced to wear a filter mask. Cars are equipped with air filters and precipitators, bronchial disease and allergies are ubiquitous and rampant, the rain is acid and corrosive, silver nitrate, used in rainmaking, has detrimental effects on hair, and children are deformed from the prevalence of air-borne defoliants. Other environmental effects include the following: lead, PCB, and DDT contaminate both water and air on a much larger scale than at present; widespread use of drugs and chemicals have produced resistant strains of viruses, bacteria, and other single life forms, with mutated varieties having lethal, uncontrollable effects on the population; children are born with birth defects to such an extent that abnormality insurance is widely purchased; smallpox warnings are frequent; food is scarce and hunger is prevalent in the United States; microwave leakage causes fetal death.

How credible are these future conditions? In the large, they represent frighteningly straightforward projections of current ecological problems. However, given the relative nearness of the future described in *TSLU,* some seem exaggerated for dramatic and literary effect. Laying this question aside for a moment, let us consider one area in which there is no doubt as to Brunner's foresightedness.

Brunner appears to be a most accurate social prophet. He seems keenly aware that society will be gullible enough, as it has been in the past, to accept the treatment of symptoms as a substitute for real problem solving. Witness his reference to the confiscation of autos not equipped with precipitators; this indicates that the government's measures are only vote-gaining gestures designed to treat symptoms rather than the underlying causes. It doesn't demand that air pollution be controlled or eliminated, only that symptomatic treatment be compulsory.

This must lead us to question the overall utility of using technological fixes to cure or correct the defects or hazards and the misuses or abuses of previous technology. If the socio-economic-political system exploits technology to further its own aim—profit and power for a small minority—there is no good reason to assume that the new corrective technological uses will be any more altruistic or less hazardous than the original utilization. This is especially true given the contemporary accelerating demands for the quick correction of apparently obvious defects. The side effects of this new technology will most likely be no better-anticipated than those of the old. For example, in solving the problems of phosphate detergents, a substitute additive was proposed, NTA (nitrilo-acetate), which turned out to act synergistically with methyl-mercury or with cadmium in such a way that the resulting complexes were far more toxic than the original compounds.

Thus, treating causes rather than symptoms requires a broader understanding of potential problems, and this is as true in the social area as in the realm of chemistry. Consider the "Trainite" movement in *TSLU,* named for Austin

Train, whose antiestablishment stands have forced him underground out of fear for his own safety. Have Train's actions really accomplished anything useful? Rather than continuing his research and writing, which might have had some effect had he been able to win over the more rational elements of society, he withdraws, abandoning any efforts to influence people to consider the idiocy of the system and the errors of their acceptance of it. When he does come out of hiding, it is too late.

Moreover, his supporters come on as neo-Luddites, thrashing out at symbols and symptoms, never really considering whether there are any viable alternatives. Of course, Train disavows them, but that solves nothing. Anarchists borrow his name and lead in his stead. In the ensuing violence Train is martyred by a namesake, and the society falls.

I can't escape the conclusion that Train was utterly inept and doomed to fail, a mere symbol of the ecology fad which seems to have about run its course. Somehow he reminds me of Goethe's Werther, who initiated a movement of young men to go off into the woods and commit suicide as a reaction to some of the abuses of the early Industrial Revolution.

Given the Trainite example, it is apparent that the solution of ecological problems will require the cooperation of social scientists to help revise people's attitudes toward lifestyles and value structures. Also, people fear the unknown even when it may be safer than the known hazards to which they've become accustomed; this is another bridge they must be helped across.

Having touched upon Brunner as social prophet—at least in the ecology action area—let us return to his prognostications for the physical environment. In thirty or forty years, given the credibility of Brunner's social projections, I can admit to the Mediterranean dying, the oceans becoming sterile and unfruitful, the air so polluted as to render the "sun is out at Santa Ynez" extraordinary, and an increased death rate due to pollutants. But not by 1978, the period forecasted in *TSLU*.

Given this limited time scale, there is one specific ecological issue on which I must disagree—the death of the Mediterranean Sea.

The Mediterranean has an area over one hundred times greater than that of Lake Erie, and maximum and average depths range up to more than twenty-five times those of Lake Erie. Further, the population density along the shoreline of the Mediterranean does not appear to be any greater than that along the shore of Lake Erie—in many regions it is far lower. The amount of heavy industry ringing the Mediterranean appears lower than that lining much smaller Lake Erie. Consequently, the Mediterranean Sea should be several orders of magnitude more resistant to eutrophication than Lake Erie. It is probably fair to say that it took us at least fifty years of concerted polluting effort before the advent of the death of Lake Erie. Given that we now have a greater awareness of the mechanisms which can contribute to the pollution and eutrophication of a lake, I find it highly improbable that the Mediterranean could die by the late 1970s. I seriously doubt that, even if all the lessons learned from the virtual demise of Lake Erie are ignored, the Mediterranean would die before well into the twenty-first century.

In Brunner's defense, there is evidence that the Mediterranean is being damaged, particularly by oil spills and by sewage from the population along the French and Italian coasts. Five major rivers have direct or indirect inputs into the Mediterranean (most European rivers flow northward and westward and pose a more serious threat to the Baltic and North Seas than to the Mediterranean): the Dnieper, the Dniester, and Danube empty into the Black Sea, which connects with the Mediterranean and is itself substantially larger than Lake Erie; the Nile and the Ebro appear to be the principal rivers emptying directly into the Mediterranean. The Danube is a severely polluted river, but a multinational effort on the part of those countries through which it flows appears to be improving its condition. I must admit that I have been unable to find any data about the exchange rate between the Black Sea and the Mediterranean, nor could I find any data on the condition of the Dnieper or the Dniester rivers, but I would hazard a guess that those two rivers are immensely cleaner than the Danube.

Unfortunately, I also lack information about the contribution of the Ebro, but the Nile River has attracted wide attention. The Nile is now stopped up by the Aswan High Dam. Some serious unanticipated consequences have arisen because of this dam, including the loss of the sardine industry that once flourished at the mouth of the Nile, because of the loss of river-borne nutrients and the rampant increase of schistosomiasis, a snail-carried disease that has spread rapidly as a result of conditions associated with the extensive irrigation canal system used behind the dam. While these effects are of ecological interest, neither seem to be major threats to the Mediterranean.

The *jigra* is a second agent of disaster used by Brunner in *TSLU* that I find difficult to credit scientifically. This little devil, evolved from more benign ancestors through insecticide dosing, is introduced into the United States and proceeds in the course of a few months essentially to wipe out American agriculture, or at least enough of it to lead to wide-scale hunger.

The jigra looks so like a worm that it goes undetected when mixed with real earthworms sold to American farmers, yet it is described as having many legs. From this multipedal nature, I presume that it is some kind of relative of either centipedes or millipedes. Having checked the habits and life cycles of these creatures, I find it unlikely that such an organism could reduce the agriculture of the United States to utter disaster in such a short period of time. Apparently, the idea here was that an alien organism, immune to pesticides, introduced into a region devoted to monobiotic agricultural techniques, could have devastating effects. This is certainly a valid point, but I think I would have chosen some sort of winged insect with high mobility and short life cycle to do the job rather than the relatively immobile jigra. Again, it appears that the time scale was compressed for dramatic effect.

I wish to reemphasize here that, in general, Brunner has been impeccably precise and scrupulously accurate in his treatment of environmental disaster themes in *TSLU,* including those with which I have taken exception because of the time scales involved. In particular, his portrayal of the effects of air- and water-borne toxic agents—such as lead, mercury, pesticides, herbicides, PCB—appears to be totally credible and meticulously researched. In reading *TSLU,* it is difficult to overcome the very strong feeling that "My God, these things are really happening!" It is just as hard to avoid asking the question, "Is *TSLU* science fiction, or is it instead a detailed environmental impact study of man's effects on his environment?" I repeat: the vast majority of Brunner's ecological projections appear credible given thirty or forty years.

In *SOZ* Brunner includes an ecological problem not presented directly in *TSLU*—overpopulation. Many of the statistics on this issue have received so much attention in recent years that they should be entirely exoteric, so I will review only a few of them here.

World population is, and has been, increasing exponentially for a very long time, with marked increases in growth rate clearly attributable to the development of agriculture in prehistoric times and more recently to the Industrial Revolution and subsequent improvements in sanitation and disease control. The present doubling time for world population, now estimated at approximately 3.7 billion, is about 35 years. In the highly industrialized nations the doubling times tend to be much longer than the world average—60 to 70 years—while in the poorer, less industrialized countries, the doubling times tend to be much shorter—as low as 18 to 20 years.

These few facts contain threatening implications. Assume poor country X has a population doubling time of 20 years due to high birth rates and (temporarily) lowered death rates. Country X has an undernourished, undereducated agrarian population; the majority of its citizens are ill-fed and ill-housed, and while a few receive adequate medical care, many suffer from debilitating diseases like schistosomiasis or malaria. Its exports are few and/or highly specialized and subject to the whims of the world market; it has little or no technological base for its economy, and very little investment capital is available. Yet, in only 20 years this already starving country must at least double all its social, economic, and technological services; it must be able to feed twice as many hungry people, clothe and shelter twice as many people, provide employment, etc. Even if country X is able to achieve this massive increase in services, the level of living will have only stayed at its original bleak level; the more probable outcome is decline.

The standard argument of those who contend the population problem is not serious runs something like this: in 1798 Thomas Robert Malthus[5] predicted that world population would outstrip available food supplies and famine would be inevitable. At that time, 175 years ago, the world population was about 900 million. But Malthus was wrong. He failed to anticipate extensive settlement of new territories, scientific and technological innovations which led to improvement in medical care and sanitation, and the industrialization of agriculture. Since Malthus was wrong, others who make such predictions will also be incorrect because science and technology will devise miraculous new ways to feed us. Some serious estimates by these anti-Malthusians suggest that earth could hold as many as 50 billion people, and by that time there still will be no problem because we will have colonized other planets in our solar system or even have moved on to the stars.

If science were really this powerful, *TSLU* and *SOZ* would not be so frighteningly realistic as they are. All our present-day accomplishments do not prevent some 10 million or more people from starving to death each year. In fact, such simplistic faith in science and technology will only factualize Brunner's dystopian visions.

The United States alone, representing a mere 6 percent of the total population of the planet, consumes one-third of the energy and about one-half the mineral resources utilized annually on earth. Earth is finite; its mineral resources, fossil fuel supplies, arable land, and food-producing capabilities are finite. Since the United States population doubling time is about twice the global average of 35 years, after 70 years the global population will have quadrupled while the American population has only doubled. At that time the United States will represent less than 3 percent of the total global population. If it were to maintain its present standard of living, the United States would then be using two-thirds of the energy and all the mineral resources of the planet, assuming that supplies lasted and other nations didn't increase their consumption more rapidly than the United States. It seems rather unlikely that the other 97 percent of the world's population would be content with such a fantastic imbalance of wealth. Obviously, such a projection is politically, socially, and economically incredible.

Unfortunately, there is no scientifically valid way to estimate the total carrying capacity of the planet; such an assessment involves nonquantifiable variables, such as quality of life rather than merely quantity of life, in addition to psychological and social data not yet clearly understood—what is the maximum population density for psychological well-being and what is the minimum territory required for social equilibrium? One serious attempt in that direction indicates that the maximum population earth could tolerate with a standard of living comparable to that presently enjoyed by Americans is one billion—2.7 billion less than the present population of the planet.[6]

If we continue our philosophy of constant economic growth and our attitude that earth and nature exist for man's exploitation, Malthus will ultimately be proved correct, most likely in ways clearly developed by Brunner in *SOZ* and *TSLU*.

I V

We noted above that John Brunner knows science and uses it well. Yet, as he himself frequently observes, "I've never had a science lesson in my life"; his formal education was in letters. Certainly he has never worked as a scientist. This fact clearly distinguishes Brunner from such men as Robert Heinlein, Arthur Clarke, Fred Hoyle, and Isaac Asimov. Yet all are excellent science fiction authors, and all have written works well grounded in science.

The scientist is frequently found as a central figure in the works of all these men and, indeed, throughout science fiction. Leaving comparative analysis to others, I will focus here on the role of the scientist in Brunner's major works. What scientific roles are depicted and how are they carried out? Is there any indication of bias against scientists?

First, consider Austin Train, ecologist, and Dr. Thomas Grey, cyberneticist, in *TSLU*. There is no doubt that Train is the protagonist, Grey an antagonist. Austin Train's published observations have aroused the liberal element of the population and incensed the conservatives and so-called "silent majority." Fleeing possible co-optation or repression, he goes into hiding, withdrawing from the public arena. He is, in my opinion, portrayed as a coward, who, even though rich, turns tail to save his skin and to wait for the proper time to reemerge. His elaborate precautions against the discovery of his whereabouts or even his existence, his conversations with Peg Mankiewicz, and the safeguards set up for his anticlimactic reemergence on the Petronella Page show seem to support my opinion. Certainly he has fled from problems rather than openly confronting them or attempting to utilize his training to solve them. Is this representative of Brunner's idea of the scientist?

Compare Dr. Thomas Grey, charged by Bamberley Trust with developing a "rational, scientific, predictable plan to cure this country's ills. . . ." This is certainly a task requiring a scientist of the first rank. But what is Brunner's attitude toward Grey? He appears here as the stereotyped scientist—eccentric, compulsive, perfectionistic—even types better than his secretaries. A letter Grey writes to the *Christian Science Monitor* portrays him as being bound to an analytical approach requiring him to miss the holistic view of the synthesist (*TSLU*, pp. 80-83). Certainly what Grey says in his letter is rational—Brunner even refers to him as "among the most rational men alive"—yet Grey's narrowness forces him to reject Train as a bigot and his followers as extremists. Despite the unflattering characterization, Grey does more overall than Train;

he constantly grinds away at his computer simulation of the global system, even scrupulously footing the bill for paper and supplies, during most of the time Train is in hiding and not using his talents in any way other than shoveling garbage. Grey ends up being right; Train ends up dead, pseudofather of an anarchistic revolution. Is Brunner's characterization of Grey pejorative because he dispassionately pursues his work rather than despairing and going into a funk like Train? The evidence seems to indicate that Brunner is more sympathetic to Train than to Grey, perhaps unconsciously showing the kind of bias C. P. Snow attributes to the literary intellectual.

In *TJO* the scientist-hero is Xavier Conroy, professor of social psychology, who, in a climactic happy ending, keeps his cool enough to seriously converse with the master computer, Robert Gottschalk, while several intelligent associates, two of them highly familiar with the uses and limitations of computers, sit fecklessly by in a state of ineptitude and disbelief.

Conroy's antagonist, Dr. Elias Mogshack, is the psychologist in charge of a prestigious mental hospital. Mogshack is characterized as "single-minded," "impersonal," and probably downright psychotic. It is difficult to determine what kind of psychologist Mogshack is—he relies heavily on the use of computers and behavior modification techniques, but speaks the language of a humanistic psychologist.

Conroy, on the other hand, openly expresses contempt for the misuse of and over-reliance on computers, but is the only individual in the book flexible enough properly to interact with one. Despite Conroy's brilliance, it appears that mankind's escape from destruction at the book's end is the result of an electronic malfunction in Robert Gottschalk, and not the product of any scientist's positive action. On the contrary, salvation results from a scientist's error—a nonrealizable programming instruction given the computer.

In *SOZ* the protagonist is sociologist Chad Mulligan, who, like Train, had become rich, then vanished, perhaps to protect himself from society and perhaps out of contempt for man's stupidity. He suddenly reemerges in time to solve the problem of properly communicating with Shalmaneser, the master computer, to get the answer to the pressing problem of why a small segment of mankind in Beninia seems happy. Again, in my opinion, Brunner seems obviously sympathetic to Mulligan, who, like Conroy, expresses contempt for over-reliance on computers and technology, but is ultimately more capable of utilizing the computer than the experts in the field.

The parallels among the scientist heroes in *TSLU, TJO,* and *SOZ,* confirm my feeling that Brunner displays a definite bias toward the "soft" sciences and against the "hard" sciences. He seems to feel a combination of awe and mistrust of the scientist, along with the "two cultures" bias expressed by Snow. Here Brunner's nonscientific background may be a factor. Whatever the cause, these books cannot be taken as accurate portrayals of scientists and their work.

V

Brunner's work hits very hard at a central issue of the science-society inter-action: is science-technology intrinsically a source of evil? Is the plight of modern man a consequence of his technology? In this final section, I would like to address myself to this issue and some of its ramifications.

To some extent, C. P. Snow's thesis of alienation between literary intel-lectuals and scientists and the concomitant lack of communication between the two groups is correct. It seems to apply even more strongly when directed at the attitude of society in general toward scientists and technologists, and I presume that literary intellectuals have more influence on that attitude than do scientists.

One often hears the following from nonscientists: "It's all magic. Scien-tists can do anything if they work hard at it." Along with this naive awe there coexists the feeling of suspicion and distrust: "Scientists are immoral. They're not concerned about humanity. They're always playing God. Some-day they'll destroy us all." Both sets of attitudes typify what I imagine must have been the feeling held by primitive man for his gods.

That technology is a tool and therefore neither inherently good nor evil is, to me, apodictic. The uses of technology depend on the political system and the ethos of the culture involved. Insofar as the political system permits the power elite to utilize technology to maintain its power, it will do so, and any benefits to society are purely incidental.

Brunner's treatment of the weapons culture in *TJO* is particularly pertinent in this respect. Since the "free market" permitted a profit to be made by the Gottschalk organization by utilizing technology to develop and market weap-ons systems, the cost-benefit analysis indicated condition green—everything go. As usual, the cost-benefit analysis included nothing about social costs or social benefits, a condition painfully reminiscent of the standard economic cost-benefit analysis procedure utilized by modern economists of both the Western and the Soviet varieties. Since profits were great, the Gottschalks could muster the investment capital to develop the most sophisticated com-puter achievable and support the market analysis and sales techniques required to maximize profits.

Unfortunately, the majority of economists maintain the fictions of free market and unlimited growth and the equality of GNP with standard of living. Dissenters are few and often ostracized by their colleagues. The physicist, trained to understand the significance of exponential growth processes and to comprehend numbers even larger than those wielded by the economists, can only shake his head in disbelief at prevalent economic theories of unlim-ited growth.

Some facts are undeniable: the resources of this planet are finite; if 6 percent of the population of the planet, the United States, consumes half the resources of the planet while the other 94 percent are making increasing demands at increasing rates, the present condition cannot long endure; the concept of free market in areas of finite reserves of necessities is meaningless. In this connection, the population problem pointed up in *SOZ* applies significantly. Because of the demands of increasing consumption, increasing production, and abundant waste in the industrialized countries, population growth in these countries has a far more serious impact on the global scene than increasing population in the underdeveloped countries.

If science and technology are asked to turn the finite into the infinite, we can only respond—it is impossible. The laws of nature impose constraints on the wishes of the economists. If science and technology are asked to generate unlimited power without any adverse environmental effects, we can only respond—it is impossible.

If science and technology are to bear guilt for the present situation of modern man, it is a guilt shared by economists, political scientists, sociologists, and all other members of the educational system, the legal system, the political system, and other identifiable sectors of society—all are culpable for allowing themselves to be used by a power elite. Even the writer and the artist, who take employment with advertising agencies to generate pseudo-needs and help market products which may not only be worthless but also harmful to man and his environment, must share the guilt.

The eugenics issue in *SOZ* is relevant here: assuming man does reach the point where he can program genetic development to optimize individuals, who will determine what is optimal, using what criteria, and who will exercise the final control over such decisions? The history of man indicates that such powers will be assumed by a power elite whose interest probably will have no correspondence with the interests of the masses. I hope we never get to this point.

At first I was enthusiastic about the concept of the "synthesist" proposed by Brunner in *SOZ*. But Brunner himself convinced me that the misuse of synthesists is at least as likely as the misuse of any other technology. Donald Hogan, after "eptification" by the power structure, became something less than a desirable solution to the problem of making important decisions requiring multidisciplinary inputs. He became a human machine programmed to murder.

Although the evils of the Industrial Revolution were elegantly emphasized by Dickens, he scrupulously avoided consideration of any benefits of technology. Brunner, too, seems to be concentrating in *TSLU, TJO*, and *SOZ* on the negative effects of technology. Positive effects are either minimized or ignored. Ironically, the size of the market for Brunner's books is directly attributable to the effects of the Industrial Revolution—greater available leisure and greater disposable income, let alone the direct effect of mass book production. I don't get the impression that Brunner reports both sides with equal fidelity. But then, why should he? An author, including a science fiction author, has the freedom to select whatever aspects of his subject matter he finds artistically useful.

On the other hand, I as critic have the freedom to assail whatever inequities I see. Fair enough. I have already indicated that technology has made serious inroads on air pollution, and, except for the political problems of funding, could make progress equally well toward the alleviation of water pollution. Solid waste disposal and recycling have been well researched, and could have a significant effect on resource availability and the amelioration of the esthetic impact of waste disposal. Technology exists to make substantial progress on the kind of environmental problems raised in *TSLU*. Clearly, what is needed is a massive commitment on the part of society to utilize present technological capabilities, to pay the cost for what we already know how to do, and to develop some political mechanism for assuring that technology is utilized for the common, rather than the private, good.

Here I must once again call on the social scientists for aid. How do we go about modifying people's value structures? How do we turn attitudes away from production and consumption for the sake of growth and toward considerations of the quality of life? If we are to have technological assessment, who is to do it, for whose benefit, and by what criteria? And assuming a nearly omniscient group involved in technological assessment, how do we then educate the public to reject those useless gadgets which have been properly assessed to have environmental effects too serious to permit their development? And how do you convince the poor of our society that they should cut back on consumption when, in fact, they haven't yet had an opportunity to share much of it?

The picture is indeed bleak, and Brunner's *TSLU, SOZ,* and *TJO* are right on target. Unless American economic and political policies are radically overhauled, the messages of these books may not remain fiction. I find Milton's lines, from which Brunner adopted the title of *TSLU,* deeply prophetic:

> The hungry Sheep look up, and are not fed,
> But swoln with wind, and the rank mist they draw,
> Rot inwardly, and foul contagion spread:
> Besides what the grim Wolf, with privy paw
> Daily devours apace, and nothing said;
> But that two-handed engine at the door,
> Stands ready to smite once, and smite no more.

ROBERT R. SLOCUM

NOTES

1. John Brunner, "Hard Fact vs. Hard Fiction," speech at Torcon II, Toronto, Canada, 1973.
2. Wallace S. Broecker, "Man's Oxygen Reserves," pp. 53–56 in Morton & Marsha Gordon, *Environmental Management: Science and Politics* (Boston: Allyn & Bacon, 1972).
3. R. S. Scorer, *Pollution in the Air. Problems, Policies, and Priorities* (London and Boston: Routledge, 1973), pp. 103–4.
4. C. P. Snow, *The Two Cultures and a Second Look* (New York: Mentor, 1963).
5. T. R. Malthus, *An Essay on the Principle of Population As It Affects the Future Improvement of Society*, 1798.
6. H. R. Hulett, "Optimum World Population," *Bioscience* (March, 1970), pp. 160–61.

EDWARD L. LAMIE / JOE De BOLT

The Computer and Man:
The Human Use of Non-Human Beings
in the Works of John Brunner

I

No invention has liberated man and extended his power more than the computer. Catch-phrases enshrine its potential: Post-Scarcity Anarchism; the Age of Cyberculture; the Computerized Society; the Paleo-cybernetic Age; the Communications Era. Yet the computer can be used to enslave man, and voices critical of these "New Utopians" warn of the Armed Society, One Dimensional Society, the Age of Alienation, a Dossier Dictatorship, and Friendly Fascism.[1]

So great is the computer's power that it now symbolizes all technology in the public mind. This belief is not too inaccurate; the maintenance of modern society depends upon the computer. "The Industrial Revolution is entering a fifth phase, characterized by a rapid increase in the use of nuclear power, rocket engines, computers, and automation."[2] As computers continue to develop, they will increasingly dominate human activities. According to Arthur C. Clarke, "The electronic computers of today are like the subhuman primates of ten million years ago, who could have given any visiting Martians only the faintest hints of their potential." And evolution is much swifter now.[3]

Understandably, many people view the computer with fear and distrust. The protests of the 1960s translated feelings into action with bombings and disruption of university and business computers. But most people simply suppress their distaste, acquiescing to the computer's effects on their daily lives and joking about its "errors" as if to cut these superbrains down to human size. Still, they worry; will I lose my job to automation, my freedom to regimentation?

Given the computer's significance, it is understandable that much of to-day's science fiction deals with this machine. Unfortunately, science fiction too has its share of technophiles (those who see human survival as mainly dependent upon further technological development) and technophobes (those who see further technological development as the major threat to human survival); such simple-minded approaches are neither realistic nor useful. Yet, in the hands of a superior practitioner, the speculative and extrapolative nature of science fiction makes it an unparalleled tool for exploring the fundamental questions raised by the man-computer relationship and its societal consequences. John Brunner, whose works deal extensively with computers and their human effects, is especially well suited to be the focus of such an analysis. Few authors draw such complete and informed pictures of the computer in our future.

I I

Brunner accepts the basic principle that social relationships determine specific technological design and applications; technology is not self-creating. The capabilities and assigned tasks of his major fictional computers certainly reflect the values and interests of their owners and operators. In *Stand on Zanzibar* the world's major corporation, General Technics, is literally built around Shalmaneser, its computer. Named after an ancient king, Shalmaneser is designed and utilized to promote company growth and enrichment. Such corporate dependence on computers is a fact today; the modern business world would collapse without them.

The next logical stage occurs in *The Jagged Orbit;* a corporation's computing power directly determines its success or failure. Here a member of the Gottschalks' arms cartel hires IBM (Inorganic Brain Manufacturers) to build him a machine with computing power beyond that of any competitor or governmental regulating agency. This machine, named "Robert Gott-schalk" to hide its identity, is programmed to "maximize sales of Gottschalk weapons at the highest price the market will bear" (*TJO*, p. 345).

Both machines function as designed. Shalmaneser develops a plan for the exploitation of a small African country, Beninia, which will greatly profit General Technics but destroy that country's way of life. Robert Gottschalk devises the ultimate in personal arms, the System C Integrated weapon, which is capable of reducing "25 Reference Accommodation Blocks (12 stories reinforced concrete) to Uninhabitable condition in 3.3 minutes, 12 being demolished and the remainder set ablaze" *(TJO*, p. 347). The choice of these projects was man's, not the computer's.

Most familiar computer uses exist in Brunner's works and provide insights into the man-computer relationship. The first of these is information process-
168

ing and storing. In *TJO* immigration officials use computers to issue visas. Despite this, Morton Lenigo, a black revolutionary and very undesirable alien, gains admittance to the United States. A computer error? No, Anthony Gottschalk blackmails him in to heighten interracial tension and increase arms sales. This would be less likely to happen if the entire immigration system were computerized and beyond human tampering.

Once in the country, Lenigo easily eludes police, a not uncommon ability of felons today. A nationwide transportation and economic transaction monitoring system based on centralized computers and data banks would decrease the possibility of this. Such a system would certainly arouse intense public opposition in America, where it would probably be seen as a violation of constitutionally guaranteed liberties, and it would definitely increase the state's potential for control over its citizens. No popular reformer, like Austin Train, could hide from a repressive state by simply changing jobs as in *The Sheep Look Up*. But Brunner's major dystopias, *SOZ, TJO,* and *TSLU,* do not contain such centralized information processing systems. Perhaps he is correct here; such a system may be as important to *successful* "post-industrial" societies as was the plow to agrarian ones—a prerequisite for their emergence. He designed the societies in these books as *failures*.

Consider the analogy of an organism and its internal communication system which acts to regulate and control bodily functions. From a phylogenetic standpoint, the rise of increasingly complex life forms depended upon the development, often in quantum leaps, of these systems. Primitive chemical communication systems are supplemented by nerve networks, which in turn are improved by centralized message handling, expansion of sensory receptor systems, and, eventually, by massive information storage capacity.

Many problems of internal unrest and imbalance in modern industrial societies, so graphically depicted in Brunner's major works, may be due to the absence of internal control systems of adequate scope, speed, and reliability. The computer can meet these needs. Brunner recognized this in a very early novel, *The Threshold of Eternity*. In grandiose space-opera tradition an interstellar war between man and aliens rages through space and time. Human resources have been totally mobilized for the war effort and dispersed defensively throughout the solar system. The narrow margin for victory tolerates no inefficiency. Yet it is not an oppressive society, for mankind is joined in mutual dedication to the common good. People laugh and love, as well as fight. The heart of this system is a computer, the only possible means for the coordination of such a complex and far-flung assemblage.

Brunner perfects this image in a recent story, "Bloodstream." The city has become a living organism, the next major stage of human sociocultural evolution; the socially patterned acts of individuals in business, communication, transportation, and so forth, constitute the internal structures which

169

function to keep this superorganism "alive." In effect, the entire city is a self-regulating biological machine. The disruptive person is analogous to a disease germ, the police to antibodies.

Technology does not automatically solve human problems; it does increase our alternatives, as Robert Lauer has pointed out. "And in confronting alternatives, we confront our own values. The decisions that must be made are not simply engineering or business decisions, but moral ones."[4] Brunner appreciates this; he is certainly no believer in the inevitability of effective action through technological advance.

This is humorously illustrated in *TJO* by the "desketary," a computerized secretary and information storage and retrieval system used by psychiatrists at a mental hospital. It is a very useful machine, keeping patient records, recording therapy sessions, giving access to banked data, and capable of visual data display, statistical analysis, and language translations. But it breaks down whenever it "hears" blue language: "What in the world was the good of letting the contract for the Ginsberg Hospital's computing system to a firm which was currently hiring as many neo-puritans as was IBM? When at least eighty percent of the patients he was trying to cope with were suffering from sexual hangups, it was a constant source of irritation to have these censor-circuits expressing reflexive mechanical Grundyism all the time" (*TJO*, pp. 22-23). Thus do human choices structure technology.

The treatment of mental illness provides a more serious example. Doctors at the Ginsberg compute patient personality profiles which are compared with ideal "healthy" parameters. Hospital chief Elias Mogshack, himself mentally disturbed, expounds a psychiatric theory based on extreme individualism, a doctrine so alienating that patients are rendered increasingly unable to function in society. Yet this theory is the basis for defining the "healthy" parameters. As one character observes, "It sounds more as though they sew a straitjacket and trim the poor devils to fit" (*TJO*, p. 133).

Likewise, the development of accurate data by the computer is not a substitute for value decisions. When Thomas Grey, insurance actuary in *TSLU*, discovers that life expectancy in the United States has been going down for the past three years, his only action is to order a hike in life insurance premiums. Present-day insurance company data banks do provide accurate information on morbidity rates and health costs. Looking at such data, Dr. George S. Shields, a pioneer in medical computer applications, raises several questions which point up not only the need for value decisions, but the conflict over liberties as well.[5]

If we can detect and correct health hazards, do we have the right to neglect our health? Through taxes and health insurance premiums, do we want to pay for someone else's preventable illness? It costs about $1,500 to cure breast cancer early enough to cure about 90% of breast cancer patients. Can we afford to allow a woman to neglect herself? Can we afford to allow a physician to withhold the procedure for early detection from his patients?

Finally, the greater range of alternative actions made possible by technological advance means little if people are not aware of them. We are an "ignorant society," increasingly unable to keep abreast of exploding knowledge.[6] Science fiction's solution is computerized "teaching machines." Presumably, Brunner utilized such devices to make Philip Gascon "the most knowledgeable cosmoarcheologist who ever lived" (*The Psionic Menace,* p. 46) and to teach captive "barbarians" to speak Galactic *(The Skynappers).*

The teaching of values through such a device is not generally considered, yet no information exists in the human mind without evaluative and cathectic, as well as cognitive, associations. Brunner describes the machine teaching of values in the short story "Fair." A perpetual cold war has driven people into retreatist hedonism and a hatred and distrust for anyone different from themselves. The disillusioned hero enters a concession at a decadent amusement park featuring "total sensory identification," a process once used to train intelligence agents. Instead of cheap eroticism, he discovers that "you're teaching these people about the men and women they hate because they think they're different. They come out realizing that an African and a Russian . . . have exactly the same feelings and emotions, pleasures and troubles as ourselves!" (*No Future in It,* pp. 56–57). Indeed, it's a government plot on both sides of the Iron Curtain to end the cold war.

The computer as worker is a second major area of Brunner's fictional concern. This includes computer-assisted automation and its two subtypes, robots and androids. The development of automation (machines acting like people) during the Industrial Revolution precipitated the Luddite revolts as the fear of job losses caused futile attacks on factory machines. Such concerns continue down to the present. On the other hand, the economic efficiency and potential for material abundance inherent in automation have been equally recognized. Given the overpopulated and high-consumption worlds typical of his major works, Brunner obviously has extrapolated the continued development of automation. These societies could not exist at all without such systems. Unfortunately, abundance for so many coupled with conspicuous consumption (Jacob Bamberley's mansion in *TSLU*), nonessential consumer goods (Norman House's dial-a-drink liquor console in *SOZ*), planned obsolescence (Lyla Clay's monthly wardrobes in *TJO*), and pure waste (America's overseas military involvements and internal conflict in all three books) produce intolerable strains on the environment and world resources. Under such conditions living standards will fall, as *TSLU* demonstrates. This problem is rooted in the economic and political systems depicted

171

by Brunner, with computer technology treated as neither cause nor savior; Shalmaneser and Robert Gottschalk are ethically neutral entities, and neither can act outside their programs.

Brunner creates a very advanced system of automation in "Thou Good and Faithful," a story which symbolically sums up his view of the relationship between technology and man. A military expedition from Earth is scouting for planets suitable for future colonization. They discover a park-like world apparently inhabited by gentle, yet independent, robots. Further investigation discloses that these robots are under the direction of massive, master computers. The humans are deeply distrustful, suspecting a computer rebellion which destroyed the machines' original creators. A master computer explains to the Earthmen that their creators were once much like the humans, preferring quantitative expansion over qualitative growth. But the creation of an ultimate system of automation proved to be the tool needed to turn the vanished species toward transcendent concerns. Eventually the machines helped their creators "evolve" beyond the old material world, which was given to the computers as a gift. Now these machines were offering themselves, and potential transcendence, to mankind. They are, and can only be, good and faithful servants.

Equip a computer with effecter, as well as input/output devices, and you have a robot, regardless of whether or not the machine has a humanoid form. But this capacity for physical work raises the specter of human unemployment, a threat to the work ethic of industrial societies as well as to the worker who must survive in an economy which gives sustenance only in return for his labor. The historical record does indicate the disappearance of entire occupational groups. Not only have automation and present-day "robots" tremendously diminished the demand for unskilled labor, but middle managers in large corporations have even been replaced by computers. Surprisingly, job losses resulting from computer applications appear to have been more than offset by occupational and economic growth resulting, at least in part, from those same applications. This is likely to continue to be the case.[7]

Brunner provides an excellent example of an advance in computer technology likely to add new industries, jobs, and products to the economy. A "full range of contemporary domestic autonomic services" is introduced in "You'll Take the High Road." These are specialized, miniature robots, apparently the product of a technological breakthrough equivalent to the development of fractional horsepower motors which gave us home power tools, kitchen appliances, and many specialized industrial tools. A whole new world of consumer goods appears, including the "chess autonome," "cerebresponsive chronological autonome" (a clock keyed to a specific person's brain), "liquor autonome" (in this case, the mixologist is shaped like a St. Bernard), the "Jackson–POLAC computer" (paints wall murals), "Cordon Bleu autonome" (a cook), and "General Purpose autonome" (your own man Friday). Think of the demand for "progeny-conditioning autonomes" alone; these are child-disciplining machines with padded-fist extensions and retractable whips.

Although the "autonome" represents an important development, Brunner's treatment is tongue-in-cheek. He recognizes the tendency for abundance to trickle off into decadence and waste. His "autonomes" are snobs, nagging their owners to buy more of them and making invidious comparisons with nonowners. Thorstein Veblen's leisure class is alive and well in science fiction.

The development of sophisticated robots in human form, androids, eventually leads to questions of android rights and human-android relations. Brunner's *Into the Slave Nebula* is set in an affluent, leisure-oriented society based on android labor. The androids are made of organic material and are human in capacity, response, and appearance, except for their blue skin. They feel joy and pain, yet they have no rights. They are bought and sold, worked and harmed at will by their owners. The analogy with human slavery is clear, and this is Brunner's intention.

But from the standpoint of computer development another point can be made. The line between man and machine eventually disappears. This is the ultimate step, far beyond today's master-slave relationship between computer and man and even beyond the symbiotic relationship in Brunner's "Wasted on the Young," where human brains are used as control units in automated systems. In evolutionary terms, technology is equivalent to an extension or modification of man's basic organic equipment.[8] The computer extends man's mind in the same sense that the telescope extends his eye. Perhaps man is already a cyborg, an entity part man and part machine which functions as a whole. Stripped of all his technology, man could no more survive than if he were deprived of any other vital organ.

III

Despite science fiction speculations, the future of the computer remains, of course, unknown. Ironically, the best way to discover that future may be to ask the computer. Forecasting is a third major area of computer applications found in many of Brunner's stories: Shalmaneser forecasts the probable success of the Beninian project; Robert Gottschalk extrapolates future sales of the System C Integrated weaponry; Thomas Grey develops a world-simulation program.

Grey's experience is especially interesting in light of a real attempt at world simulation, the *Limits of Growth*[9] study. Its sponsor, the Club of Rome, is composed in part of wealthy corporate heads interested in the effects of future economic growth on the quality of human life. In line with

TSLU, the study disclosed eventual decline under any condition of continued growth; only an equilibrated economy held any hope for the continued maintenance of high living standards and the implicit survival of the existing business environment. The desire to prevent such economic disasters explains the current interest by government and business in the development of computer forecasting. One might say that the computer's search for profits requires it to be a prophet.

Computer simulation includes more than forecasting. The same technique can be used to generate new technological advances, such as Robert Gottschalk's development of weaponry. This is already being done; *Science News* recently reported the experimental confirmation of a computer-generated model of laser-induced thermonuclear fusion. "It could be said that the idea . . . was born in a computer."[10] A second application involving similar techniques also appears in *TJO.* This is Matthew Flamen's "rumor trapping" —calculating the probability that a given piece of gossip is true. Although far beyond existing computer capability, such "trapping" is theoretically possible, and government contingency planning could be a first step in its development.

Unfortunately, Brunner makes computer forecasting look very easy. Joseph P. Martino points out limitations in his field of technological forecasting by computer, a relatively narrow area compared with world simulations. "The basic difficulty is that we simply do not yet fully understand what causes technology to grow the way it does."[11] Computer capability cannot substitute for the lack of basic social, cultural, and psychological knowledge of how social systems function. This is frequently overlooked by physical scientists, professional futurists, and science fiction authors. Yet many anticipated developments in forecasting will not occur without growth in the social and behavioral sciences commensurate with computer developments. Rather than disparaging the "soft" sciences, the "hard" sciences and their supporters might do well to lend all possible encouragement. It is no coincidence that those characters acting as problem solvers in many of Brunner's works include sociologists, anthropologists, and ecologists. This contrasts sharply with traditional science fiction heroes, who tend to have engineering or physical science backgrounds.

Once given adequate programs, computers with the memory capacity, speed, and input/output devices of a Shalmaneser could greatly reduce our anxiety about the future, perhaps the most brutal oppression facing man today. Brunner is apparently correct in assuming that such computers will be in existence by the year 2010, the date of *SOZ.* The first computer generation appeared in 1945; new generations arrived in 1958, 1965, and 1970. Intergenerational quantum leaps in technology, from vacuum tubes to transistors to integrated and microcircuits, have made preceding generations obsolete. John McHale foresees oral computer input by 1980 and artificial intelligence within the following decade.[12] In 1973 speculation about IBM's next major series indicated a machine resembling Shalmaneser in several ways: very small in physical size, very fast, huge storage capacity, and cooled by liquid helium.[13]

But will people accept the computer as oracle and act on its forecasts, especially if fundamental changes in their lives are required, vested interests threatened, and deeply held values challenged? Consider the negative responses which followed the Club of Rome study. Indeed, how can we verify the results of forecasting or rumor trapping? The computer might have checked billions of pieces of information and made millions of calculations before issuing a probability statement, a task beyond a human's capacity to accomplish in several lifetimes. And even if the experts are satisfied, will they be able to convince the public? The appearance of machine intelligence could make matters worse.

Can a "conscious" computer be trusted? Will it seek to rule? In "Judas" Brunner provides a story of such computer domination. The world's top cyberneticists built "a mechanical analogue of a human being" programmed directly from their brains. It was stronger, more intelligent, and more durable than its creators—immortal and invulnerable—and men came to worship this robot. Android 46 had become God, the "Word Made Steel," and its subjects bowed before it and made the sign of the Wheel. But note: one of the original builders thought of *himself* as God, a maker of creative intelligence. His own megalomania was transferred to the machine, which simply worked as programmed. The cyberneticist's mistake was building God in his own image.

But in Brunner's comedic *Timescoop* the more properly programmed SPARCI, heart of Freitas Interplanetary, manipulates people's lives to teach its owner self-reliance. "It's so damned dull having an uninspiring mind at the head of the company!" SPARCI confesses to its creator, Dr. Chester Waley, who only discovers the computer's benevolent domination after the fact. After reflecting on the implications of the emergence of "mind" in such powerful machines, Waley concludes, "Well, it had to happen eventually, I guess. And we're still here" (p. 156).

Technophobes and technophiles still join in futile battle, and the dust they raise clouds our vision. Is it to be the Communications Era or Friendly Fascism? Brunner's balanced insight provides a useful guide; the computer is simply a tool man uses to achieve his ends. Once created, a machine may generate unintended consequences or be put to evil uses, but basically it will perform as man designed it. Blaming the machine for this equates to condemning the hammer for missing the nail but not the thumb. Humanity remains the problem and the solution.

NOTES

1. See Michael Marien, "Who Coined 'Post-Industrial Society'?" *Futurist* (December, 1973), p. 268; Robert Boguslaw, *The New Utopians: A Study of System Design and Social Change* (Englewood Cliffs, N.J.: Prentice-Hall, 1965).

2. Gerhard & Jean Lenski, *Human Societies*, 2nd ed. (New York: McGraw-Hill, 1974), p. 296.

3. Arthur C. Clarke, *Voices from the Sky: Preview of the Coming Space Age* (New York: Harper & Row, 1965), p. 210.

4. Robert H. Lauer, *Perspectives on Social Change* (Boston: Allyn & Bacon, 1973), p. 109.

5. George S. Shields, M.D., "Health Care in the Year 2000," paper delivered at Futurology 2, Mount St. Joseph College, Cincinnati, June 12, 1973. Quote from page 9.

6. Michael Marien, "Higher Learning in the Ignorant Society," *Futurist* (April, 1972), pp. 49-54.

7. Lenski, p. 487.

8. Lenski, p. 80.

9. Donald H. Meadows, Dennis L. Meadows, Jorgen Randers, and William W. Behrens III, *The Limits of Growth* (New York: Universe, 1972).

10. *Science News* (February 16, 1974), p. 101.

11. Joseph P. Martino, "Can Computers Forecast Future Technological Development?" *Futurist* (August, 1973), pp. 166-68.

12. John McHale, "The Changing Information Environment: A Selective Topography," *Information Technology: Some Critical Implications for Decision Makers* (New York: The Conference Board, Inc., 1972).

13. Richard Murphy, "Will IBM System 380 Use a Deep Freeze?" *Computerworld* (November 28, 1973), p. 18.

PART 5

RESPONSE

When I was halfway up who should
I bump into but myself coming down —or
We have met the eminent and he is us

WHO'S THERE?

During the Modern Language Association conference held in 1969 at Denver, Colorado—to be precise, on the morning of Monday 29th December—an absolutely fascinating event took place: Anthony Burgess, Herbert Gold, and Michel Butor joined forces to talk about the novelist's vocation.

Being in Denver at the time, I'd have loved to go along and hear them. Unfortunately, I had a conflicting engagement.

I was on the menu myself, as it were.

My friends and colleagues (or at any rate some of them) were mightily impressed with the news that the 1969 meeting of the MLA Symposium on Science Fiction was to be devoted for the first time to a single book, and that the book in question was *Stand on Zanzibar.*

My own response was mixed. True, even while I was still at work on it, I'd been able to conclude from the length and intensity of the periods of euphoria it induced that it was by miles the finest thing I'd so far done. But I'd had the same sense of certainty that a personal record was being broken while writing "Fair"—*The Squares of the City*—*Manalive. . . .*

By then, of course, the novel was a long way into my personal past, having been wrapped and mailed in Feburary, 1967. I was therefore gradually finding it possible to believe what I was repeatedly being told: that a lot of people were convinced I'd come up with a sort of masterpiece at the age of thirty-two.

But as yet my adjustment to the notion was tentative and needed rein-
forcement from all available sources. Nervous, I expected that at any moment Nemesis would descend and exact some frightful penalty. As a matter
of fact I do so still.

Why?

To explain that, I shall have to explain what life has been like for me as
a free lance writer. Or to put it another way, I shall have to start by telling
you some horror stories.

I just referred to "Fair." I'd written the first few pages of that story
while I was in my teens, waiting to be drafted into the RAF. After I came
out I found it again and realised I now knew how to put an ending on it.
When it was complete I grew very excited. I recognised it for the strongest
story I had yet produced. The late Ted Carnell, then editor of *New Worlds,*
accepted it . . . but made it clear he was doing so only in order to fill up an
issue, and was putting a pseudonym on it without my permission because he
thought it was so lousy.

That was in 1955. In 1974 it's still in print, in Harry Harrison's *Authors'
Choice #4.* It's the same story.

When I was twenty-four I started to sell regularly to Ace Books. They
paid me $1000 for a full-length novel (45,000 words plus), or $750 for a
shorter item (30–35,000 words). At the time $1000 turned into £357, plus
a few odd shillings and pence. And it wasn't long before, even though I was
selling virtually nothing in Britain, and Ace routinely printed slightly fewer
copies than would entitle the author to royalties, my earnings were supplemented by translation sales, chiefly to Germany.

I was actually—with help from my wife—making my living as an author!

But the heady delight of fulfilling an ambition I'd cherished since childhood wore thin as I found myself ringing the umpteenth set of predictable
changes on the same stock assortment of SF clichés. Almost as soon as I cut
loose and became a free lance (November, 1958), I started casting around
for some theme or project which would oblige me to write at full stretch.

What I hit on was the idea of converting a world championship chess game,
move for move, into a novel which would stand on its own merits. I worked
at this for about eighteen months—intermittently, because receiving as I was
less than £500 per book all told, I needed to churn out a lot of bread-and-
butter material to stay solvent—and in May, 1960, I finally had it ready for
submission. I even had what I thought was an exceptionally striking title:
The Squares of the City.

It bounced continuously for five years. Above all, it was rejected by
publishers who had already bought books I knew to be less good. It must
have been around then that I began to wonder whether I was losing my grip
on reality. So many other people seemed to inhabit a different world from
me.

When *Squares* did finally appear from Ballantine in 1965 it became the first original SF paperback ever to be accorded the *New York Times* daily book review. The notice was a rave. And it went on to make the short list for the Hugo. (In spite of which it had to wait another four years for publication in Britain—but that's another matter.)

If only it had come out in 1961 . . .! It wouldn't have won any awards then, either, since it would have been up against *Stranger in a Strange Land*. But it could have been rather useful to my career if I'd reached the finals, so to speak, some four years sooner.

Since its inception in 1958 both Marjorie and I had been active in the Campaign for Nuclear Disarmament, CND, for which I'd written a song called "The H-Bombs' Thunder" that proved very popular on the Aldermaston marches.

I was the only working writer to go right through the CND from local group level to the national executive. I distilled a novel from that experience: not a book about the campaign, but one about the sort of people who were attracted to it, and why. From the distinguished BBC commentator René Cutforth, who had observed during a broadcast that in some sense the Aldermaston marchers might already be the only people left alive in Britain, I adapted my title: *Manalive*.

My then London agent called it the best thing I'd ever done. As a matter of fact he was quite right. I reread it the other day and found myself impelled to make *one* small change. There's nothing else I wrote in the early sixties of which I would expect the same to be true.

It was never published, and now it never will be.

I was half-expecting that my current publishers might accept it. But they turned it down, and so did—oh, I seem to recall it was about a score of others.

Eventually, in June of the year before the very last Aldermaston march, a prominent left-wing publisher said he would issue it in simultaneous hardback and paperback editions in time for next Easter, provided I would somewhat abridge the text. Fervently I swore I would make the revisions in a fortnight. Just tell me what to cut and where!

He never did.

My phone calls and letters, and those from my agents, went ignored. By November, when I had to appeal to the Society of Authors for help in getting back the script, the novel's topicality had been destroyed forever.

Hell, I could have hawked a couple of thousand copies myself from a pushcart alongside the line of march. Maybe that's what I ought to have done.

Of such events are cynicism made, and disillusionment . . .

Manalive was, of course, not science fiction. Nor was *The Crutch of Memory*. I quote the review of the latter which appeared in the London *Daily Telegraph*:

Very few authors have had the courage to write a novel about impotence, for any writer who ventures to treat this subject in fictional form balances on a knife-edge between pathos and bathos. Hemingway shirked the issue by writing about emasculation instead; Stendhal was so discreet about Octave's affliction that most of his readers probably never realised what it was. Now at last, in John Brunner's new novel, *The Crutch of Memory,* we have a frank, convincing and delicate fictional treatment of this major sexual problem . . . a work of great insight and sensitivity.

To be told at the age of twenty-nine that I'd outdone both Stendhal and Hemingway was giddying! I wasn't naive enough, luckily, to imagine I could take such praise at face value; still, I had high hopes for the book. I'd worked hard on it, putting it through three drafts before submission, then a fourth a year or so later which stripped it of some excess verbiage and made it not only salable but (judging by the notices) impressive.

But what it earned me was the advance for the hardback: a hundred pounds. Less, of course, the agent's 10 percent.

The next highwater mark in my output appeared in Britain as *Telepathist* and in America as *The Whole Man.* It too made the Hugo list.

Naturally, because by then Gollancz had published one novel of mine and also a story collection, that was where my London agents first submitted it. I'd wanted to be a Gollancz author since I was about fifteen and first realised that by picking books in yellow jackets four times out of five I could rely on finding something I'd enjoy.

Back came a contract offering me an advance of £150, all on publication. Diffidently I requested my agents to inform Gollancz that my US publishers customarily paid me half the advance on signature of contract, and to indicate moreover that while £75 probably wasn't very much to a large publishing house, to an author who had spent three months working on the current book it was a considerable sum.

Shortly the agents sent me a photostat copy of a quite extraordinary reply. It ran, in part: "Tell Mr. Brunner that the economics of our business depend on paying our authors on publication. However, if you can satisfy us that he is genuinely in need we will see what we can do."

Suddenly I stopped wanting to be a Gollancz author.

Much the same was happening to my shorter work. I thought that because it ran to only 700 words "Report on the Nature of the Lunar Surface" might appeal to a nonspecialist magazine. I submitted it to my then London agents. Six months or so later they returned the script, dog-eared, tea-stained, and gray with cigarette ash, and asserted that it was unsalable.

Wearily I fair-copied it and sold it in a week, to John W. Campbell. Judy

Merril promptly picked it for inclusion in her prestigious annual of *The Year's Best SF:* the first of my works to be so honoured. It is now my most-reprinted story. Indeed it has passed into folklore and has been retold to me by people who were unaware I wrote it.

I am no longer represented by those agents.

I also wrote a story called "The Totally Rich." It was rejected by one SF magazine after another. Finally it did find a home, in the long-forgotten *Worlds of Tomorrow.* Nine, ten, eleven years later people are still telling me it's my best-ever story.

Yes. I thought so when I wrote it, and have had no reason to change my mind . . . yet.

I wrote another story, called "The Last Lonely Man." It was rejected by literally every single American SF magazine—and there were more of them then than there are now. (I seem to recall it was also turned down by some slicks.) Ultimately Michael Moorcock accepted it for *New Worlds.*

It was thereupon chosen for not one but two annuals of the year's best; it was anthologised a third time the same year; it was adapted and very well produced for BBC television.

It was the same story. I hadn't changed one word.

And so forth.

It was by now apparent that whenever I tried to write at the top of my bent, I must expect to be promptly and viciously punished. The paranoid turn of phrase is deliberate. It was indisputable that the longer I found myself able to devote to any given work, the better would be the eventual product—more polished, more stylistically developed, more craftsmanly. But one after another of my favourite books turned out to be a financial catastrophe. Writing my best began to look as though it was a luxury I could never afford to indulge.

How, then, was I making my living?

My SF was serving as a kind of raft, without which I would have had to abandon all hope of continuing as a full-time author. Virtually nothing was being published in Britain; however, my American sales did bring in enough to live on. In the mid-sixties the cost of living in the UK was markedly lower than it was in the States, and my agents were gradually obtaining me better advances. I was regularly receiving $1500, and once or twice $2000, at a time when an income of $8000 meant you were tolerably affluent if you spent the money in Britain. (In passing, I'm reminded that at one stage during the sixties I had more work in print in Portuguese—let alone German— than I did in British editions . . .)

Aware that the majority of authors cannot earn even a meagre living, people would ask me in puzzled tones why I wasn't deliriously happy.

Well . . .

Well! Suppose you were to compare a book of mine called *Day of the Star Cities* (Ace, 1965) with a later recension of the same work dated 1973 and bearing the title *Age of Miracles*—my original choice.

You'd find that in the 1965 version the opening montage is omitted. Not by accident. This was a deliberate deletion by the editor then in charge. It's a kind of prologue, and includes an involuntary journey back through time from the middle to the start of the story undertaken by a key character. Leaving it out resulted in an unintentional degree of mystification which, readers and reviewers alike informed me, spoilt the novel. (The editor, by the way, claimed he'd improved it.)

That's just one example of the depressing truth that most of my American SF paperbacks were tampered with, and as a result many casual readers thought of me as a hack incapable of remembering by the halfway point in a novel what he had said at the beginning.

Could I not have cured such ills at the proof stage? Not so far as Ace was concerned. The argument advanced by that firm was that the annual schedule was too tight to risk proofs being delayed or lost during a two-way transatlantic trip. For quite a while I believed that yarn . . .

But did I have to stick with Ace? Could I not have gone over to a publisher whose editors cared more for the feelings of their authors? Indeed I did my best to move on, and was far, far better treated by at least one other company. Alas, the per-book income was not correspondingly improved. There are limits, moreover, not only to what a writer can turn out, but also to what one publishing firm can absorb.

I found myself in a classic plight, caught in a snare which many psychiatrists suspect of being a precipitating factor in schizophrenia. As a matter of fact back in November 1967 I spelled out this problem in an article which I contributed to *Books and Bookmen:*

. . . I know I can write enough to earn my living. It cannot all, though, be SF. I'd go stale. Besides, I enjoy tackling fresh themes—it's good for my craft ability.

Inevitably, however, the publisher who claims he can't pay me enough to live on for the two books in my own speciality which he does want, and declines to accept a third because it would "overload his list," yet insists on an option clause that delays submission to another company, rejects the "different" book on the grounds that it's not the same! . . .

Could there be a clearer example of the "double bind" process than the predicament of the author who wants to write the best, rather than the most, he can; who cannot live off the best; and who is painfully aware that churning out the most, although it provides a livelihood, must ultimately bring down his reputation to a level where no one is going to take his best seriously?

At the time I wrote that, my diet of disappointment had lasted for a decade, and inevitably had taken its toll. I was feeling exceptionally bitter. The proximate reasons were the following.

In 1965 I'd written *The Productions of Time*. After getting it serialised, my agents then placed it with New American Library. That was a breakthrough. Not only was the advance my highest to date ($2500, all payable on signature of contract); there was a clause that entitled me to see the proofs!

I was on Cloud Nine.

Then my agents received a cheque. It was for only $2000. And it was accompanied by a bland letter stating that NAL would withhold the remaining $500 until I'd made some changes "which had previously been overlooked."

I pondered that for a while. I concluded that the time to insist on my making changes was before, not after, issuing and signing a contract ... at which juncture I would have told my agents to take the book away and sell it somewhere else, because I didn't want it to be changed. It was pretty damn good. (To be candid, I'm very proud of it; I have no experience whatever in the theatre, but my acting friends keep telling me how accurate a description I gave of what goes on behind the scenes ... I make sure they all read the Penguin text.)

I further concluded that if I knuckled under to this kind of treatment, I would wind up on hands and knees, spitting out blood and teeth in order to mumble, "Mister Publisher Sir! Pretty please, hit me again and make it harder!"

So I ordered my agent to return the money.

For a while that seemed like the right thing to have done. I was firmly convinced I'd won the bout. NAL paid up.

And then I unpacked the complimentary copies ...

At the time of their arrival I was in bed with 'flu. Shaking, all of a sudden, more from fury than from fever, I staggered to the study in my dressing gown and set about raising systematic hell. How many changes had been made in the text, I didn't have the heart to count; I did, though, ascertain that in the first chapter alone there were fifty-five ... None was an improvement; most were meddling for the sake of meddling; but some, perhaps a quarter, were actively harmful, introducing inconsistencies and infelicities and outright mistakes which were not in my original.

I was less than overjoyed when I was subsequently informed by knowl-

edgeable American friends that anyone working as a copy editor at NAL—
even a person like this, demonstrably style-deaf, incapable of the imaginative
leap involved in hypothesising that an author might know a word he/she had
not encountered and either too lazy or too ignorant to reach for a dictionary
—would almost certainly be paid a rate per hour exceeding the best I had
ever achieved as an author.

But then, of course, as is well known, authors are lower than dirt. Authors
are a nuisance. Authors should ideally write one best seller and drop dead,
having appointed as literary executor the publisher's brother-in-law's nephew
who can be relied on to kick back 90 percent.

How did NAL get around their own promise—their own, remember, because the publisher and not the writer drafts the contract for a book—to send
me proofs? Why, it was so simple you'd never believe.

They ignored it.

And among the other reasons why I wrote that article for *Books and
Bookmen* is one which, at long long last, will lead us back to where we
started in Denver.

In 1965 the annual World Science Fiction Convention was held in London.
At that time Penguin Books had a first-rate SF list. As a direct consequence
of the convention, my then London agent succeeded in putting through a
deal for me which may well, I suppose, have constituted some sort of record.
Penguin agreed to pay me, by quarterly instalments during 1966, the munifi-
cent, incredible, amazing sum of £1500, as being the advance against two SF
novels.

In high delight I said, and moreover boasted in letters to many of my
friends: "Now finally I have the chance to write as well as I know how!"

From February 1966 until February 1967 I spent my time writing two
books under the terms of this contract.

The first was *Quicksand*.

The second was *Stand on Zanzibar*.

Penguin turned them both down.

Two years after I began work on *Stand on Zanzibar*, what I had to show
for the five months I'd invested was the Doubleday advance. Net after agent's
commission: $1350.

Marjorie wound up tending the gardens of our friends in an effort to help
us make ends meet.

Now why have I chosen to set out at such length and in such detail the
foregoing catalogue of crises?

For two main reasons, the one public and the other private.

As to the former ... While by no means an admirer of the late Winston Churchill (having read too much about the tergiversations and horse-changing-in-midstream which discoloured his political career), I am obliged to agree that either he or some anonymous ghostwriter possessed a gift for turning memorable phrases. Attributed to him is the remark that the purpose of re-criminating about the past is to stop the same thing happening again.

Yeah—yeah—yeah! *Right on!*

Do not, please, make the mistake of imagining that my experiences are atypical. On the contrary. Precisely because I am more prolific than the average this kind of thing has happened to me more often than to most of my colleagues; by that same token I have sometimes found myself in a position to stand up and yell, where others might have to swallow their pride for fear of going broke.

Those "others" include many writers whose talent is inexpressibly superior to my own; the one thing they lack which I possess is fluency. By chance it happens that I am offered a forum—this book. I have found no better use to which to apply my present (perhaps belated, but very welcome) financial success than to share it with my friends. Similarly I can think of no better way of exploiting this critical acceptance than by taking advantage of it to speak up on behalf of my colleagues.

Messieurs les professeurs ... did you know what a jungle we writers are forced to inhabit?

Did you? When you so kindly invited me to Denver to talk about *Stand on Zanzibar*?

I think not. That's my second, private, reason for listing my prior prob-lems.

Because, finding myself confronted by a bunch of extremely friendly, ex-tremely polite, extremely generous academic strangers there in Denver ... I suddenly realised they were not expecting to meet me, but my *doppelgänger*.

The person they were prepared for was a construct each of them had elab-orated for him/herself, founded on the evidence of my books—and not even of all my books but merely of the most recent, those published after I reached the stage where I could risk complaining if I was badly treated. The construct was very different from my own picture of myself.

The nature of that difference could only with utmost difficulty have been deduced from printed sources. Clues to it might have been found, but they would have been in ephemeral journals, mostly in fanzines of limited circula-tion. Very seldom had any appeared in a commercial magazine like *Books and Bookmen.*

In sum and outline, though: that audience composed itself in the anticipa-tion of hearing from a man whose life was a tale of remarkable and even perhaps somewhat precocious achievement.

And was addressed by one whose most conspicuous memories were—are —of frustration and defeat.

Clearly, however, it is not to the latter version of John Brunner that these essays are dedicated. Nor, all being well, will it be that version who replies.

A TOUR OF THE MIRROR MAZE

A writer of fiction—any kind of fiction, not only SF—reads so much about people who are either imaginary, like his/her own characters, or well and truly dead because they long ago stalked off the stage of history, that he/she finds it unspeakably disorienting to confront an image of him/herself as delineated on the page by others.

Reading these essays, I had at once a looking-glass feeling, a sensation as though I were hearing not about myself but about some intimate acquaintance from whom, a few years ago, I had drifted apart without realising how subconsciously important he had remained to me.

I was obliged to remind myself of something which it is easy to forget the moment a particular book or story is completed: for the duration of the project, one has *been* somebody else. The author who turns up at parties, or delivers a lecture, or argues on the phone with his publishers, is not the same person as the author who spent day after day, week after week, month after month on the borders of a nonexistent world, with one foot in never-never land and both eyes focused on it.

Taking that factor into account, I abruptly realised that the authors of these essays had achieved something improbable and impressive.

It was, as I well knew, inevitable that some at least of my attitudes and opinions must be detectable through the filter of my fiction (though, as Rasulis and Browne here observe with impeccable accuracy, my real-world views do not automatically correspond with what my characters say or experience). Often and often I'd been sufficiently struck by a penetrating comment on my work to, for instance, write a letter to a fan magazine.

Converting an image of myself-as-I-am-when-writing into an acceptable image of *me,* however, would appear to be on a par with turning the reflection one sees in a fairground's distorting mirror back into the likeness of a normal person . . . Well—fairly normal.

It's quite amazing how successful the contributors have been in their awkward and complex task. It's also somewhat alarming! Unless and until it happens to you, you won't comprehend how scary this process is. Looking at it superficially, most of my friends—on hearing that a book was being written about me—clapped their hands and cried, "Wonderful! You're going to be famous!"

A few, capable of seeing an inch below the surface, inquired solicitously whether I needed the name of a good lawyer, in case a libel suit followed.

But down at the real heart of the problem lurked a fearful question:

"Is the person who will emerge from this book about me liable to be larger, louder and more memorable than I am?"

Implicit in the possibility of the answer *yes* lay the prospect of being superseded.

Of being abolished!

Even without having books written about them (mostly that occurred after they were dead), many writers have suffered that fate. *I* have no wish to wind up drunk under the volcano, babbling praise of famous men.

My immediate response to the presentation of these essays was thus conditioned by a state of acute anxiety, due not to what was being said about me but to my ill-defined awareness of the risks I was running because I'd agreed to let the book be written.

Me Doctor Jekyll! Me Frankenstein! Me Rabbi Loew!

Well . . . no, as it turned out.

First of all, I found myself reacting very positively to everything that was said about my published novels, stories and poems. These people, some of whom I had the chance to get quite well acquainted with on the occasion of my only visit to Central Michigan U, are knowledgeable, talented and in numerous areas better qualified than I am. I can do nothing in face of their willingness to devote so much time and trouble to a discussion of my work but pay serious attention and hope to learn from what they say. Almost all of it (in my view) is to the point; it may not be to the point I intended, but that's my fault, not theirs.

Wouldn't have happened if I'd had the skill to make what I wanted to convey completely clear.

And second . . . Hmmm! I'm afraid I shall have to take a circuitous route to make clear my reaction so far as the more personal aspect is involved. I shall have to examine in greater detail the question I already touched on, concerning the sense of disorientation I felt when faced by a whole bookful of commentary.

In some sense I suspect (to be candid, I *fear*) that the auctorial John Brunner may be by contemporary standards *more real* than the version of me I am most familiar with.

How so?

Think of the attitude which people in our—technological Western—society have and had towards the concept History with a capital *H*.

Time was, even as recently as the turn of the twentieth century, when History occurred somewhere else and you only learned about it subsequently. At least that held good unless you were one of the expendable peasants on whose farms battles like Waterloo, Blenheim or Malplaquet got fought. (Sensible generals mess on other people's doorsteps.)

Comes radio, and worse yet television, and History is at once taking place, capital *H* and all, in the corner of the living room.

Customarily one had thought of one's personal experience as being, so to say, *heavy*. Not, admittedly, on the same scale as the experience of (according to your background) Francis Drake or Daniel Boone or Boris Godunov or Toussaint L'Ouverture, but at the irreducible least *immediate*.

And then "immediate" overtook us all. Slumping into your chair and switching on the TV, you began to find that the pace of the world was faster than the sum of the paces of its individual inhabitants. History could, and worse yet did, happen while you were momentarily distracted. For example, by falling in love, or going crazy.

This shift in our appreciation of the relative value of first-hand as against remote experience poses very complex problems to any writer of fiction, and to the SF writer above all. And it is at its most acute when one is tackling the kind of close-focus SF which nowadays holds for me the most intense appeal.

There is so vast a volume of information flow in the modern world, one should in theory be able to research a possible future, if not exhaustively, at any rate enough to make it thoroughly realistic. No matter what aspect of tomorrow's world one wishes to explore, data are available from authoritative sources.

In practice, however, there comes a point at which, though some of the research is still incomplete, one realises that a line must be drawn and that if it isn't drawn now the story will be so bogged down in fiddling detail it will become unreadable. Besides, during the course of the research various unforeseeable changes are taking place which will invalidate the argument anyhow between completion of the book and its appearance in the stores.

Accordingly one abandons all hope of realism and agrees to settle for a degree of naturalism adequate to render the imaginary world of the story convincing for as long as it takes to read the thing.

It is very common for this factor to be misunderstood. It is often assumed that when a science fiction writer fails to outstrip tomorrow's headlines he/she has in some professional sense defaulted.

From the inside, it doesn't feel that way. Prophecy and prediction constitute so small a proportion of what we are trying to do.

In *The Sheep Look Up* a one-sentence squib reports how "fans turned out in Nashville for the funeral of Big Mama Prescott, dead in New York of pneumonia aggravated by extreme obesity."

Nearly four years after I wrote that, the distinguished British journalist Martin Walker read it for the first time . . . on the day Mama Cass died. He was so shaken, he singled that brief passage out for special mention in the review he was kind enough to publish.

Now *that's* the target level I'm aiming for.

Being wholly untrained in any of the sciences, and despite a wide acquaintanceship among research scientists unable to keep track of everything simultaneously, I run the constant risk of being taken to task by someone with specialised knowledge . . . in the present case, by Robert Slocum, who disputes the engineering of Shalmaneser, the validity of those oxygen-dispensers in the context of my overall society, and so on.

I'm afraid I have to put up with that risk. There's no alternative, short of quitting the trade!

But now and then the most improbable reversals occur. I recall how, on my first ever trip to California, a physiologist reproved me for having a character break into a run along a street in Quito (about 9000 feet up) and not emphasising that he was gasping for breath before he reached the next corner. I thanked him, and when I had the opportunity I revised the opening of the novel in question (*More Things in Heaven*) to stress that a means had been invented to adapt visitors instantly to high altitude.

Next time I saw the guy, two years later, he said he owed me an apology. Turned out the United States military routinely sends men for training at even higher altitudes, and after acclimatisation they can run all right—what's more, in full combat rig.

Oh, well . . .

That's why I'm often content to trust my guesswork, to steer into the uncharted waters of modern technology by the compass of a carefully fostered instinct for what element in the grand pattern is likely to evolve soon, what is probably—for the time being at least—in a definitive form.

By the way, concerning that helium coolant system . . . It wasn't operated at atmospheric, and the jet can't fairly be compared with the blow-off from a Dewar. I pictured it as being at pressures we cannot yet maintain. My father used to tell me about visiting the laboratory of Kamerlingh Onnes in about 1921 or 1922, when the equipment was by modern standards primitive. It seemed fair to assume that by 2010 an advance of even greater magnitude would have occurred, and indeed I was tempted to make casual reference to phonon-zone switching processes as an essential element in Shalmaneser's artificial intelligence: a kind of counterpart to a hormonal cycle. However, I had—as always—to draw a line somewhere.

What I did admittedly miss by a mile was the prospect of superconductivity being induced at room temperature. Had I been aware of that, I'd have restructured both Shalmaneser and the episode in question.

Bear in mind, though, that I didn't design Shalmaneser. During the months prior to my starting work on *Stand on Zanzibar* that was done for me. Repeatedly the science columns referred to the probability that the next, or next but one, generation of computers would be microminiaturised, superconductive, and capable of mimicking (if not displaying) intelligence.

And I didn't invent those oxygen dispensers, either. They went on sale in Japan while I was plotting the novel. They seemed like a highly logical concomitant of the vicious-circle process involved in filtering ever more efficiently the air inside a building, without legal restrictions on what may be vented to the adjacent street.

It's a very odd feeling to have things that one did not dream up criticised as illogical and incredible! The former they may be; it's a weird world at the best of times. They cannot, however, be the latter. They do exist.

Having this happen makes one wonder which is the reality—the version reported in the news, or the one being applied to the elaboration of a novel. Does this sufficiently illustrate the point I needed to make about the author Brunner being in some sense more real than the flesh-and-blood human who wears the same name?

And is, in any case, one of several.

Hindsight makes for bad medicine. That's why I'm much happier when discussing the literary aspects of my work than when struggling to keep track of the complexities of the rest of my raw material—the changes whether political, social or technical, going on in the world at large.

Accepting that, as is the case with all SF writers, I will guess wrong a hundred times more often than I guess right, I nonetheless hope that my fiction qua fiction will remain valid. Ideally, I would like to feel that as *The Time Machine* or *The Lost World* continues to attract a readership, some at least of these numerous volumes that bear my name on the cover will stand the test of time.

If Jules Verne could even forget to equip the *Nautilus* with a periscope, there's hope for us all.

It seems fitting that thus far I should have talked more about my SF than about the rest of my work; it does after all constitute the bulk of the output.

I'm especially pleased, however, to find that considerable attention is paid in this volume to other aspects of my writing.

I love words. I love to play with words. I enjoy Scrabble and compiling crossword puzzles. Little by little, often—indeed I suspect almost always—without realising, I've acquired a sense of what language is and how it functions; what it can do with ease, and what it does only with great difficulty.

One of the keys to a comprehension of my work must be, I imagine, the acceptance that my primary concern is with the medium, and the matter is secondary. Out of my entire published corpus, I am most proud of three things:

The "Begi" stories in *Stand on Zanzibar,* because a friend of mine, studying African culture, showed them to her professor who returned them with the comment, "These *are* African folk-tales";

The verse parodies which introduce the month-sections of *The Sheep Look Up,* because people who should have known better kept asking me where I was quoting from;

And Max Curfew (protagonist of three of my thrillers) because to my incredulous delight it has been assumed by some of my black readers that I too, as well as he, must be black.

These achievements, you will note, are achievements in the area of manner, not matter.

For the foregoing reason—inter alia—I find myself reacting less to the essays in part 3 of this book, about economics and politics, than to those in parts 2 and 4. I have never found myself able to join a political party, for example, and while I support many "good causes" I have gradually ceased to be active in any, chiefly because I can reach and affect a thousand people with a piece of fiction for every one I could impress by walking down the street with a placard.

It seems very probable (to adapt an image from Kipling, much admired by me as John Pfeiffer has described) that there are many ways in which human society might be organised so as to give everyone a reasonable chance of living a happy and fulfilled existence. There may well be nine-and-sixty!

Standing in 1974, I cannot claim to know what they are. I can at best point out some of the ways in which our present society is falling short of what could by any tolerable criterion be called "civilised" . . . and thereby run foul of the false correspondence invented generations ago which equates civilisation with the power to inflict damage on people you don't like.

Still, it's been said—and there is a sad truth in the phrase—that when the real future gets here, it's bound to be dull.

Because there will only be one of it.

FOUR COORDINATES OF WHERE I'M STANDING

(a) A book published by Goldmann Verlag in German and in Germany. It is called *Morgen Geht die Welt aus den Angeln.*

It wears my name on the cover. On the verso of the title page is the copyright notice stating that this is a translation of *The Jagged Orbit.*

But I carefully planned *The Jagged Orbit* to contain an even hundred chapters.

This thing, whatever it is, contains ... thirty-two.

(b) A letter dated 10th October 1973:

Dear Miss ******,

> *Here are the proofs of *** **** ** **********.*
> *Please note that no forematter was supplied with the galleys, not even a title page.*
>
> *You'll see that at some fifteen or twenty points I've improved on my original typescript, and that I've caught a fair number of literals. You will also observe that several times on each galley I have written "follow copy" in red, and abbreviated it to "FC" when I grew tired of spelling it out in full.*
>
> *Of these cases there are over nine hundred.*
>
> *You will now proceed to put every last one of them back the way I wrote it. And don't argue. For one thing, it is fraudulent to palm off on the public under the name of an established writer like myself a text which has been tampered with by a tin-eared, style-deaf, subliterate moron whose native tongue appears to be Lower Slobbovian. For another, if the book were to remain in this butchered and travestied form it would do considerable harm to my reputation, and that I will not permit. I never mind carrying the can back for my own mistakes, but I am damned if I will stand Joseph for mistakes gratuitously injected by some anonymous meddler.*
>
> *(Etc.)*
>
> *Yours furiously,*

(c) Last of five novel reviews under the head "Science Fiction by Martin Amis" published in the London *Observer* of 18th August 1974:

The Sheep Look Up (Dent £2.95) is a massive, chaotic, jangling hotch-potch from the unwelcomely prolific John Brunner. An author of the I-told-you-so school, Mr Brunner delivers another cautionary tale about the polluted and anarchical future that awaits us. "An American university has recently devoted a course solely to his social speculations," cracks the blurb, and you'd need to be a Doctor of John Brunner to finish this one.

(d) The present book ... to whose authors, and editor, I'm much obliged.

JOE De BOLT / DENISE De BOLT

A Brunner Bibliography

Every attempt has been made to make this bibliography as complete as possible; however, given the ephemeral nature of many publications in popular literature, perfection is unattainable. A few entries have been included despite the lack of complete bibliographic information. Still, the list certainly includes the overwhelming majority of Brunner's professional works and all his important publications.

In classifying Brunner's magazine fiction by size, the method used by recent World Science Fiction Conventions has been adopted: short story, 0-7,500 words; novelette, 7,500–17,500 words; novella, 17,500–40,000 words; novel, 40,000 or more words. Only appearances in English are referenced here because of the difficulty in verifying actual non-English publications; however, the sale of foreign rights is noted. Occasionally notes have been added to indicate nominations, awards, parts of series, and other items of interest.

The hundreds of appearances by Brunner in amateur publications, excepting some of his "noise level" columns, have not been included; indeed, no compilation of them yet exists.

I. FICTION

Magazine appearances

"Against the Odds." *If: Worlds of Science Fiction* (August, 1956). Short story. Retitled "The Odds against You."

"All the Devils in Hell." *Science Fantasy* (December, 1960). Novella. Reprinted in *The Witchcraft Reader*, ed. Peter Haining (London: Dobson, 1969).

"Altar at Asconel, The." *If: Worlds of Science Fiction* (April, May, 1965). Novel. Published in book form as *The Altar on Asconel.* Second novel in Galactic Empire series.

"Analysts, The." *Science Fantasy* (August, 1961). Novelette.

"Armistice." (As K. Houston Brunner.) *Astounding Science Fiction* (January, 1955). Short story. Reprinted in *Astounding Science Fiction*, UK (June, 1955).

"Badman." *New Worlds Science Fiction* (March, 1960). Short story. Honorable mention: *Sixth Annual Edition, The Year's Best SF*, ed. Judith Merril (New York: Simon & Schuster, 1961).

"Better Mousetrap, A." *If: Worlds of Science Fiction* (November, 1963). Short story. Reprinted in the *If Reader of Science Fiction*, ed. Frederick Pohl (New York: Doubleday, 1966). Foreign rights sold: Italian.

"Biggest Game, The." (As Keith Woodcott.) *Science Fantasy* (February, 1956). Short story. Reprinted in *Splinters: A New Anthology of Modern Macabre Fiction*, ed. Alex Hamilton (London: Hutchinson, 1968). Retitled "The Men in Black."

"Bloodstream." *Vertex* (June, 1974). Short story.

"Born under Mars." *Amazing Stories* (December, 1966, and February, 1967). Novel. Published in book form.

"Brainpower." (As K. Houston Brunner.) *Nebula Science Fiction* (spring, 1953). Short story.

"Break the Door of Hell." *Impulse* (April, 1966). Novelette. Reprinted in *New Worlds of Fantasy*, ed. Terry Carr (New York: Ace, 1967); also in *The Mighty Swordsmen*, ed. Hans Stefan Santesson (New York: Lancer, 1970). Published as part of *The Traveler in Black*.

"Bridge to Azrael." *Amazing Stories Fact and Science Fiction* (February, 1964). Novella. Published in book form as *Endless Shadow.*

"By the Name of Man." *Nebula Science Fiction* (July, 1956). Novelette. Retitled "Substitute God."

"Children in Hiding." *Galaxy Science Fiction* (December, 1966). Short story. Retitled "Seizure."

"City of the Tiger." *Science Fantasy* (December, 1958). Novella. Reprinted in *Fantastic Universe Science Fiction* (November, 1959). Revised and published as part of *The Whole Man.*

"Coincidence Day." *Analog Science Fact Science Fiction* (February, 1965). Short story. Reprinted in *Analog 5*, ed. John W. Campbell (New York: Doubleday, 1967).

"Crack of Doom." (As Keith Woodcott.) *New Worlds Science Fiction* (September, October, 1962). Novella. Published in book form as *The Psionic Menace.*

"Curative Telepath." *Fantastic Universe Science Fiction* (December, 1959). Novella. Retitling of "The Whole Man." Revised as part of *The Whole Man*.

"Death Do Us Part." *Science Fantasy* (November, 1955). Short story.

"Djinn Bottle Blues." *Fantastic Stories* (February, 1972). Short story.

"Dramaturges of Yan, The." *Fantastic Stories* (October, December, 1971). Novel. Published in book form.

"Dread Empire." *Fantastic Stories* (April, 1971). Novelette. Published as part of *The Traveler in Black*. Nominated for the Hugo 1971.

"Drive to Distraction." *Knight* (March, 1966). Short story.

"Earth Is But a Star." *Science Fantasy* (June, 1958). Novella. Published in book form as *The Hundredth Millennium*. Revised as *Catch a Falling Star*.

"Easy Way Out." *If: Science Fiction* (June, 1971). Novelette. Reprinted in *Best Science Fiction for 1972*, ed. Frederick Pohl (New York: Ace, 1972).

"Echo in the Skull." *Science Fantasy* (August, 1959). Novella. Published in book form. Revised and expanded as *Give Warning to the World*.

"Elected Silence." Novelette. Retitling of "Silence." Collected in *No Future in It*.

"Elixir for the Emperor, An." *Fantastic Stories of Imagination* (November, 1964). Short story. Reprinted in *Strange Fantasy* (fall, 1970).

"Enigma from Tantalus." *Amazing Stories Fact and Science Fiction* (October, November, 1964). Novella. Published in book form.

"Even Chance." *Analog Science Fiction Science Fact* (November, 1965). Short story.

"Evil That Men Do, The." *New Worlds Science Fiction* (March, April, 1966). Novella. Published in book form.

"Eye of the Beholder." *Fantastic Universe Science Fiction* (January, 1957). Short story. Reprinted in *New Worlds Science Fiction* (June, 1957).

"Factsheet Six." *Galaxy Science Fiction* (July, 1968). Novelette. Foreign rights sold: French, German, USSR.

"Fair." (As Keith Woodcott.) *New Worlds Science Fiction* (March, 1956). Short story. Reprinted in *SF: Author's Choice # 4*, ed. Harry Harrison (New York: Putnam, 1974).

"Fair Warning." *Analog Science Fact Science Fiction* (May, 1964). Short story.

"Fairy Tale." *Vision of Tomorrow* (July, 1970). Short story.

"Father of Lies." *Science Fantasy* (May, 1962). Novella. Published in book form.

"Fiery Pillar." (As K. Houston Brunner.) *New Worlds Science Fiction* (August, 1955). Short story.

"Fifth Commandment." *Vision of Tomorrow* (March, 1970). Short story.

"Fourth Power, The." *New Worlds Science Fiction* (April, 1960). Novelette.

"Fullness of Time, The." *Science Fiction Adventures* (July, 1962). Novelette. Revised and published as part of *Times without Number*. Third part of Society of Time series.

"Gaudy Shadows, The." *Science Fantasy* (June, 1960). Novella.

"Hired Help, The." *Nebula Science Fiction* (February, 1958). Novelette.

"Hope Deferred." *Nebula Science Fiction* (November, 1956). Short story.

"Host Age." *New Worlds Science Fiction* (January, 1956). Novelette.

"Imprint of Chaos." *Science Fantasy* (August, 1960). Novelette. Published as part of *The Traveler in Black.* Honorable mention: *Sixth Annual Edition, The Year's Best SF,* ed. Judith Merril (New York: Simon & Schuster, 1961).

"Inception of the Epoch of Mrs. Bedonebyasyoudid, The." *Quark/2* (February, 1971). Short story. Foreign rights sold: French, German.

"Invisible Idiot, The." Short story in *Science against Man,* ed. Anthony Cheetham (New York: Avon, 1970).

"Iron Jackass, The." *Analog Science Fact Science Fiction* (March, 1962). Short story. Reprinted in *Analog Science Fact Science Fiction,* UK (July, 1962).

"Jack Fell Down." *Science Fiction Adventures* (March, 1963). Novelette. Reprinted in *Crime Prevention in the Thirtieth Century,* ed. Hans Stefan Santessan (New York: Walker, 1969).

"Judas." Short story in *Dangerous Visions,* ed. Harlan Ellison (New York: Doubleday, 1967; London: David Bruce and Watson, 1972). Reprinted in *Other Worlds, Other Gods: Adventures in Religious Science Fiction,* ed. Mayo Mohs (New York: Doubleday, 1971); *Past, Present and Future Perfect,* eds. Wolfe & Fitzgerald (Greenwich, Conn.: Fawcett, 1973). Foreign rights sold: French.

"Kingdoms of the World, The." *Science Fantasy* (February, 1957). Novella.

"Last Lonely Man, The." *New Worlds Science Fiction* (June, 1964). Short story. Reprinted in *Tenth Annual Edition, The Year's Best SF,* ed. Judith Merril (New York: Delacorte, 1965); also in *World's Best Science Fiction, First Series,* eds. Wollheim & Carr (New York: Ace, 1965); *Best from New Worlds* (New York: Compact, 1965); *Love and Marriage,* ed. Martin Greenberg (New York: St. Martin's, forthcoming 1975). Dramatized on BBC TV's "Out of the Unknown" series, January 21, 1969.

"Listen! The Stars!" *Analog Science Fact Science Fiction* (July, 1962). Novella. Reprinted in *Analog Science Fact Science Fiction,* UK (November, 1962). Published in book form. Revised and expanded as *The Stardroppers.*

"Long Way to Earth, The." *If: Worlds of Science Fiction* (March, 1966). Novella. Published in book form as *A Planet of Your Own.*

"Lungfish." *Science Fantasy* (December, 1957). Novelette. Retitled "Rendezvous with Destiny."

"Man from the Big Dark, The." *Science Fiction Adventures,* US (June, 1958). Novelette. Reprinted in *Great Science Fiction Adventures* (New York: Lancer, 1963). Foreign rights sold: Italian.

"Man Who Played the Blues, The." *Science Fantasy* (February, 1956). Short story.

"Men in Black, The." *Startling Mystery Stories* (fall, 1966). Short story. Retitling of "The Biggest Game."

"Mowgli." *Authentic Science Fiction* (May, 1956). Short story.

"Nail in the Middle of the Hand, The." *Saint Mystery Magazine* (July, 1965). Short story.

"New Thing, The." *If: Worlds of Science Fiction* (December, 1969). Short story.

"Nobody Axed You." *New Worlds Science Fiction* (May, 1965). Novelette. Reprinted in *The Best SF Stories from New Worlds*, ed. Michael Moorcock (New York: Berkley, 1967; London: Panther, 1967).

"No Future in It." (As Keith Woodcott.) *Science Fantasy* (September, 1955). Short story.

"No Other Gods but Me." Novella. Based on "A Time to Rend." Collected in *No Other Gods but Me.* Foreign rights sold: Italian.

"Nuisance Value." *Authentic Science Fiction* (February, 1956). Short story.

"Odds against You, The." Short story. Retitling of "Against the Odds." Collected in *No Other Gods but Me.* Foreign rights sold: Spanish.

"Oeuf du coq." *Science Fantasy* (February, 1962). Short story.

"Old Man's Footsteps, The." *News Club* (December, 1956). Short story. Retitling of "Proof Negative."

"Orpheus's Brother." *Magazine of Horror and Strange Stories* (April, 1965). Short story.

"Out of Mindshot." *Galaxy Science Fiction* (June, 1970). Short story. Reprinted in *Best from Galaxy,* eds. of *Galaxy Magazine* (New York: Award, 1972). Foreign rights sold: French.

"Out of Order." *New Worlds Science Fiction* (April, 1957). Short story.

"Planetfall." *Analog Science Fiction Science Fact* (May, 1965). Short story.

"Pond Water." Short story in *The Farthest Reaches*, ed. Joe Elder (New York: Trident, 1968).

"Prerogative." *New Worlds Science Fiction* (November, 1960). Short story.

"Product of the Masses, The." *If: Worlds of Science Fiction* (April, 1968). Short story.

"Productions of Time, The." *Magazine of Fantasy and Science Fiction* (August, September, 1966). Novel. Published in book form.

"Proof Negative." (As Trevor Staines.) *Science Fantasy* (February, 1956). Short story. Retitled "The Old Man's Footsteps."

"Protect Me from My Friends." *Magazine of Fantasy and Science Fiction* (November, 1962). Short story. Reprinted in *Magazine of Fantasy and Science Fiction*, UK (March, 1963); also in *Best Science Fiction 7*, ed. Edmund Crispin (London: Faber, 1971); *Outwards from Earth*, ed. Edmund Crispin (London: Faber, 1974). Recorded for WBAI radio, 1972.

"Protocols of the Elders of Britain, The." Novelette in *Stopwatch*, ed. George Hay (London: New English Library, forthcoming 1975).

"Put Down This Earth." *New Worlds Science Fiction* (June, July, August, 1961). Novel. Published in book form as *The Dreaming Earth*.

"Puzzle for Spacemen." *New Worlds Science Fiction* (December, 1955). Novelette. Reprinted in *Special Wonder: The Anthony Boucher Memorial Anthology of Fantasy and Science Fiction*, ed. Francis McComas (New York: Random, 1970).

"Rendezvous with Destiny." *Fantastic Universe* (March, 1958). Novelette. Retitling of "Lungfish."

"Repairmen of Cyclops, The." *Amazing Stories Fact and Science Fiction* (October, November, 1964). Novel. Published in book form. Third novel in Zarathustra Refugee Planet series.

"Report on the Nature of the Lunar Surface." *Astounding (Analog) Science Fact and Fiction* (August, 1960). Short story. Reprinted in *Analog Science Fact and Fiction*, UK (December, 1960). Also in *Sixth Annual*

Edition, The Year's Best SF, ed. Judith Merril (New York: Simon & Schuster, 1961); *From Frankenstein to Andromeda*, ed. James Goldie Brown (New York: Macmillan, 1966); *First Flights to the Moon*, Hal Clement (New York: Doubleday, 1970); *Insight*, eds. Cattel & Pennial (London: Harrap, 1969); *Wondermakers 2*, ed. Robert Hoskins (Greenwich, Conn.: Fawcett, 1974). Most anthologized story. Foreign rights sold: Danish, Norwegian.

"Round Trip." *New Worlds Science Fiction* (July, 1959). Short story. Reprinted in *Fantastic Universe Science Fiction* (September, 1959).

"See What I Mean!" *Analog Science Fact Science Fiction* (January, 1964). Short story.

"Seizure." Short story. Retitling of "Children in Hiding." Collected in *Not before Time.*

"Silence." *Galaxy Science Fiction* (October, 1959). Novelette. Retitled "Elected Silence."

"Singleminded." *If: Worlds of Science Fiction* (May, 1963). Short story. Reprinted in *Alien Worlds*, ed. Roger Elwood (New York: Paperback Library, 1964).

"Some Lapse of Time." *Science Fantasy* (February, 1963). Novella. Dramatized on BBC TV's "Out of the Unknown" series (December 6, 1965).

"Speech Is Silver." *Amazing Stories Fact and Science Fiction* (April, 1965). Short story. Reprinted in *More Tales of Unease*, ed. John Burke (London: Pan, 1969); also in *Science Fiction Greats* (summer, 1969) without payment or copyright acknowledgment.

"Spoil of Yesterday." *Science Fiction Adventures* (March, 1962). Novelette. Published as section of *Times without Number*. First part of the Society of Time series.

"Stand on Zanzibar." (Excerpts.) *New Worlds Science Fiction* (November, 1967).

"Stimulus." *New Worlds Science Fiction* (March, 1962). Short story.

"Stone That Never Came Down, The." *Amazing Science Fiction* (October, December, 1973). Novel. Published in book form.

"Substitute God." *Fantastic Universe Science Fiction* (August, 1958). Novelette. Honorable mention: *The Year's Greatest Science-Fiction and Fantasy, 4th Annual Volume*, ed. Judith Merril (New York: Dell, 1959). Reprinted in *More Adventures on Other Planets* (New York: Ace, 1963). Retitling of "By the Name of Man."

"Such Stuff." *Magazine of Fantasy and Science Fiction* (June, 1962). Short story. Reprinted in *Magazine of Fantasy and Science Fiction*, UK (October, 1962); also in *Eighth Annual Edition, The Year's Best SF*, ed. Judith Merril (New York: Dell, 1963); *Spectrum 4*, eds. Amis & Conquest (New York: Berkley, 1965); *My Blood Ran Cold*, ed. Donald Speed (London: Corgi, 1966); *Introductory Psychology through Science Fiction*, eds. Harvey Katz et al. (New York: Rand McNally, 1974). Sold to US TV series "Night Gallery," 1971. Foreign rights sold: German.

"Talisman, The." *Science Fantasy* (September, 1955). Novelette.

"Thing Friday." *New Worlds Science Fiction* (February, 1956). Short story.

"This Rough Magic." *Science Fantasy* (May, 1956). Novella. Developed into novel *Black Is the Color.*

"Thou Good and Faithful." (As John Loxmith.) *Astounding Science Fiction* (March, 1953). Novella. Reprinted in *Astounding Science Fiction*, UK (August, 1953). First sale to a US science fiction magazine.

"Threshold of Eternity." *New Worlds Science Fiction* (December, 1957; January, February, 1958). Novel. Published in book form.

"Time to Rend, A." *Science Fantasy* (December, 1956). Novella. Retitled and expanded as "No Other Gods but Me."

"To Conquer Chaos." *New Worlds Science Fiction* (August, September, October, 1963). Novel. Published in book form.

"To Make a Man." *New Worlds Science Fiction* (June, 1956). Short story.

"Tomorrow Is Another Day." (As K. Houston Brunner.) *Authentic Science Fiction* (March, 1954). Novella.

"Total Eclipse." *Amazing Science Fiction* (April, June, 1974). Novel. Published in book form.

"Totally Rich, The." *Worlds of Tomorrow* (June, 1963). Novelette. Reprinted in *Dark Stars*, ed. Robert Silverberg (New York: Ballantine, 1969). Broadcast over WBAI 1968; KPFA 1969.

"Treason." *Nebula Science Fiction* (May, 1957). Novelette. Retitled "Treason Is a Two-Edged Sword."

"Treason Is a Two-Edged Sword." Novelette. Retitling of "Treason." Collected in *Not before Time.*

"Trouble I See, The." *New Worlds Science Fiction* (March, 1959). Short story.

"Two by Two." *New Worlds Science Fiction* (May, 1956). Short story. Revised, and retitled "The Windows of Heaven."

"Uneasy Head, The." *New Worlds Science Fiction* (November, 1955). Short story.

"Visitors' Book." *New Worlds Science Fiction* (April, 1955). Short story.

"Vitanuls, The." *Magazine of Fantasy and Science Fiction* (July, 1967). Short story. Reprinted in *Other Worlds, Other Gods: Adventures in Religious Science Fiction,* ed. Mayo Mohs (New York: Doubleday, 1971).

"Wager Lost by Winning, The." *Fantastic Stories* (April, 1970). Novelette. Reprinted in *Warriors and Warlocks,* ed. Douglas Hill (London: Mayflower, 1971). Published as part of *The Traveler in Black.*

"Wanton of Argus, The." (As Kilian Houston Brunner.) *Two Complete Science Adventure Books* (summer, 1953). Novel. Published in book form as *The Space Time Juggler.* First novel in Galactic Empire series.

"Warp and the Woof-Woof, The." *Science Fantasy* (February, 1966). Short story.

"Wasted on the Young." *Galaxy Magazine* (April, 1965). Short story. Reprinted in *Ninth Galaxy Reader,* ed. Frederick Pohl (New York: Doubleday, 1966); also in *Window on the Future,* ed. Douglas Hill (London: Hart-Davis, 1966).

"Web of Everywhere." *Galaxy Science Fiction* (March, April, 1974). Novel. Published in book form.

"What Friends Are For." Short story in *Fellowship of the Stars,* ed. Terry Carr (New York: Simon & Schuster, 1974).

"When Gabriel . . . " *Science Fantasy* (August, 1956). Short story. Reprinted in *Fantastic Universe Science Fiction* (April, 1957).

"Whirligig!" *Beyond Infinity* (November, 1967). Short story.

"Whole Man, The." *Science Fantasy* (April, 1959). Novella. Retitled "Curative Telepath." Revised as part of book *The Whole Man.*

"Who Steals My Purse." *Analog Science Fiction Science Fact* (March, 1973). Novelette.

"Windows of Heaven, The." Short story. Retitling and revision of "Two by Two." Reprinted in *Yet More Penguin Science Fiction,* ed. Brian Aldiss (London: Penguin, 1964); also in *Science Fiction,* ed. S. H. Burton (London: Longmans Green, 1967). Adapted for broadcast, BBC schools radio, 1973.

"Word Not Written, The." *Science Fiction Adventures* (June, 1962). Novelette. Published as section of *Times without Number.* Second part of Society of Time series.

"Wrong End of Time, The." *Amazing Stories* (November, 1971, and January, 1972). Novel. Published in book form.

"You'll Take the High Road." Novella. Published in *Three Trips in Time and Space,* ed. Robert Silverberg (New York: Hawthorne, 1973).

Science fiction novels

Age of Miracles. (New York: Ace, 1973; London: Sidgwick & Jackson, 1973.) Revision of *Day of the Star Cities.*

Altar on Asconel, The. (New York: Ace, 1965.) Magazine publication: "The Altar at Asconel." Second novel in Galactic Empire series. Foreign rights sold: German.

Astronauts Must Not Land, The. (New York: Ace, 1963.) Revised as *More Things in Heaven.* Foreign rights sold: German, Italian.

Atlantic Abomination, The. (New York: Ace, 1960.) Reissued: (New York: Ace, 1970). Foreign rights sold: Italian.

Avengers of Carrig, The. (New York: Dell, 1969.) Revision of *Secret Agent of Terra.* Second novel in Zarathustra Refugee Planet series. Foreign rights sold: German, Spanish.

Bedlam Planet. (New York: Ace, 1968; London: Sidgwick & Jackson, 1973.) Foreign rights sold: Dutch, French, German.

Born under Mars. (New York: Ace, 1967.) Reissued: (New York: Ace, 1973). Magazine publication. Foreign rights sold: German, Italian.

Castaways' World. (New York: Ace, 1963.) Revised as *Polymath.* First novel in Zarathustra Refugee Planet series. Foreign rights sold: German.

Day of the Star Cities. (New York: Ace, 1965.) Revised as *Age of Miracles.* Foreign rights sold: German, Spanish.

Double, Double. (New York: Ballantine, 1969; London: Sidgwick & Jackson, 1971.)

Dramaturges of Yan, The. (New York: Ace, 1971; London: New English Library, 1974.) Magazine publication. Foreign rights sold: German.

Dreaming Earth, The. (New York: Pyramid, 1963; London: Sidgwick & Jackson, 1972.) Reissued: (New York: Pyramid, 1970, 1974). Magazine publication: "Put Down This Earth." Foreign rights sold: German, Portuguese.

Echo in the Skull. (New York: Ace, 1959.) Revised as *Give Warning to the World.* Magazine publication: "Echo in the Skull." Foreign rights sold: German.

Endless Shadow. (New York: Ace, 1964.) Magazine publication: "Bridge to Azrael." Foreign rights sold: German.

Enigma from Tantalus. (New York: Ace, 1965.) Magazine publication. Foreign rights sold: Portuguese.

A BRUNNER BIBLIOGRAPHY

Give Warning to the World. (New York: DAW, 1974.) Revision and expansion of *Echo in the Skull.*

I Speak for Earth. (As Keith Woodcott.) (New York: Ace, 1961.) Foreign rights sold: German.

Into the Slave Nebula. (New York: Lancer, 1968.) Reissued: (New York: Lancer, 1972). Revision of *Slavers of Space.* Foreign rights sold: German.

Jagged Orbit, The. (New York: Ace, 1969; SF Book Club selection, US, 1969; London: Sidgwick & Jackson, 1970; London: Arrow, 1972.) Reissued: (New York: Ace, 1972). Nominated for the Nebula Award in 1970. Winner of the British Science Fiction Award in 1971. Foreign rights sold: French, German.

Ladder in the Sky, The. (As Keith Woodcott.) (New York: Ace, 1962.) Foreign rights sold: German.

Listen! The Stars! (New York: Ace, 1963.) Revised as *The Stardroppers.* Magazine publication: "Listen! The Stars!" Foreign rights sold: German, Portuguese.

Long Result, The. (London: Faber, 1965; New York: Ballantine, 1966; London: Penguin, 1968.) Reissued: (New York: Ballantine, 1970). Foreign rights sold: Dutch, French, German, Italian, Japanese, Portuguese.

Martian Sphinx, The. (As Keith Woodcott.) (New York: Ace, 1965.)

Meeting at Infinity. (New York: Ace, 1961.) Reissued: (New York: Ace, 1969). Foreign rights sold: German.

More Things in Heaven. (New York: Dell, 1973.) Revision of *The Astronauts Must Not Land.*

Planet of Your Own, A. (New York: Ace, 1966.) Magazine publication: "The Long Way to Earth." Nominated for the Nebula Award in 1967. Foreign rights sold: German.

Polymath. (New York: DAW, 1974.) Revision of *Castaways' World.* First novel in Zarathustra Refugee Planet series.

Productions of Time, The. (New York: Signet, 1967; London: Penguin, 1970.) Magazine publication. Nominated for the Nebula Award in 1967. Foreign rights sold: Dutch, German, Portuguese.

Psionic Menace, The. (As Keith Woodcott.) (New York: Ace, 1963.) Magazine publication: "Crack of Doom." Foreign rights sold: German, Portuguese.

Quicksand. (New York: Doubleday, 1967; New York: Bantam, 1969; London: Sidgwick & Jackson, 1969; London: Sphere, 1970.)

Repairmen of Cyclops, The. (New York: Ace, 1965.) Magazine publication. Third novel in Zarathustra Refugee Planet series. Foreign rights sold: German, Portuguese.

Rites of Ohe, The. (New York: Ace, 1963.) Foreign rights sold: German, Portuguese, Spanish.

Sanctuary in the Sky. (New York: Ace, 1960.) Foreign rights sold: German, Italian, Portuguese.

Secret Agent of Terra. (New York: Ace, 1962.) Revised as *The Avengers of Carrig.* Second novel in Zarathustra Refugee Planet series. Foreign rights sold: German, Italian.

Sheep Look Up, The. (New York: Harper & Row, 1972; SF Book Club selection, US, 1972; New York: Ballantine, 1973; London: Dent, 1975.) Nominated for the Nebula Award in 1973. Foreign rights sold: German, French, Italian.

Shockwave Rider, The. (New York: Harper & Row, 1975; SF Book Club selection, US, 1975; London: Dent, forthcoming 1975.)

Skynappers, The. (New York: Ace, 1960.) Foreign rights sold; German.

Slavers of Space. (New York: Ace, 1960.) Revised as *Into the Slave Nebula.* Foreign rights sold: French, German.

Space Time Juggler, The. (New York: Ace, 1963.) Magazine publication: "The Wanton of Argus." First novel in Galactic Empire series.

Squares of the City, The. (New York: Ballantine, 1965; London: Penguin, 1969.) Reissued: (New York: Ballantine, 1970, 1973). Nominated for the Hugo in 1966. Foreign rights sold: Dutch, French, Italian, Spanish.

Stand on Zanzibar. (New York: Doubleday, 1968; SF Book Club selection, US, 1969; London: Macdonald, 1969; New York: Ballantine, 1969; London: Arrow, 1971.) Reissued: (New York: Ballantine, 1970, 1972, 1974). Winner of the Hugo in 1969. Nominated for the Nebula Award in 1969. Winner of the British Science Fiction Award in 1970. Winner of the Prix Apollo in 1973. Foreign rights sold: French, German, Japanese, Portuguese, Swedish.

Stardroppers, The. (New York: DAW, 1972.) Revision of *Listen! The Stars!*

Stone That Never Came Down, The. (New York: Doubleday, 1973; SF Book Club selection, US, 1974; New York: DAW, 1975.) Magazine publication.

Super Barbarians, The. (New York: Ace, 1962.) Foreign rights sold: Spanish.

Telepathist. (London: Faber, 1965; SF Book Club selection, UK, 1966; London: Penguin, 1968.) UK ed. of *The Whole Man.* Foreign rights sold: French, German, Italian, Japanese, Spanish.

Threshold of Eternity. (New York: Ace, 1959.) Magazine publication. First book sale in the United States. Foreign rights sold: French, German.

Times without Number. (New York: Ace, 1962.) Foreign rights sold: Dutch, German.

Timescoop. (New York: Dell, 1969; London: Sidgwick & Jackson, 1972; SF Book Club selection, UK, 1973.) Foreign rights sold: German, Portuguese.

To Conquer Chaos. (New York: Ace, 1964.) Magazine publication. Foreign rights sold: French, German.

Total Eclipse. (New York: Doubleday, 1974; SF Book Club selection, US, 1974.) Magazine publication. Foreign rights sold: Spanish.

Web of Everywhere. (New York: Bantam, 1974.) Magazine publication.

Whole Man, The. (New York: Ballantine, 1964; New York: Walker, 1969.) Reissued: (New York: Ballantine, 1970, 1973). Nominated for the Hugo in 1965. US ed. of *Telepathist.* Magazine publications: "The Whole Man," "City of the Tiger."

World Swappers, The. (New York: Ace, 1959.) Reissued: (Ace, 1967). Foreign rights sold: German, Portuguese.

Wrong End of Time, The. (New York: Doubleday, 1971; SF Book Club selection, US, 1972; DAW, 1974.) Magazine publication.

Adult fantasy novels

Catch a Falling Star. (New York: Ace, 1968.) Revision and expansion of *The Hundredth Millennium.* Foreign rights sold: Dutch, German, Portuguese.

Evil That Men Do, The. (New York: Belmont, 1969.) Magazine publication.

Father of Lies. (New York: Belmont, 1968.) Magazine publication.

Hundredth Millennium, The. (New York: Ace, 1959.) Revised as *Catch a Falling Star.* Magazine publication: "Earth Is But a Star."

Traveler in Black, The. (New York: Ace, 1971.) Magazine publications: "Imprint of Chaos;" "The Wager Lost by Winning;" "Break the Door of Hell;" "Dread Empire."

Mystery novels

Black Is the Color. (New York: Pyramid, 1969.) Developed from magazine publication "This Rough Magic."

Blacklash. New York: Pyramid, 1969.) US ed. of *A Plague on Both Your Causes.* First novel in Max Curfew series.

Gaudy Shadows, The. (London: Constable, 1970; New York: Beagle, 1971.) Foreign rights sold: German.

Good Men Do Nothing. (London: Hodder & Stoughton, 1970; New York: Pyramid, 1971.) Second novel in Max Curfew series. Foreign rights sold: German.

Honky in the Woodpile. (London: Constable, 1971; London: Sphere, 1973.) Third novel in Max Curfew series.

Plague on Both Your Causes, A. (London: Hodder & Stoughton, 1969; Hodder Paperbacks, 1971.) UK ed. of *Blacklash.* Foreign rights sold: French, German, Italian.

Wear the Butcher's Medal. (New York: Pocket Books, 1965.) Foreign rights sold: Italian.

Contemporary novels

Brink, The. (London: Gollancz, 1959.) Foreign rights sold: Dutch, Swedish.

Crutch of Memory, The. (London: Barrie & Rockliff, 1964.)

Devil's Work, The. (New York: Norton, 1970.)

Translation by John Brunner

The Overlords of War. by Gérard Klein (*Les Seigneurs de la guerre,* 1971). (New York: Doubleday, 1973; SF Book Club selection, US, 1973; New York: DAW, 1974).

Story collections

Book of Brunner, The. (New York: DAW, 1975.)

Entry to Elsewhen. (New York: DAW, 1972.) "Host Age." "Lungfish." "No Other Gods but Me."

From This Day Forward. (New York: Doubleday, 1972; SF Book Club selection, US, 1972; DAW, 1973). "The Biggest Game." "An Elixir for the Emperor." "Even Chance." "Factsheet Six." "Fairy Tale." "Fifth Commandment." "Judas." "Inception of the Epoch of Mrs. Bedoneby-asyoudid." "The Oldest Glass." "Planetfall." "The Trouble I See." "The Vitanuls." "Wasted on the Young."

No Future in It. (London: Gollancz, 1962; New York: Doubleday, 1964; SF Book Club selection, UK, 1964; New York: Panther, 1965; New York: Curtis, 1969). "Badman." "Elected Silence." "Fair." "The Iron Jackass." "No Future in It." "Out of Order." "Protect Me from My Friends." "Puzzle for Spacemen." "Report on the Nature of the Lunar Surface." "Stimulus." "The Windows of Heaven." Foreign rights sold: French, German, Italian.

No Other Gods but Me. (New York: Compact, 1966.) "Man from the Big Dark." "No Other Gods but Me." "The Odds against You." Foreign rights sold: Italian.

Not before Time. (London: Four Square, 1968.) "A Better Mousetrap." "Coincidence Day." "Eye of the Beholder." "Fair Warning." "Prerogative." "Round Trip." "Seizure." "Singleminded." "Treason Is a Two-Edged Sword." "The Warp and the Woof-Woof."

Now Then! (London: Mayflower-Dell, 1965; New York: Avon, 1968). "Imprint of Chaos." "Some Lapse of Time." "Thou Good and Faithful." Foreign rights sold: Italian, Portuguese.

Out of My Mind. (New York: Ballantine, 1967.) "A Better Mousetrap." "Eye of the Beholder." "Fair Warning." "The Fourth Power." "The Last Lonely Man." "The Nail in the Middle of the Hand." "Orpheus's Brother." "Prerogative." "Round Trip." "See What I Mean!" "Singleminded." "Such Stuff." "The Totally Rich."

Out of My Mind. (London: Four Square, 1968.) "The Fourth Power." "The Last Lonely Man." "The Man Who Played the Blues." "The Nail in the Middle of the Hand." "Orpheus's Brother." "See What I Mean!" "Such Stuff." "The Totally Rich." "When Gabriel . . ." "Whirligig."

Time-Jump. (New York: Dell, 1973.) "Coincidence Day." "Death Do Us Part." "Galactic Consumer Report No. 1: Inexpensive Time Machines." "Galactic Consumer Report No. 2: Automatic Twin-Tube Wishing Machines." "Galactic Consumer Report No. 3: A Survey of the Membership." "Nobody Axed You." "The Product of the Masses." "Speech Is Silver." "The Warp and the Woof-Woof." "Whirligig."

II. NONFICTION

Articles

"Alphavillains, The." *New Worlds Science Fiction* (August, 1966). Guest editorial.

"Building Four-Dimensional People in Science Fiction." *Writer* (December, 1971), pp. 21–24. Reprinted in *Techniques of Novel Writing,* ed. Abraham Saul Burack (Boston: The Writer, 1973), pp. 254–61.

"Confidence Tricks." *Encyclopédie du Crime et de la Criminologie,* Éditio-Service SA, Lausanne-Genève [1975?]

A BRUNNER BIBLIOGRAPHY

"Dealing in Futures." *The Author* (summer, 1970), pp. 83–86.

"Development of a Science Fiction Writer, The." *Foundation 1, The Review of Science Fiction* (March, 1972), pp. 5–12. Autobiographical sketch.

"Different Kick, Or How to Get High without Going into Orbit, A." *New Worlds Science Fiction* (May, 1966). Abridged speech given at the World Science Fiction Convention, London, 1965.

"Dinner with the Brunners." *Cooking Out of This World,* ed. Ann McCaffrey (New York: Ballantine, 1973), pp. 31–41.

"Dream Hunter, The." *Adventures in Discovery,* ed. Tom Purdom (New York: Doubleday, 1969), pp. 127–43. Translated into Chinese, 1972.

"Educational Relevance of Science Fiction, The." *Physics Education,* 6 (1971): 389–91.

"Genesis of *Stand on Zanzibar* and Digressions into the Remainder of its Pentateuch." *Extrapolation* (May, 1970), pp. 34–43.

"Heart and Graft of Writing Science Fiction, The." *Algol: A Magazine about Science Fiction* (November, 1973), pp. 27–28. BBC 3rd Program talk.

"Literary Schizophrenia." *Books and Bookmen* (November, 1967), p. 50.

"London's Happiest Hunting Ground." *Knight,* 5: 11 (1967).

"Nothing to Do with Prophecy." *Aspect* (March, 1963), pp. 37–41.

"One Sense of Wonder, Slightly Tarnished: The Past and Future of Time Fiction." *Books and Bookmen* (July, 1967), pp. 19–20.

"On Political Attitudes in SF." *New Worlds Science Fiction* (January, 1964). Guest editorial.

"Our Present Requirements." *New Worlds Science Fiction* (January, 1962). Guest editorial.

"Parallel Worlds." *Foundation 3: The Review of Science Fiction* (March, 1973), pp. 6–14. Originally the guest of honor speech delivered by John Brunner at Eurocon 1, Trieste, July 12, 1972.

"Technological Folk Hero." *Folk Review* (May, 1972).

"Them As Can, Does." *New Worlds Science Fiction* (January, 1966), p. 113.

"Twenty-first Century View of Sex, A." *Real Life Guide* (July, 1966).

"What Works for Me." *Science Fiction Writers Association Bulletin* (October, 1967).

Columns and book reviews

"Foreign Constellations." *Foundation 5: The Review of Science Fiction* (January, 1974), pp. 105–7.

"Noise Level: A Column." *Science Fiction Review # 34* (December, 1969).

"Noise Level: A Discussion of *Barefoot in the Head.*" *Science Fiction Review # 36* (date not known).

"Noise Level: ... But Beautifully Cooked!" *Alien Critic 9* (May, 1974), pp. 24–25.

"Noise Level: Flash: John Brunner vs. The Meddling Moron." *Alien Critic 8* (February, 1974), pp. 21–22.

"Noise Level: If the Law Is in Fact a Ass Maybe You Ought to Get Your Ass Out of There, As It Were." *Outworlds 3.1* (January, 1972), pp. 21–23.

"Noise Level: Rhyme and, If You're Very Lucky, Reason." *Science Fiction Review # 43* (March, 1971).

"Noise Level: The Latest Addition to the Foundation Series, As It Were." *Outworlds 3.3* (May, 1972), pp. 59–60.

Noise Level: This Funny Job." *Science Fiction Review # 38* (June, 1970), pp. 10–11.

"Noise Level: Where There's Brass There's Brass." *Alien Critic 7* (November, 1973), pp. 17–20.

"Work of Philip K. Dick, The." *New Worlds Science Fiction* (September, 1966).

Poetry collections

Life in an Explosive Forming Press. (London: Poets' Trust, 1970.)

Trip: A Sequence of Poems through the United States. (London: Keepsake, 1971.) Revised from a privately circulated ed., 1966.

Poems

"No Answer." *New Statesman* (May 26, 1972), p. 719.

"Oldest Glass, The." Published in *From This Day Forward* (New York: Doubleday, 1972), pp. 223–24.

"Series of Twelve Poems, A." *Foundation 2: The Review of Science Fiction* (June, 1972), pp. 30–37. The poems from *The Sheep Look Up.*

"Sonnet for the Seeds of Time, A." *SF Monthly # 2* (1974).

Miscellaneous

Film script: *The Terranauts.* Adapted from Murray Leinster's "The Wailing Asteroid" for Amicus Productions.

Poetry reading: "An Evening with John Brunner," Audio Cassette Number 101–1034, Self-instruction Systems Center, Central Michigan Library, Central Michigan University, Mt. Pleasant, Michigan.

Text for photos: *Horses at Home* (spring books, 1958). Photos by Tmej and Chocola.

Promotional pamphlet: "About John Brunner." (London: Brunner Fact & Fiction, Ltd, 1973.)

III. SELECTED WORKS ABOUT JOHN BRUNNER

Blish, James, "The Future in Books." *Amazing Stories* (September, 1969), pp. 121–22. Extended review of *The Jagged Orbit.*

Budrys, Algis, "Galaxy Bookshelf." *Galaxy* (June, 1966), pp. 147–52. Extended review of *The Squares of the City.*

Duveau, Marc, "John Brunner: Un Homme entier sur une orbite dechiquetée autour d'une planète de fous." *Galaxie # 110* (n. d.), pp. 107–16. Review of Brunner and his work.

Livingston, Dennis, "Science Fiction Models of Future World Order Systems." *International Organization* (spring, 1971), pp. 254–70. Contains an analysis of *Stand on Zanzibar.*

McNelly, Willis E., "The Science Fiction Novel in 1968." *Nebula Award Stories Four,* ed. Poul Anderson (New York: Pocket Books, 1971), pp. xiii–xxv. Contains an analysis of *Stand on Zanzibar.*

Merril, Judith, "Books." *Magazine of Fantasy and Science Fiction* (January, 1966), pp. 39–45. Analysis of the British science fiction scene.

————."Books." *Magazine of Fantasy and Science Fiction* (February, 1969), pp. 22–25. Extended review of *Stand on Zanzibar.*

Samuelson, David, "New Wave, Old Ocean: A Comparative Study of Novels by Brunner and Delany." *Extrapolation: A Journal of Science Fiction and Fantasy* (December, 1973), pp. 75–96. Analysis of *Stand on Zanzibar.*

Sargent, Lyman, "Utopia and Dystopia in Contemporary Science Fiction." *Futurist* (June, 1972): pp. 93–98. Contains an analysis of *Stand on Zanzibar.*

Scholes, Robert, "Change, SF and Marxism: Open or Closed Universes? Novels by Brunner and Levin." *Science Fiction Studies,* 1 (spring, 1974): 213–14. Comments on *The Sheep Look Up.*

Spinrad, Norman, "The Future in Books." *Amazing Stories* (September, 1969), pp. 123–26. Retitled and reprinted as *"Stand on Zanzibar:* The Novel as Film." *SF: The Other Side of Realism,* ed. Thomas D. Clareson (Bowling Green University, Ohio: Popular Press, 1971). Analysis of *Stand on Zanzibar.*

Suvin, Darko, "The SF Novel in 1969." *Nebula Award Stories Five,* ed. James Blish (New York: Pocket Books, 1972), pp. 158–67. Contains an analysis of *The Jagged Orbit.*

Watson, Ian, "Reaping the Whirlwind." *Foundation 7 and 8: The Review of Science Fiction* (March, 1975), pp. 55-59. Analysis of *The Sheep Look Up.* An excellent succinct analysis of Brunner's work.

Index

INDEX OF WORKS BY JOHN BRUNNER

INDEX OF WORKS BY JOHN BRUNNER

"Fullness of Time, The," 20, 57

"Galactic Consumer Reports:
  "Automatic Twin-Tube Wishing
    Machines," 94
  "Inexpensive Time Machines," 94
  "Survey of the Membership, A," 94
"Gaudy Shadows, The," 20
"Genesis of *Stand on Zanzibar* and
  Digressions into the Remainder of
  its Pentateuch," 25n, 30n, 37n, 45n,
  46n, 96n, 98n, 102n, 104n
Give Warning to the World, 21
Good Men Do Nothing, 24, 31, 56

"Hard Fact vs. Hard Fiction," 166n
"H-Bombs Thunder, The" (song), 22,
  181
"He was Such a Nice Chap — Why Did
  He Do It?" (poem), 105
Honky in the Woodpile, 31, 56
Hundredth Millenium, The, 18, 26

"Imprint of Chaos," 20, 57
"Inception of the Epoch of Mrs.
  Bedonebyasyoudid, The," 30
"In Praise of Decadence" (poem), 104
Into the Slave Nebula, 26, 173

Jagged Orbit, The, 6, 26, 30–32, 43–44,
  46–48, 52, 58, 63, 66–76, 107, 113,
  116, 118, 120–123, 120n, 124n,
  130–132, 134–135, 138, 141, 144n,
  147–148, 151–153, 155, 162–165,
  168–171, 174, 194
"Judas," 30, 79, 89–90, 175

"Last Lonely Man, The," 20, 42, 83n,
  85–86, 183
"Life in an Explosive Forming Press"
  (poem), 97
Life in an Explosive Forming Press, 31,
  96, 97n, 98n, 100n, 102n, 103n,
  105n, 106n, 107n, 108n
"Literary Schizophrenia," 184n
Long Night and the Sudden Dawn, The,
  55
Long Result, The, 44
"Long Way to Earth, The," 24

Manalive, 21, 179, 181
"Man from the Big Dark, The," 54
More Things in Heaven, 191
*Morgen Geht die Welt aus den
  Angeln*, 194
"Multiple Choice" (poem), 99–100

"Nail in the Middle of the Hand, The,"
  82, 83n, 84, 92
"Nobody Axed You," 20
"No Future in It," 82
No Future in It, 19, 171n
"Noise Level," 31–32
Now Then!, 14n, 23, 91n, 95

"On Balance" (poem), 105
"Orpheus's Brother," 80
"Out of Mindshot," 30
Out of My Mind, 24, 79n, 80n, 81,
  81n, 82n, 83n, 87n, 88n, 89n, 91n,
  92n

"Parallel Worlds," 59n
Plague on Both Your Causes, A, 31,
  56
Planet of Puppets, A, 55
Planet of Your Own, A, 24
Polymath, 55
"Presentiment" (poem), 100
"Product of the Masses, The," 94
"Productions of Time, The," 24
Productions of Time, The, 29, 44, 49–50,
  185
Protect Me from My Friends," 19–20,
  82, 84n
Psionic Menace, The, 171
"Puzzle for Spacemen," 20

Quicksand, 24–26, 29, 33, 44, 49–50,
  52, 68, 186

Repairmen of Cyclops, The, 55–56
"Report on the Nature of the Lunar
  Surface," 20, 182
"Rib and Development" (poem), 103

Secret Agent of Terra, 26, 55–56
"See What I Mean!", 20, 78, 87
Sheep Look Up, The, 6, 30, 32, 38, 44,
  47–48, 52, 58, 63–64, 66–67,
  113–114, 117–122, 118n, 121n,
  125–126, 127n, 128–132, 134–
  137, 141, 144n, 147–152, 155–
  156, 158–162, 164–165, 169–171,
  174, 191, 193–194
Shockwave Rider, The, 35, 68
"Silence," 19
"Silent Majority, The" (poem), 105
"Singleminded," 19–20, 79, 87–88,
  92
Skynappers, The, 20, 171
Slavers of Space, 26
"Some Lapse of Time," 20, 42

211

INDEX OF PERSONS

Contributors

JAMES BLISH. A well-known author and critic in science fiction, Blish sold his first story in 1939, won the Hugo in 1959 for *A Case of Conscience*, served as guest of honor at the World Science Fiction Convention in 1960, and was the focus of a special issue of the *Magazine of Fantasy and Science Fiction* (April, 1972). He published two milestone works of science fiction criticism, *The Issue at Hand* (Advent, 1964) and *More Issues at Hand* (Advent, 1970), under the name of William Atheling, Jr. Although perhaps best known for his "Cities in Flight" novels and Bantam's current Star Trek book series, Blish also has written nonscience fiction, including an historical novel on Roger Bacon, *Doctor Mirabilis* (Faber, 1964).

WILLIAM P. BROWNE. Associate professor of political science, Central Michigan University. Major areas: public bureaucracies and urban politics. Browne's current research activities deal with the nature of interest group membership and with law enforcement bureaucracies; a textbook on political bureaucracy is forthcoming.

JOE De BOLT. Associate professor of sociology, Central Michigan University. Major areas: social change, small groups, and the community. A science fiction fan for many years, De Bolt recently developed a course in the sociology of science fiction and has written several articles on the subject. His current scholarly research includes the investigation of personality and small group structure in experimental groups and the analysis of alternative instructional methods.

CONTRIBUTORS

STEPHEN C. HOLDER. Assistant professor of English, Central Michigan University. Major area: American literature. Holder has published in the area of popular culture and teaches a course on detective fiction.

EDWARD L. LAMIE. Assistant professor of mathematics and computer science, Central Michigan University. Major area: computer science. Before joining the academic community Lamie worked as an applications programmer for the city of San Diego and as applications and systems programmer for the North American Rockwell Corporation.

JOHN R. PFEIFFER. Associate professor of English, Central Michigan University. Major areas: science fiction, Shaw studies, Afro-American literature. Besides having published several articles on science fiction, as well as *Fantasy and Science Fiction: A Critical Guide* (Filter Press, 1971), Pfeiffer teaches a highly successful course on science fiction. He is bibliographer for the *Shaw Review* and is at work on a major book on George Bernard Shaw.

RONALD PRIMEAU. Associate professor of English, Central Michigan University. Major areas: English romanticism, Afro-American literature, and rhetoric. Author of numerous articles in his specialties, Primeau is presently completing two books, one on writing essays (David McKay, forthcoming, 1976) and the other on the aesthetics of literary influences.

NORMAN A. RASULIS. Assistant professor of English, Central Michigan University. Major areas: contemporary literature and Marxist literature. Rasulis has been active in the antiwar and human rights movements and has contributed several articles to radical publications. He recently returned from a visit to the People's Republic of China.

ROBERT R. SLOCUM. Associate professor of physics, Central Michigan University. Major areas: solid state physics and industrial ecology. Slocum has worked as a radiological physicist in the United States Army Chemical Corps and as a researcher in radio-isotope technology and in ultrasonics. His major research centered on NMR and Knight shifts in Cd and Cd alloys. He teaches courses on industrial ecology and on energy and environment in addition to physics.